CARDOZO
AND FRONTIERS OF
LEGAL THINKING

Beryl Harold Levy is professor of philosophy at Hofstra University. He is the author
of *Our Constitution: Tool or Testament?* and
Corporation Lawyer: Saint or Sinner?

BERYL HAROLD LEVY

CARDOZO
AND FRONTIERS
OF LEGAL THINKING

WITH SELECTED OPINIONS

REVISED EDITION

THE PRESS OF
CASE WESTERN RESERVE UNIVERSITY
CLEVELAND AND LONDON 1969

Revised Edition.
First edition published by Oxford University Press, 1938.

Copyright © 1938 by Beryl Harold Levy.
Copyright © 1969 by
The Press of Case Western Reserve University,
Cleveland, Ohio 44106.

Printed in the United States of America.
Standard Book Number: 8295–0147–9.
Library of Congress Catalogue Card Number: 69–17682.

PREFACE TO THE
1969 EDITION

CHIEF Justice Stone once wrote me, in answer to a question about the drastic change in his views in later years, that he owed this development of his thought to the influence of Holmes and Cardozo. The vast impact of the Holmes-Cardozo philosophic approach—the Great Tradition of American law—was the most vital force in shaping the 'frontiers of legal thinking' in the first half of this century. That Cardozo's suasion has not dimmed with the passage of time is shown by his stimulus to subsequent analyses. I have chosen for discussion some contributions which seem to me addressed most significantly to those fundamentals which were Cardozo's catalytic concern, especially ways of handling the non-routine type of case. Omissions and oversights are egregious. But by this inevitable judgment of exclusion and by the subordination of my own views I have sought to avoid the intellectual congestion which so often afflicts this subject.

The book was designed for the general reader. It was my hope that the inter-related issues of philosophy and law could be made clear to the layman without loss of professional integrity incurred by simplification. I thought then, and think now, that the disciplines of law and philosophy have too much effect on people's lives to be left shrouded in esoteric terms. The houses of intellect of both law and philosophy have many mansions; and it has been my good fortune and design to live in more than one of them. Thus, however inadequately, I aspired to reach the kind of audience that Zechariah Chafee's review invoked: the 'layman' who might 'read the book with pleasure' as well as the 'wide-awake' lawyer. As it turned out, the book has been maintained in print almost continuously since its initial publication, and it is a source of modest satisfaction to find it included in the *Deans' List of Recommended Reading for Prelaw and Law Students,* edited by Julius J. Marke (New York, 1958).

A book is entitled to a life and character of its own. In this new edition I have not presumed to give the reader a different book from the one I originally wrote. I have left the first edition as it was, with only minor alterations, preferring to incorporate my further reflections and updating in the Afterword to this edition. Specifically, I have not attempted to corrupt the passage of time by correcting allusion to events that were current when the book was first brought into print. Moreover, Justice Cardozo is often treated as the living person he was when the original edition was written. This ineluctable anomaly is in one sense not an anachronism at all—for he still lives through the vitality of his extraordinary influence.

September 1968   B. H. L.

ACKNOWLEDGMENTS

I have much pleasure in acknowledging aid and encouragement in the germination and preparation of this new edition. My thanks and indebtedness go to Cleveland State University for a special grant; to its library and stenographic pool; to Mrs. Evelyn M. Hamilton, Mrs. Diana F. Gamble, and Miss Laurel L. Rhyand for unfailing courtesies; to my life-long friends Professor Elliott Cheatham, Professor Abraham Edel (who also read the manuscript of the original book), and Bruno Schachner, Esq., legal scholar, philosopher, and fellow-realist, respectively; to David Berks, Arthur Miller, and Wilton Sogg, jurisprudentially sophisticated lawyers; to my friends and students Dr. and Mrs. Gerald Marshall; and, most especially, to my wife, Phyllis, who was not only all that an author's wife must staunchly be, but more than prose can be entrusted adequately to express.

CONTENTS

I

CARDOZO IN CONTEMPORARY JURISPRUDENCE

The judge should no doubt, like our own great Chief Judge, be both lawyer and philosopher of the highest grade, blessed with saving common sense and practical experience as well as sound and comprehensive learning, but such men are rare.

Judge Cuthbert W. Pound
Defective Law—Its Cause and Remedy
I BULLETIN NEW YORK STATE BAR ASSOCIATION (1929) 285

I

CARDOZO IN CONTEMPORARY JURISPRUDENCE

Steering the Course

No dramatic crises mark the life of Benjamin Nathan Cardozo unless they be quiet crises of the mind. There is an even inevitability in the ripening of his career.

He was born in New York City on 24 May 1870. His ancestry in America goes back to colonial times. His maternal great-grandfather, Benjamin Mendes Seixas, helped drill Revolutionary troops. His great-great-uncle, Rabbi Gershom Mendes Seixas, participated in the inauguration of George Washington. On the paternal side, we find his great-great-grandfather, Aaron Nunez Cardozo, a merchant, arriving from London in the middle of the Eighteenth Century. The best of the patriot—his concern for the welfare of the state; the best of the business man—his sturdy grip on everyday realities; the best of the minister—his zeal to actualize ideals, combine, as we shall see, in Mr. Justice Cardozo.

The imagination of many a youth has been fired by *Fame and Fortune* and *From Canal Boy to President*. Their author was Justice Cardozo's boyhood tutor.

'My preparation for college,' wrote the Justice in response to an inquiry, 'was the work of Horatio Alger. He did not do as successful a job for me as he did with the careers of his newsboy heroes.'[1]

1. Letter to Milton H.Thomas, curator of Columbiana, Columbia University in the City of New York, 20 March 1936.

In 1889, at the age of nineteen, Cardozo graduated from Columbia College. His interest in governmental theory was displayed at this early date with a Commencement oration on *The Altruist in Politics* and with a B.A. thesis on *Communism*. The deliberative and philosophic habit of mind and the concern for moral fundamentals, which have been so notably cultivated, are already present in this thesis.[2]

By twenty he had earned an M.A. in political science. After two years at the Columbia Law School he was admitted to practice in 1891. His arguments won notice. His memory for cases was famed. He spent two decades specializing in appellate practice, which is the work of a 'lawyer's lawyer,' arguing complex points of law before a higher court of review.

Then in November 1913, he was elected a Justice of the Supreme Court in New York City in the course of the Fusion movement which elected John Purroy Mitchel mayor. 'As an independent Democrat, Judge Cardozo would probably never have been put forward for his first candidacy either by Tammany Hall or by the Republican organization,' William M.Chadbourne has pointed out.[3] And indeed, Charles C. Burlingham, chairman of the committee on judicial nominations of the Fusion Committee of 107, has related how the Republican organization held back for a time, preferring to place in nomination the name of one of its stalwarts.[4] Concerning the credit for Cardozo's nomination, Mr. Burlingham recently made the following disclosure at the memorial meeting for Dr. Henry Moskowitz:

'Seven cities claimed Homer's birth and about seventy different people claim to have nominated Cardozo. I know the

2. Cardozo, *Communism* (Unpublished thesis in the library of Columbia University in the City of New York, 1889).
3. Letter to the editor of the *New York Times*, 27 February 1932.
4. *New York Times*, 25 May 1930.

story. I have told it as Henry [Moskowitz] would never have told it himself. Henry was not the chairman, but he was behind the scenes and determined to help in every way possible. And one day he came to me and said: "I think I have just the man for a judge—Benjamin Cardozo."

'Some years before, at the request of Mr. Wickersham, Attorney General of the United States, I had asked Cardozo whether he would accept a Federal judgeship. He said that he could not do so at that time. This time he accepted our nomination for Justice of the New York Supreme Court, and the result you all know.'[5]

The extraordinary details are not generally known. Within a month, and even though he had not served in the Appellate Division, which is the intermediate court, he was appointed by Governor Glynn to serve temporarily as Associate Judge of the highest court of the state, the Court of Appeals, where additional help was needed. The Governor had asked the Court to name its candidate and Cardozo was unanimously chosen. The Governor pointed to his brief judicial experience and the fact that he had been in the trial court only. The Court repeated its request and it was granted. Few indeed are the lawyers whose abilities are so outstanding that they have been drafted for high judicial office in this way.

In 1916 Samuel Seabury resigned from the Court to run for governor. On 15 January 1917, Cardozo was appointed a regular member by Governor Whitman. In the following Fall he was duly elected, running with the joint endorsement of the two major parties. In 1927 he became chief judge. The frequency with which the Court agreed, the fewness of Cardozo's dissents,[6] and the sovereign reputation of

5. Address at Town Hall, 4 April 1937.
6. From volume 210 of the New York Reports, where his opinions begin.

the Court in this period are testimony to his leadership.

'Four to three decisions have been rare,' Henry W.Taft has observed, 'and the occasional dissenting opinion has not often been so copiously buttressed or so unrestrained in expression as to impair the force of the prevailing opinion. It is this accord in the court that has given to its decisions weight and authority in all jurisdictions.'[7]

Cardozo's leadership had really begun long before. On Chief Judge Hiscock's retirement, it is said that Judge McLaughlin, who had differed with Cardozo as much as any man on the Court, wept when the rumours ran that Cardozo might not become chief judge. Cardozo has declared, however, that he was almost dismayed to discover the additional authority in the Court which came to him by virtue of his holding that office.

In 1927 he declined an appointment to the Permanent Court of Arbitration at The Hague. But in 1932 came a more urgent call. President Hoover invited him to serve on the Supreme Court of the United States because 'the whole country demanded the one man who could best carry on the great HOLMES tradition of philosophic approach to modern American jurisprudence.'[8] The appointment was unanimously confirmed by the Senate, which had subjected two of Hoover's previous nominees to attack. On 14 March 1932, he took his place on the country's highest tribunal.

Aristotle speaks of the peculiar *telos* of the acorn to become

to volume 252 (February 1930), there were, in round figures, 470 prevailing opinions by Cardozo for the Court, which was unanimous in 375 cases. There were fifteen concurrences by Cardozo and fifteen dissents. Bernard L.Shientag, 'The Opinions and Writings of Judge Benjamin N.Cardozo ' (1930) 30 *Col.L.Rev.*597.

7. Taft, 'One Aspect of Judge Cardozo's Noteworthy Career' (1932) 18 *American Bar Association Journal* 172.

8. Judge Cuthbert W.Pound at the close of the last consultation of the Judges of the New York Court of Appeals, 3 March 1932, 258 N.Y.vi.

an oak, of the boy to become a man. It is as though with the same steadiness Cardozo's course was steered to judicial eminence. As far back as 1903, he had turned his scholarly attention upon the Court of Appeals, writing a book on its jurisdiction.[9] Felicitously at home in the more rarefied circles of the law, he has the meditative temper of the appellate judge who must pass on questions of law and who is not bothered with straightening out the facts of a case in the thick of a trial. As he sits now among the Nine he is the judge authentic and undeflected.

Despite his eminence of intellect and position, the Justice is renowned for his warm, amiable friendliness. The 'stuffed-shirt' formalities which so often accompany success at the bar are foreign to him. How many distinguished lawyers would answer a letter of simple inquiry on the day it is received, and in their own handwriting? How many can count their corridor acquaintances by the legion? 'For sheer loveableness,' says one writer, 'the Justice sets some sort of record. And the protective tenderness is so communicable that newspaper, magazine, and free-lance writers are immediately affected by it.'[10]

Not a little of Cardozo's vast influence—from the bench, among his colleagues, on the bar, and with a large section of the public—may be ascribed to the charm of his personality. Evidence on that score pours in from every side, from practising lawyers, New York judges, university professors, law teachers, his former law secretaries, Washington officials. 'In this summary of the judge,' as Cardozo has said of another, 'one must not be forgetful of the man, for indeed the two

9. Cardozo, *The Jurisdiction of the Court of Appeals of the State of New York* (Banks & Company, Albany, first edition 1903, second edition 1909).
10. 'The Honorable Supreme Court,' 13 *Fortune* (May 1936) 80.

were of a piece.'[11] No greater tribute could be paid to the man than that which comes from Oliver Wendell Holmes, whom Cardozo succeeded not only on the United States Supreme Court but as the bearer of the grand tradition, the philosophic approach to American law. In a recently published letter to the Chinese jurist Dr. John C.H.Wu, Holmes wrote in 1929:

'Cardozo I am sure that I should really love if I knew him better. I not only owe to him some praise that I regard as one of the chief rewards of my life, but have noticed such a sensitive delicacy in him that I tremble lest I should prove unworthy of his regard. All who know him seem to give him a superlative place. I have seen him but once, and then his face greatly impressed me. I believe he is a great and beautiful spirit.' [12]

At the end of another letter to Wu in 1932, he added:

'Since I began this I have had a call from Cardozo. I think you would love him as I do and have from the first moment I saw him—a beautiful spirit.'[13]

One is reminded of another great Jew of Sephardic origin. Benedict Spinoza too served the cause of morals and philosophy, of goodness in society. About the outward incidents of Cardozo's life there is little more to relate than about Spinoza's. Life's adventures for both men have been in the study. Many an arctic in the realm of mind each has explored. Both are champions of civil rights, Jews who moved to serve a wider community and bathed in the best intellectual currents

---

11. Cardozo, 'Memorial of Nathan Bijur,' *Yearbook* 1931 *Association of the Bar of the City of New York* (New York, 1931) 354.
12. Letter from Beverly Farms, Massachusetts, 1 July 1929. *Justice Oliver Wendell Holmes: His Book Notices and Uncollected Letters and Papers* (edited by Harry C.Shriver, Central Book Co., New York, 1936) 201–2.
13. *Ibid.* (Letter of 14 March 1932) 206.

of their day, thinkers with a peculiar sense of dedication—not distracted, even to the extent of being married, from an ascetic untiring persistence in their work.

'The submergence of self in the pursuit of an ideal,' Cardozo has avowed, 'the readiness to spend oneself without measure, prodigally, almost ecstatically, for something intuitively apprehended as great and noble, spend oneself one knows not why— some of us like to believe that this is what religion means. True, I am sure, it is that values such as these will be found to have survived when creeds are shattered and schisms healed and sects forgotten and the things of brass and stone are one with Nineveh and Tyre.'[14]

Those among our younger generation of lawyers, who have been trained in a university law school in today's 'case system' and who have been taught to see the law as flowing and shifting in an age of dynamic and far-reaching change, are sometimes a little disturbed by the smoothing of doctrinal currents to which Cardozo's opinions are frequently devoted, often in the very process of changing law. Zeal for stability of law combines in him with zeal for progress.[15] It may be relevant, in this connection, to recall that he started his study under Dwight, using the old textbook method, and only in the latter period of his student days was he exposed to the then radical Harvard case method, according to which, instead of just learning textbook principles, students encounter actual law cases.

'I went to Columbia Law School,' he tells us, 'in the transition days when it was passing from the old method of instruc-

14. Cardozo, 'Values,' delivered at Exercises of the Jewish Institute of Religion on 24 May 1931, 2 *News Bulletin of the Jewish Institute of Religion* (June 1931) 6.
15. Cardozo, *The Growth of the Law* (Yale University Press, New Haven, 1924) 1–3.

tion by textbook—itself a long advance over the method of Mansfield's time—to the case method now in vogue. I had been there more than a year under Dwight and Chase and their associates when Prof. Keener, fresh from Harvard, descended on a bewildered class.'[16]

It is as if he has kept these elements of his training in equal mixture since. While he is strongly inclined toward settling the law in terms of its basic and undercutting principles, at the same time he is alertly aware that changes prompted by a consideration of the individual case and especially by new social and economic conditions are necessary. Recent reformers have stressed the change. A further genetic explanation for Judge Cardozo's equally firm insistence on a rounded finality, so far as may be, can be sought in the fact that the function of the New York Court of Appeals, his early subject of study and his later place of work, is to settle the law of the state.

'The court exists not for the individual litigant but for the indefinite body of litigants, whose causes are potentially involved in the specific cause at issue. The wrongs of aggrieved suitors are only the algebraic symbols from which the court is to work out the formula of justice.'[17]

16. Cardozo, 'The Comradeship of the Bar,' *Law and Literature* (Harcourt, Brace, New York, 1931) 179; originally in 5 *New York University Law Review* 1,1. *Cf.* Judge Lehman: 'Perhaps as one educated by the Harvard method, I have at times an inner sense of superiority over those educated under the Dwight method, but I must confess that this sense of superiority evaporates when I discuss legal principles with men like Justice Cardozo . . . taught under the other system.' Irving Lehman, Address delivered before the Joint Conference on Legal Education in the State of New York, 28 June 1935,5–6.

17. Cardozo, *The Jurisdiction of the Court of Appeals* 11, citing Martin, J.: 'The Constitutional convention clearly entertained the opinion that the continued existence of the Court of Appeals was justified only by the necessity that some tribunal should exist with supreme power to authoritatively declare and settle the law uniformly throughout the state . . . to the end that the people might understand the

This settling tendency, this disposition to give coherent expression to legal fundamentals, shows itself not only in his day-to-day work but in his active sponsorship of the American Law Institute in restating the law. To extremely zealous reformers, this interest, together with the concern he still expresses for certainty in the law,[18] indicates an incomplete emancipation. But Cardozo has gone as far in the direction of loosening and revising legal method, both in theory and practice, as any judge has dared. No one on the United States Supreme Court has shown more persistent liberalism. There are those who wish he might have been a bit bolder. But the canons of ordinary criticism cannot be applied to the appellate judge as if he were wholly free to express his private convictions in his judicial opinions. A man may be a liberal judge in his construction of the Constitution and still an aristocrat in economic belief and temperament, as was Holmes. A man might be a liberal judge in his conception of the ordinary common law judicial function—in the breadth of view and absence of literalism with which he construes statutes, 'follows' precedents, and embraces the various possible sources of law, and still have a personal preference for laissez-faire. There is a sad confusion which comes of using the word 'liberal' to describe both a type of judge and a progressive social attitude. The liberal in politics and economics may regard as mild-hearted the liberal in robes. In Constitutional questions, where social issues are most prominent, the conservative judge is an ultra-conservative, and the liberal judge is merely refusing to block what a legislature has already done

principles which regulated their dealing and conduct and thus, if possible, avoid litigation.'
    Cf. 'One man is made a victim to the extent of a few dollars in return for a readjustment that will save many victims in the future.' Cardozo, *The Growth of the Law*, 122.
18. See Jerome Frank, *Law and the Modern Mind* (Brentano's,1930) 237-8.

and an executive officer approved. The impatient social radical may wish to discard the entire judicial system and all the lawyers to boot, but as long as this institution continues to function in our society, the just critic will strive to estimate those who bear its responsibilities in a perspective and context appropriate to their office. Cardozo must then emerge a shining figure.

But our description, if it continues so personal and general, becomes panegyric. On the whole, there is too much formal reverence for the judge-in-office. Decked in robes, risen for, addressed as 'Your Honour,' privileged to cite for contempt—he is surrounded with a sanctity hard to justify in a nation which vaunts its democracy. Strip Cardozo of these ceremonial trappings. Reverence is still compelled for his subtlety and depth, for the exacting and imaginative performance of his job, for his devout interest in the development of the law and legal institutions, for his courtesy and gentleness of bearing. His heroic intellect has won widest acclaim in a society where money measures success and the pursuits of business are haloed. Despite possible disqualification by geography, lineage, or party lines, he is acknowledged as superlative in his profession and is buoyed to its top.

'By universal consent,' says Dean Pound, 'he is a great lawyer, a master of the principles, ideals, and technique of Anglo-American law. He has been fortunate in sitting upon the bench in the state court of most influence in the land, and later upon the highest federal court in a time of transition, quite comparable to the formative era of American law, a time when judges are called upon to shape the legal materials which took form for nineteenth-century America to the exigencies of the economically unified, urban, industrial America of the twentieth century. He has been conscious of this task and has approached it in the same creative but judicial spirit as that which characterized the great judges of the first half of the nineteenth century. He has known the tools of his craft and has known how to use them. He has shown the sound administrative judgment and discretion guided by reason characteristic of the strong common-law judge. Above all, he has shown himself a scholar of the first rank. The pressure of business in American appellate courts today does not admit of judges writing great treatises, as could Story and Cooley, nor of their teaching along with their judicial duties. But Mr. Justice Cardozo has been able to write two books which are likely to rank with the writings of Mr. Justice Holmes as formative influences in contemporary science of law. Moreover, his is an all round scholarship, and his culture, his wide general knowledge, and his command of English put him with the best of those who have sought to formulate judicial experience for the use of lawyers and litigants to come.'[19]

His career is a tribute to the truth that for real greatness sound practical judgment must be welded to theoretic knowledge and insight. Without vision, learning, and perspective, the man of affairs is precariously placed in a position of authority.

'Until philosophers are kings, or the kings and princes of this world have the spirit and power of philosophy, and political greatness and wisdom meet in one, and those commoner natures who pursue either to the exclusion of the other are compelled to stand aside, cities will never have rest from their evils—no, nor the human race, as I believe—and then only will this our state have a possibility of life and behold the light of day.'[20]

19. Roscoe Pound, Foreword, Joseph P.Pollard, *Mr. Justice Cardozo: A Liberal Mind in Action* (Yorktown Press, New York, 1935) 4–5.
20. Plato, *Republic* V.473 D.

Legal Realism

In the Seventeenth Century, when the common law courts were asserting their supremacy, a vain boast was made by Lord Coke, the great judge of the period.

'Reason is the life of law,' said Coke, 'nay the common law itselfe is nothing else but reason.'[21]

But King James I pointedly remarked that 'he and others had reason as well as the Judges.'

Whereupon Coke boldly retorted that 'causes which concern the life, or inheritance, or goods, or fortunes of his subjects, are not to be decided by natural reason, but by the *artificial reason and judgment of law*.'[22]

These assertions of Coke, important as they were in a time of powerful monarchy to protect the people against the tyranny of their king, reveal the lingering pride and prejudice of our legal tradition—the pride that the law is itself the embodiment of reason, of 'everything that's excellent,' and therefore beyond question; the prejudice that its comprehension is the exclusive prerogative of lawmen. If law proceeds only by reason, and yet only lawyers and judges are initiated into the use of this 'artificial reason,' law becomes immune from outside fertilizing and outside criticism. It finds both its sources and its standards within itself.

But even in those days Coke's insularity was challenged by a younger contemporary, the shrewd philosopher, Hobbes.

'That Law can never be against Reason,' wrote Hobbes, 'our Lawyers are agreed. . . . And it is true: but the doubt is,

21. Coke, *The First Part of the Institutes of the Laws of England; or, A Commentary upon Littleton: Not the Name of the Author Only, But of the Law Itself*, Sec.138, fol.97.b.
22. See Coke's report of this controversy in Prohibitions del Roy, Mich. 5 Jacobi I. 12 Co.Rep.64,65 (1608). Italics author's. *Cf.* Roscoe Pound, *The Spirit of the Common Law* (Marshall, Jones, Boston, 1921) 60–1.

of whose Reason it is, that shall be received for Law. It is not meant of any private Reason; for then there woud be as much contradiction in the Lawes, as there is in the Schooles: nor yet, (as Sr.*Ed.Coke* makes it,) an *Artificiall perfection of Reason, gotten by long study, observation and experience,* (as his was). For it is possible long study may encrease, and confirm erroneous Sentences: and where men build on false grounds, the more they build, the greater is the ruine . . .'[23]

And in his *Dialogue between a Philosopher and a Student of the Common Laws of England,* Hobbes has the philosopher remark of Coke that 'whether he had more or less use of reason' he 'was not thereby a judge, but because the King made him so.'[24]

It is with the same salt of matter-of-fact realism that Holmes remarked that the object of the study of law is 'the prediction of the incidence of the public force through the instrumentality of the courts.'[25]

This cynical approach, when followed through, carries significant implications. It robs lawfolk of a sense of superiority and the notion that they possess an especially sacred or eso-

23. Hobbes, *Leviathan or the Matter, Forme & Power of a Commonwealth, Ecclesiasticall and Civill* (1651)* 139–40.
24. *The English Works of Thomas Hobbes of Malmesbury* (edited by Sir William Molesworth, Bart., John Bohn, London, 1840) 14. *Cf.* 'It is not wisdom, but authority which makes a law.' *Ibid.*5. For a criticism of Blackstone's attempt to combine both of these in his definition of law as 'a rule of civil conduct prescribed by the supreme power in a State . . . commanding what is right, and prohibiting what is wrong,' (Sir William Blackstone, *Commentaries on the Laws of England,* *53), see M.R.Cohen, 'The Process of Judicial Legislation,' *Law and the Social Order* (Harcourt, Brace, New York, 1933) 137; F.S.Cohen, 'The Problems of a Functional Jurisprudence' (1937) 1 *Modern Law Review* 15.
25. Oliver Wendell Holmes, 'The Path of the Law,' *Collected Legal Papers* (Harcourt, Brace, New York, 1921) 167; originally in 10 *Harv.L.Rev.* 457. It is interesting to note that Holmes read Hobbes's *Leviathan.* See reference in Richard Walden Hale, *Some Table Talk of Mr. Justice Holmes and 'The Mrs.'* (Privately printed, Boston, 1935) 13.

teric capacity of mind or body of knowledge. It serves to stress that not reason alone, but any force or factor which will operate upon a judge's mind to make him decide a case one way or another, is a source of law—whether it be a previous decision of one of his colleagues or predecessors, whether it be a law review article, or a book on sociology or economics, or a prevailing moral or political trend, or his age or health, or whatever. It emphasizes that we must keep our eye not only on a set of legal principles but on the actions of judges. And that we must try to predict the actions of judges without being confused by moral considerations.

'If you want to know the law and nothing else, you must look at it as a bad man, who cares only for the material consequences which such knowledge enables him to predict, not as a good one, who finds his reasons for conduct, whether inside the law or outside of it, in the vaguer sanctions of conscience. . . . Take the fundamental question, What constitutes the law? You will find some text writers telling you that it is something different from what is decided by the courts of Massachusetts or England, that it is a system of reason, that it is a deduction from principles of ethics or admitted axioms or what not, which may or may not coincide with the decisions. But if we take the view of our friend the bad man we shall find that he does not care two straws for the axioms or deductions, but that he does want to know what the Massachusetts or English courts are likely to do in fact. I am much of his mind. The prophecies of what the courts will do in fact, and nothing more pretentious, are what I mean by the law.'[26]

This robust and unsentimental point of view increases the clarity of legal analysis. It approaches law in terms of its

26. Holmes, 'The Path of the Law,' *Collected Legal Papers*, 171–3.

barest effects—the penalty in dollars or in jail-time which it
exacts of its violators. Because the legal consequences of a
course of behaviour are put in these cold terms, Holmes did
not mean that men are also advised to calculate their conduct,
or that judges will decide cases, in these terms. Holmes was
here talking as a detached analyst, concerned about the exact-
ness of legal analysis, and not in the capacity of a judge ex-
pounding the common law. It is also from the *analyst's* point
of view that he remarked: 'The duty to keep a contract at
common law means a prediction that you must pay damages if
you do not keep it—and nothing else.'[27] But speaking as a
judge in his dissenting opinion in *Bailey* v. *Alabama,* he said:
'Breach of a legal contract without excuse is wrong conduct.'[28]

Holmes stirred a ferment in American jurisprudence which
has since been brewing, recently with increased vigour, among
students and moulders of legal methods.[29] It challenges the
traditional view of law in no less basic a sense than old traditions in other human activities have been shaken by present-
day 'modernistic' trends. The principal departures in law will
presently emerge in detail. At this point three widespread
general tendencies may be indicated: one, *functionalism*—the
adaptation of an object to its use; two, *individuality*—the
stress on the particular instance rather than on the general
class; and three, *frankness*—an absence of restraint both as to
what is said and how it is said. The contemporary trend of

27. *Ibid.*175.
28. 219 U.S.219,246 (1911).
29. Karl N.Llewellyn, 'A Realistic Jurisprudence—The Next Step' (1930)
    30 *Col.L.Rev.*431; Roscoe Pound, 'The Call for a Realist Jurispru-
    dence' (1931) 44 *Harv.L.Rev.*697; Llewellyn, 'Some Realism about
    Realism—Responding to Dean Pound' (1931) 44 *Harv.L.Rev.*1222, of
    which Cardozo has said: 'A temperate and withal a wise summary of
    neo-realist tendencies is to be found in the latest exposition of the new
    creed by one of the most brilliant of its teachers.' Address, 55 *Report
    of New York State Bar Association* (Albany, 1932) 273 f.n.

realism in law is the companion of these current tendencies in other areas, not all of which are necessarily good or apply to Cardozo.

Functionalism is most apparent in industrial and domestic designs, in modern architecture or furniture, in a streamlined train or airplane, but its influence extends through education, philosophy, and even mathematics and physics. While renewed today, this tendency has marks as old as the Greeks.[30] Legal functionalism, in ways that we shall see, wishes to streamline legal doctrine, to remove historical relics and formal fringes, to shape the tools of law for the smoothest performance of their present-day uses. This applies no less to legal institutions, like the mode of procuring a divorce, for example, and to statute revision, than to common law rules.

In its stress on *individuality*, the modern departs from the classic with its bias toward the type, the universal symbol. In murals by contemporary artists, for example, we are not likely to find an abstract picture of general virtues, like Lady Justice holding the scales, but specific incidents, scenes, and persons. Similarly in literary criticism, the 'genetic approach' leads to accounts of an author's writings in terms of his own individual experience. Modern scientific theory has stressed induction and experiment, the drawing of conclusions from many particular happenings, more than the previously over-stressed deduction from general principles. So, in the law, does the realist bid us look to the specific court we are to address and to the background of its judges, to measure our argument and predict our result accordingly. In relation to legal doctrine, he

30. See Gilbert Murray, 'The Value of Greece to the Future of the World,' *The Legacy of Greece* (edited by R.W.Livingstone, Oxford University Press, 1928) 9.

bids us observe the particular case and how it affects broad rules.

Frankness is especially marked in literature and it is unrestrained both as to style and subject matter. Writers like Joyce, D.H.Lawrence, or Farrell do not draw the line anywhere when it comes to telling about life as it is really seen and experienced. The realist in law, too, believes in breaking down polite conventions about the law, in looking at what is really there, and in telling plainly what he sees. This habit shocks an older generation at the Bar accustomed to more decorum and dignity, in much the same way that these literary figures would offend a Victorian purist. When truth is at stake it is always difficult to know the bounds of good taste.

'We are talking about ourselves and looking into ourselves, subjecting our minds and our souls to a process of analysis and introspection with a freedom and in a measure that to the thought of our predecessors would have been futile and meaningless or even down-right unbecoming.'[31]

Cardozo is an eminent pioneer of the 'realist' movement in law. This contemporary movement insists more specifically on freedom from formalism and an end to the idolatry of precedent-worship; on a lesser devotion to legal abstractions and a greater nearness to the push and sweat of life; on a greater regard for the consequences of the actions of legal officials, and a lesser focusing on the mere words of judges (though Cardozo does think that realists have underestimated the importance of judicial language);[32] on a concern for honest description of how the wheels of the law machine really move. Realism is not so much a school of thought as it is a trend or tendency. Generalizations concerning it must be

31. Cardozo, Address, 55 *Report of New York State Bar Association* 264.
32. *Ibid.*278.

warily taken.[33] Because this outlook was shared in basic respects, by Bentham as well as Von Jhering and Savigny abroad, and by Holmes and Dean Pound in this country, Cardozo prefers to call the strictly contemporary movement 'neo-realism.'[34] There are certain respects in which some of those in the vanguard of reconstruction would wish to qualify Cardozo's views, but, as to fundamental attitudes, they hail his singular frankness, his broad societal orientation, and his general refusal to be bossed by legal concepts.[35] For himself he has been willing to be classed as their co-believer in theory and practice.[36]

Though refusing to go along with many of the neo-realists in treating internal order in the legal system and certainty in law as comparatively unimportant if not negligible, he is in agreement with them generally, he tells us, 'in their insistence that the virtues of symmetry and coherence can be purchased at too high a price; that law is a means to an end, and not an end in itself; and that it is more important to make it consistent with what men and women really and truly believe and

33. Llewellyn, 'Some Realism about Realism' (1931) 44 Harv.L.Rev.1225. 'Realism' is a poor term because it means such different things in literature, morals, metaphysics, and epistemology. Our analysis is written from a point of view favourable to a united front of contemporary legal thinkers who are fighting Lord Coke's 'artificial reason and judgment of the law.' Common cause would be made with philosophers of law like Roscoe Pound, Morris H.Cohen, and Mortimer J. Adler, as well as with those specifically bringing to law economic, sociologic, and psychologic learning. See Robert L.Hale, 'Force and the State: A Comparison of "Political" and "Economic" Compulsion' (1935) 35 Col.L.Rev.149; Hale, Legal Factors in Economic Society (Unpublished casebook in the library of the School of Law, Columbia University in the City of New York, 1937); Huntington Cairns, Law and the Social Sciences (Harcourt, Brace, New York, 1935); Edward S. Robinson, Law and the Lawyers (Macmillan, New York, 1935). All of these are agreed in viewing law as a tool making for the social good.
34. Cardozo, Address, 55 Report of New York State Bar Association 268.
35. Cf. F.S.Cohen, 'Transcendental Nonsense and the Functional Approach' (1935) 35 Col.L.Rev.809–11.
36. Cardozo, Address, 55 Report of New York State Bar Association 270.

do than what judges may at times have said in an attempt to explain and rationalize the things they have done themselves.'[37]

In the sources of his realism, Cardozo has been inspired by Holmes, his great predecessor as a philosophic jurist, and by pragmatism, which has been described as the characteristically American philosophy, furthered by John Dewey in our day but sponsored by William James, who was a friend of Holmes [38] and perhaps had influence upon him. Holmes's approach we have already seen. The relations to pragmatism and other philosophic views will be considered as we go along. In a series of books, addresses, and notable opinions, Cardozo has carried the work of legal enlightenment into the very chambers of the judge, letting the shades up and removing his robe, so that all may see what are the ordinary human traits, the efforts and the stumblings, out of which emerge the achievements of the arts of justice. It is true that the sleeves have not been rolled up, nor the door thrown open. That job has remained for ultra-realists, unencumbered by official position. But certainly his were among the first and most significant steps taken in the United States toward a frank and easy manner and a healthy naturalness about things legal. Physicians still write prescriptions in Latin, and many a judge and jurist talk jargon beyond the understanding of the average layman and beyond the patience of the functionally trained young lawyer. But one has only to turn to the books of Cardozo to see the process shorn of its mystery.[39]

37. *Ibid.*292.
38. See *The Letters of William James* (edited by Henry James, Atlantic Monthly Press, Boston, 1920, volume I) 98ff.,124ff. *Cf.* Edward S. Robinson, Book Review (1936) 25 *Yale Review* 618.
39. *The Nature of the Judicial Process* (Yale University Press, New Haven, 1922)
   The Growth of the Law (Yale University Press, New Haven, 1924)

Philosophy and Law

CARDOZO'S writings serve, on the whole, to provide an insight into the way judges and lawyers work with their peculiar tools. Though he is concerned mainly with an explanation of method, he has also made a contribution to other phases of jurisprudence and legal philosophy, to an understanding of the functioning of law in society. Where the philosophy of the judge—which is an expression of his working ideals and methods—ends, and where the philosophy of the man— which is an avowal of the beliefs by which he lives—begins, it is impossible to tell in the case of a man whose life is as wrapped up in his work as is Cardozo's. We have undertaken no separation where he has not. The philosophy of every man betrays his occupation and to Cardozo the law has been a holy grail.

Philosophers jealous of their title might decline to embrace him. They will point out that he is a judge grown philosophical, not a philosopher who has become a judge; that his philosophic expressions do not have the direct geysering forth which Holmes's had; that they are not as clean-cut as is demanded by the logician (who is sometimes willing to sacrifice accuracy for precision); that he often quotes profusely in a manner resembling what he himself has described as the 'scissors and paste' method of composition. Technical philosophy, however, is going the way of technical law, and there are not many philosophers who would exclude from their number one whose intellectual judgments and moral attitudes have

The Paradoxes of Legal Science (Columbia University Press, New York, 1928)
Law and Literature (Harcourt, Brace, New York, 1931).
Address, 55 Report of New York State Bar Association (Albany, 1932).

been so deeply and diligently forged, whose approach is so broad and critical, and whose synthesis so clarifying, and who, besides, has made himself the champion of philosophy in the field of law.[40]

'The lawyers, I say, have been talking philosophy or what they thought was philosophy; but then on the other hand the philosophers have been talking law or what they thought was law, and some of them certainly have learned more about the law than the lawyers or the judges have learned about philosophy. So we have to-day the heartening spectacle of lectures by John Dewey on the place of logic and of ethics in legal science, and lectures by Morris R.Cohen on the meaning of law and the function of the judge, and essays and addresses by others—by psychologists on the law of evidence, by moralists on the theory of the state—till indeed it seems at times that the lawyers and the judges are playing a minor role and may soon be elbowed off the stage.'[41]

And again:

'If some of the applications of philosophy to law may not incite to emulation, the fault has been, not in supposing that philosophy is a helpful guide, but in the conception of philosophy as alien to experience and life. One must select one's guide with care, even though the candidates for employment are decked in the regalia of the schools. The student does not need to be warned against fertilizing law with the teachings of philosophy. The warning must rather be to be on the watch for the philosophy, which, disguised or unavowed, is latent in existing law, to extricate it when it is hidden, to test its truth and value, and to be ready to correct or discard it when

40. Cardozo, *The Growth of the Law*, 22–3.
41. Cardozo, Address, 55 *Report of New York State Bar Association* 265.

it is defective or outworn. The more he knows of philosophy, past and present, the quicker his eyes will be to detect and his judgment to appraise.'[42]

Men of more limited learning and breadth of mind ignore what Cardozo knows, that philosophy has long wrestled with basic issues which find illustration in some legal problem;[43] that a judge's philosophy necessarily enters into the determination of every question before him;[44] and 'that many of the most perplexing problems of the judicial process will be solved once the nature and origin of law shall be better understood.'[45] As to the deprecated frequency of quotation, it is a habit of reference to authority not easily put aside by a judge, and those who know him vouch for the deep modesty which prompts him: 'the desire to make manifest the truth that back of what I write is the sanction of something stronger than my own unaided thought.'[46] Nor will his genial and welcoming eclecticism, his warm and sympathetic attitude toward many diverse points of view, toward whatever light there may be in any source, bother those who know how ugly a rigidly conceived and rigorously excluding philosophy can be in any man, and how particularly unbecoming it is to a judge.

'Let us not exaggerate unduly the differences that divide the forces of enlightenment and truth when there is need to present a united front to the embattled ranks and outposts of prejudice and error.'[47]

42. Cardozo, *The Growth of the Law*, 131.
43. *Ibid*.128–9; *The Paradoxes of Legal Science* (Columbia University Press, New York, 1928) 4. See the discussion of causation, *Ibid*.81ff.; Silverstein v. Metropolitan Life Ins. Co., 254 N.Y.81, 171 N.E.914 (1930); reprinted in full *infra* p.215, and Palsgraf v. Long Island R.Co., 248 N.Y.339, 162 N.E.99 (1928); reprinted in full *infra* p.124.
44. *Ibid*.25–6.
45. Cardozo, Address, 55 *Report of New York State Bar Association* 267.
46. Cardozo, *The Paradoxes of Legal Science*, 101.
47. Cardozo, Address, 55 *Report of New York State Bar Association* 269.

PHILOSOPHY AND LAW

It has been frequently indicated of and by Cardozo that he is a pragmatist.[48] His many sympathetic references to James and Dewey lend support to that assertion. Of a pragmatic bent his mind surely is, if by pragmatism we mean that ideas, in James's language, 'become true just in so far as they help us to get into satisfactory relation with other parts of our experience' and: 'Theories thus become instruments, not answers to enigmas, in which we can rest.'[49] He believes that pragmatism, considered in its broad and elementary sense, is deeply influencing the law, if indeed it is not itself the central spirit of the law.

'Who would think off hand that pragmatism had a message for the judge on the bench or the lawyer at the bar? I cannot doubt, however, that the message has been heard. By emphasizing standards of utility, by setting up the adaptation to an end as a test and evidence of verity, pragmatism is profoundly affecting the development of juristic thought. Its truth, if not genuine for the metaphysician, is genuine at least for those whose thought must be translated into action, who are not merely scientists, but craftsmen, and who must ever be satisfied with something less than the perfect and complete ideal.'[50]

And elsewhere he goes as far as to say that 'the juristic philosophy of the common law is at bottom the philosophy of pragmatism. Its truth is relative, not absolute. The rule that functions well produces a title deed to recognition.'[51]

48. Cardozo, *The Growth of the Law*, 46–7,127; Hardman, 'Mr. Justice Cardozo' (1932) 38 *W.Va.L.Q.*187; Farnum, 'Justice Benjamin N. Cardozo: Philosopher' (1932) 12 *B.U.L.Rev.*590; Shientag, 'The Opinions and Writings of Judge Benjamin N.Cardozo' (1930) 30 *Col. L.Rev.*601.
49. William James, *Pragmatism* (Longmans, Green & Co., New York, 1925) 58,53.
50. Cardozo, *The Growth of the Law*, 127.
51. Cardozo, *The Nature of the Judicial Process* (Yale University Press, New Haven, 1922) 102–3.

But Cardozo's is no true-blue pragmatism as that is popularly conceived. He is more inclusive in his range. Especially does he insist too strongly on certain tacit moral absolutes.[52] Unmistakably part of his outlook is a nagging ethical reference, a concern that affairs be rightly ordered, which can scarcely be accurately described as other than Prophetic.[53] Though it would not be fair to cite passages from legal opinions as illustrative of a judge's personal views, tone and emphases are revealing. See, for example, his refusal in his dissent in *Jones v. Securities and Exchange Commission* to allow the statute and its sanctions to 'become the sport of clever knaves':

'The rule now assailed was wisely conceived and lawfully adapted to foil the plans of knaves intent upon obscuring or suppressing the knowledge of their knavery.'[54]

Or the anxiety expressed for adequate development of the individual personality:

'The Multiple Dwelling Act is aimed at many evils, but most of all it is a measure to eradicate the slum. It seeks to bring about conditions whereby healthy children shall be born, and healthy men and women reared, in the dwellings of the great metropolis. To have such men and women is not a city concern merely. It is the concern of the whole State. Here is to be bred the citizenry with which the State must do its work in the years that are to come. The end to be achieved is more than the avoidance of pestilence or contagion. The end to be achieved is the quality of men and women. . . . If the moral and physical fibre of its manhood and womanhood is not a State concern, the question is, what is?'[55]

Or the eloquent announcement, so often reaffirmed by

52. See *The Paradoxes of Legal Science*, 54.
53. See Cardozo, *The Paradoxes of Legal Science*, 120–2.
54. 297 U.S.1,33 (1936).
55. Adler v. Deegan, 251 N.Y.467,484, 167 N.E.705,711 (1929).

him,[56] of the duty of a fiduciary, one entrusted with broad discretion over the property or affairs of another:

'A trustee is held to something stricter than the morals of the market place. Not honesty alone, but the punctilio of an honor the most sensitive, is then the standard of behavior. As to this there has developed a tradition that is unbending and inveterate. Uncompromising rigidity has been the attitude of courts of equity when petitioned to undermine the rule of undivided loyalty by the "disintegrating erosion" of particular exceptions. . . . Only thus has the level of conduct for fiduciaries been kept at a level higher than that trodden by the crowd.'[57]

Bergson asks the question: 'How has justice emerged from social life, within which it had always dwelt with no particular privilege, and soared above it, categorical and transcendent?'

And he answers: 'Let us recall the tone and accents of the Prophets of Israel. It is their voice we hear when a great injustice has been done and condoned. From the depths of the centuries they raise their protest. True, justice has singularly expanded since their time. . . . None the less they imparted to justice the violently imperative character which it has kept, which it has since stamped on a substance grown infinitely more extensive.'[58]

The insistence on righteousness, which was the force of Amos and Isaiah, is quietly present in many of Cardozo's opinions, though not so militantly as it has sometimes appeared in Brandeis's.

Even more basic for Cardozo is a philosophic insight

56. See Globe Woolen Co. v. Utica Gas & Electric Co., 224 N.Y.483, 121 N.E.378 (1918); reprinted in full *infra* p.180.
57. Meinhard v. Salmon, 249 N.Y.458,464, 164 N.E.545,546 (1928); reprinted in full *infra* p.168.
58. Henri Bergson, *The Two Sources of Morality and Religion* (Henry Holt, New York, 1935) 67–8.

which prompts him to find in every problem a clash of basic opposites, a phenomenon anciently recognized by the Greek philosophers before Socrates. It is one of the curiosities of current juristic discussion in America that lawmen, who have just awakened to the existence of these fundamentals, proceed to engage in startled discussion as if no previous philosophic thoughts had ever been uttered. Rest and motion, change and permanence, absolutism and relativity, individuality and universality, the one and the many—everywhere these opposites recur, in the latest theory of Einstein as in the ancient puzzles of Zeno, in ethics as in physics. The caution which Morris R. Cohen has called the 'principle of polarity' is always relevant to remind us that these 'opposite categories . . . must always be kept together though never identified.'[59] Physical science knows that physical action is not possible without resistance or reaction, that protoplasm cannot live except by continually dying. Physical science makes progress by eliminating the vagueness of popular contrasting categories like *hot* and *cold* and substituting definite degrees of temperature. In legal discussion, too, we must avoid the uncritical grasping of simple alternatives and assume the difficult burden of finding the proper distinctions and qualifications.[60]

In that compromise which may be called 'radical conservatism' lies Cardozo's position—conservatism in the sense of conserving what criticism reveals as good; radical because, in the pristine sense of the word, it seeks to go to the roots. Those who are used to the old and tried ways might insist on stressing rather more his radicalism. His frequent appearance as a leader in the advance of law, his critical attitude

59. Morris R.Cohen, *Reason and Nature* (Harcourt, Brace, New York, 1931) Preface xi.
60. *Ibid.*165–6.

toward legal methods, his faithful stand among the liberals on the Supreme Court bench, and his lone dissent in the 'Hot Oil' case,[61] suggest primary emphasis on his departures. Labels are bromides and there is no point in quarrelling about them. But it is to be noted that his starting point is still precedent. Certainty is still a cardinal legal objective for him. Internal legal coherence has a substantial place in his view. Compared to Jerome Frank or Thurman Arnold, roaring realists,[62] he moves slowly. These facts warn us not to exaggerate as revolutionary his urge toward reconstruction.[63]

'What has once been settled by a precedent,' he affirms, 'will not be unsettled over night, for certainty and uniformity are gains not lightly to be sacrificed. Above all is this true when honest men have shaped their conduct upon the faith of the pronouncement.'

61. Panama Refining Co. v. Ryan, 293 U.S.388,433 (1935).
62. See Frank, *Law and the Modern Mind*; Thurman W.Arnold, *The Symbols of Government* (Yale University Press, New Haven, 1935) and *The Folklore of Capitalism* (Yale University Press, New Haven, 1937).
63. 'After a realistic huddle and a functional hunch,' writes a satirist of the newer movements in law, 'our younger law teachers and students decide to give up the dogmas of legal theology, bid adieu to Cardozo, Brandeis, Dean Pound, Beale, Williston and Wigmore, defenders of tradition and precedent in varying degree.' Kennedy, 'Functional Nonsense and the Transcendental Approach' (1936) 5 *Fordham L.Rev.* 272,281–2.
    Speaking of the most recent critics of legal method, Cardozo has said: 'I do, indeed, discover here and there an accent of contempt for the old ideals of symmetry and order,—a note of mere derision as if they had been supplanted altogether, made obsolete and futile by a new organon and method; but the accent and the note are not, to my thinking, of the essence of the movement.' Address, 55 *Report of New York State Bar Association* 27.
    'Certainty and regularity,' he affirms, 'have at least a presumption in their favor. They show us the well-worn ways, and as in conduct generally, so in law, what we have done in the past, we are likely to continue to do till the shock of a perturbing force is strong enough to jolt us out of the rut.' *Ibid.*284.

But see how quickly he adds, 'On the other hand, conformity is not to be turned into a fetich.'[64]

Rest and motion (or, as we mean it here, stability and progress) are not equally opposed, for the motion is 'moderated and tempered by the immemorial traditions of a professional technique,'[65] in the same way that any craftsman is limited by his roots, his materials, his co-workers, and the conditions of his work. In fact, it is the powerful and watchful presence of this tradition—though this point is not stressed by Cardozo—which affords a safeguard against arbitrary behaviour on the part of a judge who is not in the thrall of past doctrine. No judge could long defy, if his professional conscience allowed him to reach that far, the concerted disapproval of the trained bar. There is an institutional check on judicial tyranny.

Often there is more than one conflict to resolve and each specific situation is so tangled in its complexity that, in desperation, one might be tempted to adopt an *ad hoc* approach entirely, treating each case on its own merits only. But there can be no doubt that for Cardozo a search for basic underlying principles must continue. Indeed, the mathematician, whose treatment of principles can proceed with a smoother, surer hand, is an object of his envy.[66]

But there is equally little doubt that the sources of law are to be found beyond the leather-bound books. They are to be found beyond the mere pronouncements of judges and legislatures. They are to be found in the seething life of the people, in their actual doings, their ways of behaving. These are also a source of ethics, but ethics is the wider classification embracing law. There comes a time when law must give effect, by

64. Cardozo, *The Paradoxes of Legal Science*, 29–30.
65. *Ibid.*56, *cf.*59.
66. *Ibid.*1,80.

PHILOSOPHY AND LAW   31

means of its own powerful sanctions, to what ethics has wrought. Indeed, if a lawyer could reasonably predict that a court of law would so act with respect to some rule of conduct, Cardozo would go so far as to call that rule, itself, law.

'Now, personally, I prefer to give the label law to a much larger assembly of social facts than would have that label affixed to them by many of the neo-realists. I find lying around loose, and ready to be embodied into a judgment according to some process of selection to be practiced by a judge, a vast conglomeration of principles and rules and usages and moralities. If these are so established as to justify a prediction with reasonable certainty that they will have the backing of the courts in the event that their authority is challenged, I say that they are law . . .'[67]

He quotes with approval an English judge who said:

'It would not be correct to say that every moral obligation involves a legal duty; but every legal duty is founded on a moral obligation. A legal common law duty is nothing else than the enforcing by law of that which is a moral obligation without legal enforcement.'[68]

The particular case from which this quotation is drawn involved a peculiar challenge to the old doctrine that, barring a special duty of protection, one may stand by and see another perish, though there would be no peril in undertaking a rescue. The decision moves a little in the direction of the good Samaritan. Centuries after Christ, the English common law, (that great body of law which has grown up through the decisions of judges rather than acts of the legislature) grows critical of stony indifference on the part of a bystander and in

67. Cardozo, Address, 55 *Report of New York State Bar Association* 276. See also *The Growth of the Law*, 33-4,52.
68. Lord Coleridge, C.J. in Queen v. Instan (1893) I Q.B.450; quoted in *The Paradoxes of Legal Science*, 26, f.n.58.

one grave instance discovers a legal duty to help. When opportunity affords and an ethical trend is clear, persistent, sound, and widespread, Cardozo will, in the absence of strong counter factors, seek thus to bring the law into accord with morals. He is the very opposite of the juiceless legalist. As the opinions herein collected exhibit, he is the exponent of a living law. The justice of the law, as he conceives it, marches to the time of community-justice when its trumpets sound loud and steady.

II
DOING JUSTICE

My lawyer tells me, returned he, that I have Salkeld and Ventris strong in my favor, and that there are no less than fifteen cases in point. 'I understand,' said I, 'those are two of your judges who have already declared their opinion.' Pardon me, replied my friend, Salkeld and Ventris are lawyers who some hundred years ago gave their opinions on cases similar to mine; these opinions which make for me my lawyer is to cite, and those opinions which look another way are cited by the lawyer employed by my antagonist: as I observed, I have Salkeld and Ventris for me, he has Coke and Hales for him, and he that hath most opinions is most likely to carry his cause. 'But where is the necessity,' cried I, 'of prolonging a suit by citing the opinions and reports of others, since the same good sense which determined lawyers in former ages may serve to guide your judges at this day? They at that time gave their opinions only from the light of reason: your judges have the same light at present to direct them, let me even add a greater, as in former ages there were many prejudices from which the present is happily free. If arguing from authorities be exploded from every other branch of learning, why should it be particularly adhered to in this? I plainly foresee how such a method of investigation must embarrass every suit, and even perplex the student: ceremonies will be multiplied, formalities must increase, and more time will thus be spent in learning the arts of litigation than in the discovery of right.'

Oliver Goldsmith,
The Citizen of the World or *Letters from A Chinese Philosopher Residing in London to his Friends in the East.* Letter XCVIII (1762).

II

DOING JUSTICE

IN *The Nature of the Judicial Process*, which appeared in 1922, Cardozo began to present his thoughts on ways of legal development. His ideas were elaborated in *The Growth of the Law*, which was published in 1924, while more philosophic analysis emerged four years later in *The Paradoxes of Legal Science*.

It was as though he had leaned back and focused into clear awareness and generality of statement the ultimate bases and elements of technique marking his daily routine on the bench. Being no detached critic, but already an experienced judge, he was, of course, engaged in no mere academic study. It was a philosophic effort to help himself and his colleagues of bench and bar to do their work more understandingly and effectively. An unexamined profession, he might have paraphrased Socrates, is not worth pursuing. At the same time he was revealing to the public the inside workings of law. Ten years after the appearance of his first book, in an address in which he sought to bring his views into line with the writings of the neo-realists, he confessed:

'If I have not lost the road altogether, if my feet have not sunk in a quagmire of unco-ordinated precedents, I owe it not a little to the signposts and the warnings, the barriers and the bridges, which my study of the judicial process has built along the way.'[1]

1. Cardozo, Address, 55 *Report of New York State Bar Association* 307. This address, together with Cardozo's three books, his essays collected

What Cardozo calls the 'judicial process' is one which every lawyer must master. The skilful lawyer by his brief and argument may swerve in his direction the line of a judge's decision. The well-prepared lawyer often finds opportunity to instruct the judge. To the extent that, in general, he knows how much and how strategically to lean on the various factors described by Cardozo, a lawyer is so much the more assured of success. A trained capacity to estimate these factors facilitates his arrival at a sound opinion (*i.e.*, prediction) on the law in a complicated matter.

Of course, the greatest part of a lawyer's work is office work which never reaches a court and often has no direct reference to a trial.

'In the literature of the law there has been a tendency to underestimate the importance of the role that is played by the office adviser, not merely in keeping his client out of jail or in avoiding civil liability, but even in shaping and directing the institutions of the law itself. He is much more than a traffic officer, warning of obstructions and keeping travellers to the travelled path. He is a creative agent just as truly as the advocate or the judge. In our complex economic life, new problems call from day to day for new methods and new devices. The lawyer in his office formulates a trust receipt, or stock certificate with novel incidents, or bonds, municipal or corporate, with privileges or safeguards till then unknown to the business world. . . . The courts do no more than set the *imprimatur* of regularity upon methods that have had an origin

in *Law and Literature* [see footnote 39, chapter I] and his opinions in the New York Court of Appeals and the United States Supreme Court should be chiefly consulted for a fuller presentation of the Justice's views than is possible or desirable in a selective appraisal and critique.

in the creative activity of an adviser, working independently
of courts in the quiet of an office.'[2]

Even when the first motions leading toward a trial are commenced, one side or the other usually surrenders after no more
than a series of grimaces. But Cardozo's writings, flowing
from his appellate court experience as counsel and judge, are
concerned with the rationale of that phase of law work with
which the youthful aspirant to the bar and the general public
naturally associate the process of law: a case in the courts.

'I feel quite certain,' he writes, 'that it is the court, and not
the office, that is the attraction for ambitious youth. The
struggle for justice would lose its zest if law could be turned,
as I believe medicine is turning in some degree, into a pro-
phylactic science ordered with such nicety that litigation
would become as catastrophic as the plague.'[3]

Emphatic attention to justice in the work of the courts is
critically imperative today, not for the sake of the word's
emotive value, of course, but operationally to denote the
responsibility of law to ethics. The cynical slant of recent
jurisprudence has led to a scorn of 'justice' as too loose and
hazy a concept, one by which a court ought not be beguiled.

'I have said to my brethren many times that I hate justice,'
Holmes remarked in a letter to Dr. Wu, 'which means that I
know if a man begins to talk about that, for one reason or
another he is shirking thinking in legal terms.'[4]

As to which general attitude Cardozo has entered the
caveat:

2. Cardozo, Memorial of John D.Milburn, *Yearbook* 1931 *Association of
   the Bar of the City of New York* (New York, 1931) 439–40.
3. 'The Comradeship of the Bar,' *Law and Literature*, 181–2.
4. Letter to Dr. John C.H.Wu, 1 July 1929, Shriver (ed.), *Justice Oliver
   Wendell Holmes: His Book Notices and Uncollected Letters and Papers*,
   201.

'The constant insistence that morality and justice are not law, has tended to breed distrust and contempt of law as something to which morality and justice are not merely alien, but hostile.'[5]

It has been said that under Cardozo the Court of Appeals ceased to be a court of law and became a court of justice.[6] Surely there is less wit in this remark than there is cause for anxiety that such a transformation might be said to have been necessary. It is true that pompous talk about justice can cover a multitude of sins, especially in a society in which, critics are quick to point out, the forms of democracy often conceal the power of some oligarchical group. But the high-minded judge, who is aware of the realities of the situation and concerned to right them, is liberated and directed by Cardozo's view of the place of justice in the judicial process. For fruitful results the objectivity and expertness, the *frankness* and *functionalism* of the cynical realist must be made significant by an awareness of the ends to be attained and of how to arrive at worthy ends.

If such be our concern and perspective, we turn favourably disposed to a critical examination of the judge as law-maker and of Cardozo's account of the ways of doing justice.

5. Cardozo, *The Nature of the Judicial Process*, 134. See also Llewellyn: 'I have said before that this tendency of our teaching has caused me worry, in its aspect as developing the technician at the cost of the whole man. It gives me double pause in this connection—in its effect on young men already disillusioned beyond the portion of young men.' Llewellyn, *The Bramble Bush* (Tentatively printed for the use of students at Columbia University School of Law, New York, 1930) 128. *Cf.* Milton, who speaks of 'some allured to the trade of law, grounding their purposes not in the prudent and heavenly contemplation of justice and equity, which was never taught them, but on the promising and pleasing thoughts of litigious terms, fat contentions, and flowing fees.' John Milton, essay 'Of Education.'
6. 'You may chain the law down with all manner of clamps and bonds. The wizard Justice has a queer way of setting the victim free.' Cardozo, *The Paradoxes of Legal Science*, 27–8.

A Dying Myth

ONE of the conventional myths about law—akin to the other widely held notions that law is certain and clearly defined and that our government is one of laws not men—is that only the legislature makes the law. Every lawyer knows, even though it may not always be clear to the client, that in the pseudo-science of law we deal with predictions in a mist of contingent, equivocal, and doubtful elements. Every lawyer knows that, though ours is not professedly, as in China, a government by 'gentlemen' unrestricted by law, the personal equation enters at every point.[7] So too it is apparent to a sophisticated observer that Francis Bacon was calling for the impossible in the opening sentence of his essay 'Of Judicature':

'Judges ought to remember that their office is *jus dicere*, and not *jus dare*; to interpret law, and not make law, or give law.'

The very fact that Bacon felt obliged to give the warning would lead us to suspect, even had we not known of his rivalry with Lord Coke,[8] that there were vigorous judges in those days too. Indeed, even the more acquiescent judge makes law, for in resting upon past decided law, he has made the decision to align with the already-done, to use his power to remake the law in its own image. As Thomas Reed Powell remarked of the United States Supreme Court, it does what it prefers to do when it prefers to do as nearly as possible what it has done before. Any one glancing at a long succession of decisions (even decisions interpreting statutes) over a period

7. See Howard Lee McBain, *The Living Constitution* (Workers Education Bureau Press, 1927) 3–6.
8. See Cuthbert William Johnson, *The Life of Sir Edward Coke* (second edition, volume I, Henry Colburn, London, 1845) 150ff.,284ff.

of years in a particular field could see at once that the judge's
work in an appellate court has an essentially creative element.
Still the myth that judges merely *announce* what the law 'is'
has persisted down to our own day, even though Dicey,
Gray, Corbin, and M.R.Cohen exposed it decades ago.[9]

Note for its conventionality (without considering whether
or not the judge was right) the recent statement in a decision
granting an injunction:

'*This court* has previously stated *he* must take the law as *he*
finds the law, and *he* must interpret and follow that law. If
there is to be a change in the laws it is legislative function to
make those changes, and *the court* perforce must follow the
mandates of the Legislature relative thereto, but *the court*
cannot legislate, *the court* can but interpret and enforce.'[10]

9. A.V.Dicey, *Law and Public Opinion in England* (Macmillan, New
York, 1905) 359ff.; John Chipman Gray, *The Nature and Sources of
Law* (Macmillan, New York, first edition 1909; second edition 1927)
93–101; Arthur L Corbin, 'The Law and the Judges' (1914) 3 *Yale
Review* 235; Morris R.Cohen, 'The Process of Judicial Legislation,'
Law and the Social Order 112. [The major part of this essay was read
at the first meeting of the Conference on Legal and Social Philosophy,
26 April 1913, and published under this title in 48 *American Law Review* (1914) 161. Portions of the essay are taken from a paper presented
at the thirty-eighth annual meeting of the New York State Bar Association, 22–3 January 1915, and published under the title 'Legal Theories
and Social Science' in 25 *International Journal of Ethics* (1915) 469.]
10. Gadola, J., *New York Times*, 3 February 1937. Author's italics to indicate also how in the same sentence this Michigan judge slips from
the impersonal cloak to the personal pronoun.
The conventional view is thus well described by Jerome Frank:
'Law is a complete body of rules existing from time immemorial
and unchangeable except to the limited extent that legislatures have
changed the rules by enacted statutes. Legislatures are expressly em-
powered thus to change the law. But the judges are not to make or
change the law but to apply it. The law, ready-made, pre-exists the
judicial decisions.
'Judges are simply "living oracles" of law. They are merely "the
speaking law." Their function is purely passive. They are "but the
mouth which pronounces the law." They no more make or invent new
law than Columbus made or invented America. Judicial opinions are
evidence of what the law is; the best evidence, but no more than that.

Several reasons for the persistence of the myth that judges do not make law have been advanced and discussed:

1. For a simple routine case some rule can often be found to govern. What is overlooked is that the important case is usually out of the ordinary; and that a previous rule rarely, if ever, *precisely* governs.

2. The division of power—legislative, executive, judicial—in our form of government is said to necessitate judicial impotence to legislate. But this division is not absolute. The framers of the Constitution gave the president a share in legislation through his veto power and the Senate a share in executive appointments through the power of confirming them. The executive now makes detailed laws in the form of departmental regulations, and the legislature, by controlling appropriations, determines many an executive policy. Through the power of determining what is a reasonable return on an investment in public utility cases, judges practically fix gas and railway rates.

3. The abhorrence of *ex post facto* law—law which though made today is extended to govern a past happening—leads to

When a former decision is overruled, we must not say that the rule announced in the earlier decision was once the law and has now been changed by the later decision. We must view the earlier decision as laying down an erroneous rule. It was a false map of the law—just as a pre-Columbian map of the world was false. Emphatically, we must not refer to the new decision as making new law. It only seems to do so. It is merely a bit of revised legal cartography.

'If a judge actually attempted to contrive a new rule, he would be guilty of usurpation of power, for the legislature alone has the authority to change the law. The judges, writes Blackstone, are "not delegated to pronounce a new law, but to maintain and expound the old law"; even when a former decision is abandoned because "most evidently contrary to reason," the "subsequent judges do not pretend to make new law, but to vindicate the old one from misrepresentation." The prior judge's eyesight had been defective and he made "a mistake" in finding the law, which mistake is now being rectified by his successors.' Frank, *Law and the Modern Mind*, 32–3.

an unwillingness to admit the fact of judicial legislation. For the parties involved such law is indeed retroactive.[11] But 'in the vast majority of cases the retrospective effect of judge-made law is felt either to involve no hardship or only such hardship as is inevitable where no rule has been declared.'[12]

4. The Puritan view of human nature, that man is a sinner not to be entrusted with great power, ran through our early institutions.[13]

5. A man rarely grows fully emancipated from his youthful dependence upon his father. According to a suggested application of Freudian theory, a source of unquestioned authority similar to the parent is found in the law. The feeling is engendered that the law is something fixed, absolute, and unwavering, like the wisdom ascribed to its father by the child. The judge's sole task is supposed to be to announce this law.[14]

6. Especially when a judgment is difficult or harsh, judges are comforted by the feeling that they have authorities upon which they are really leaning to support their decisions.[15]

7. The prestige of the courts is better maintained, in the face of results which must always displease at least one of the parties, if litigants are hoodwinked into thinking that the judge himself is merely a creature of the law performing its behests.

Despite such reasons Holmes bluntly remarked twenty years ago: 'I recognize without hesitation that judges do and

11. Gray, *The Nature and Sources of Law*, 99–100.
12. Cardozo, *The Nature of the Judicial Process*, 146. 'I think it is significant,' he adds, 'that when the hardship is felt to be too great or to be unnecessary, retrospective operation is withheld.' *Ibid.*146–7.
13. See Pound, *The Spirit of the Common Law*, 55–6. For a fuller consideration of these four reasons and other phases of this problem, see M.R.Cohen, 'The Process of Judicial Legislation,' *Law and the Social Order*, 112–15.
14. *Cf.* Frank, *Law and the Modern Mind*, 13–21.
15. *Cf.* Walton H.Hamilton, 'Judicial Process,' 9 *Encyclopedia of the Social Sciences* (Macmillan, New York, 1932) 454.

must legislate, but,' he took pains to add in a famous qualifying phrase, 'they can do so only interstitially; they are confined from molar to molecular motions.'[16] There are times when even the most liberal judge will feel that he should consign a needed change, when it is drastic, to the attention of the legislature. An interesting development which can be traced through three tort opinions which Cardozo wrote, and in which he finally reached a point where he would go no further, illustrates when the judge may feel obligated to stop short and refer an evil to the legislature. In *MacPherson* v. *Buick Motor Company*,[17] Cardozo forcefully extended an earlier New York trend, and held the Buick Company liable to an *ultimate buyer* for injuries caused by a defective wheel. A few years later in *Glanzer* v. *Shepard*,[18] a public weigher was requested by a seller to submit a copy of the finding of weight to a buyer for his use. In reliance thereon the buyer overpaid. The actual weight was less than the weight certified and the weigher was held responsible to the buyer.[19] These brief summaries, though they do not do justice to these cases, serve our purpose, and now we come to *Ultramares Corporation* v. *Touche, Niven & Co.*[20] Here a public accountant firm was asked to prepare and certify a balance sheet, which the firm knew was to be shown to potential creditors. Cardozo declined to hold the accountants liable to the *creditors* for the negligence of an honest blunder. Such an extension of liability he pointed out, 'will so expand the field of liability for negligent speech as to make it nearly, if not quite, coterminous with that of liability for fraud. . . . Many pages of opinion

16. Holmes, J., Southern Pacific Co. v. Jensen, 244 U.S.205,221 (1917).
17. 217 N.Y.382, 111 N.E.1050 (1916).
18. 233 N.Y.236, 135 N.E.275 (1922).
19. See also International Products Company v. Erie Railroad Company, 244 N.Y.331, 155 N.E.662 (1927).
20. 255 N.Y.170, 174 N.E.441 (1931).

were written by judges the most eminent, yet the word was never spoken. We may not speak it now. A change so revolutionary, if expedient, must be wrought by legislation . . .'[21]

When the judge is faced with a Constitutional provision or a statute which is clear, it is his bounden duty to follow it, subordinating a statute to a Constitutional clause. If there is doubt about the meaning, as so often there is, the judge employs certain techniques of statutory and Constitutional construction.[22] These constitute a subject of the greatest importance which is, however, outside the scope of our present study.

An example of judicial limitation, of subservience to statutory law, is found in *Doyle* v. *Hofstader et al.*, *Constituting Legislative Committee.* Doyle refused to testify before the investigating committee, of which Samuel Seabury was counsel, concerning bribes he was alleged to have made. This was in due accordance with the privilege against self-incrimination granted by the Constitution. But counsel for the committee contended that an act of the legislature granted immunity from prosecution to those so testifying. Despite the strong feeling which the press had aroused, Cardozo's court declined to read this statute as wide enough to protect Doyle against prosecution for a mere *conspiracy* to bribe, and thus the court justified the refusal to answer questions concerning a conspiracy. Said Cardozo:

'We are not unmindful of the public interests, of the insistent hope and need that the way of bribers and corruptionists

---

21. 255 N.Y.170,185–7, 174 N.E.441,447. The author is not necessarily concurring in Cardozo's opinion here or elsewhere when illustrations are given. It is no part of his purpose to criticize Cardozo's cases as to the conclusion which they reach, but only to use them to indicate a type of approach and technique and theory of judicial method.
22. See Henry Glass & Co. v. Misroch, 239 N.Y.475, 147 N.E.71 (1925) and Tauza v. Susquehanna Coal Company, 220 N.Y.259, 115 N.E.915 (1917); reprinted in full *infra* at pp.258 and 272 respectively.

shall be exposed to an indignant world. Commanding as these interests are, they do not supply us with a license to palter with the truth or to twist what has been written into the statutes into something else that we should like to see. Historic liberties and privileges are not to bend from day to day "because of some accident of immediate overwhelming interest which appeals to the feelings and distorts the judgment" (HOLMES, J., in *Northern Securities Co.* v. *United States*, 193 U.S.197,400), are not to change their form and content in response to the "hydraulic pressure" (HOLMES, J., *supra*) exerted by great causes. A community whose judges would be willing to give it whatever law might gratify the impulse of the moment would find in the end that it had paid too high a price for relieving itself of the bother of awaiting a session of the Legislature and the enactment of a statute in accordance with established forms.'[23]

In most of his discussion of method, however, Cardozo's mind is on the situation where no statute governs and a judge may truly go one road or another, or hew a new path. His conscientious candour has led him, more than any other judge, to dwell at length on the judge as law-maker. He is mainly interested in the cases on the border where ground is broken.

'These are the cases,' he declares 'that have a maximum of interest for the student of legal methods. These are the cases in which neo-realism, as I view it, has its maximum of truth and also its maximum of utility. It is here that mere logic or consistency, though never negligible forces, have a minimum of compulsion.'[24]

23. 257 N.Y.244,268, 177 N.E.489,498 (1931); reprinted in full *infra* p.279.
24. Cardozo, Address, 55 *Report of New York State Bar Association* 278.

These cases constitute a much narrower area than need be when once judges grow more aware of the powers that they exercise willy-nilly, and when once they become more accustomed to a direct and deliberate facing of their problem. We have reason to expect, partly as a result of Cardozo's realistic analysis, that this process of growth will be speeded.

How important it is that we should have a more rational and realistic judicial procedure becomes clear when we consider that, in Harold Laski's words:

'In England and America . . . what is called, and rightly, judge-made law probably covers an area wider than that of statute; and, in America, the fact that all legislatures are non-sovereign in character, since their authority is derived from written constitutions which they cannot change, gives to the judges who interpret those constitutions, as in cases where the authority either of a statute or an executive is challenged, a power that is greater than that of the legislature itself, since the judicial will is the chief factor in deciding the limits of legislative competence.'[25]

'Standing on' Precedent

DOES the common law proceed by induction, drawing conclusions from many instances, or by deduction, following out the implications of general principles? The question is an idle one.[26] Without certain general ideas from which to start, the judge, like any other thinker, would be groping in a maze. If he failed to check these ideas against the legal sources in the reports of cases or in social behaviour, he would become the

25. Harold J.Laski, *Politics* (J.P.Lippincott, Philadelphia and London, 1931) 85–6.
26. See Cardozo, Address, 55 *Report of New York State Bar Association* 286, 306; *The Growth of the Law*, 91.

victim of irresponsible fancies. In his first book Cardozo tells us that the method of the common law is inductive. At the same time, he avers that back of the precedents from which conclusions are drawn are the 'basic juridical conceptions which are the postulates of judicial reasoning,'[27]—conceptions like 'contract,' 'ownership,' 'possession,' 'testament.' Though he does not inquire where these come from,[28] it is clear that they are a starting point for deriving various consequences.

More attention could profitably be devoted to a critical re-examination of such concepts. If 'property' is analysed, its essential nature as a form of control or sovereignty—as the power to exclude—emerges. The tendency in our law to extend the public interest in private property then becomes more intelligible and defensible.[29] Some concept, if not 'contract,' would always be required to cover the relations into which men enter in that area where the government has not fully determined their relations. But the distinctions between property and contract, as well as liberty, coercion, and sovereignty, are not hard and fast. These categories overlap in mutual interdependence. To have a right under a contract (which means someone else has a duty toward you) is to have property which can be traded at some future date, if not now. To have property is to possess a greater liberty to do things you could not otherwise do. You may now exercise sovereignty over others who are coerced into acting as you wish them to—into selling you something, say, or into working for you, or otherwise deferring to your wishes—in order that they may procure a share of what you have.[30]

27. Cardozo, *The Nature of the Judicial Process*, 19.
28. *Ibid*.47–8.
29. *Cf.* Helvering v. Davis, 301 U.S.619 (1937); reprinted in full *infra* p.300, and People ex rel. Lehigh Valley R.Co. v. State Tax Commission, 247 N.Y.9, 159 N.E.703 (1928); reprinted in full *infra* p.235.
30. Robert L.Hale's early analysis, 'Coercion and Distribution in a Sup-

Such concepts being given for the judge to operate with, the first thing which he does, according to Cardozo and according to popular notions, is to compare the case before him with the precedents. Not that he will necessarily follow the precedents, but that they are to be regarded as having an initial persuasion in the absence of more peremptory factors.[31] From the precedents is distilled an underlying principle (*ratio decidendi*).[32] Here already the judge's discrimination has entered. Certainly thereafter, in the critical step of choosing the direction along which the principle is to move, ample scope for selective emphasis is afforded. There are four lines of directive force which are available. Cardozo calls them the methods of *philosophy* (symmetry),[33] *history*, *custom*, and *sociology* (ethics).[34] We must consider each in turn.

Cardozo opens with a discussion of the method of philosophy, not because it is most important but because it has the 'primacy that comes from natural and orderly and logical succession.'[35] This succession is achieved by extending a principle to new cases which are within the bounds of its 'unifying capacity.' The method is the commonplace one thrice familiar to lawyers. Its essence, in Cardozo's words, is 'the derivation of a consequence from a rule or a principle or

posedly Non-Coercive State' (1923) 38 *Pol.Sci.Q.*470, cuts under the surface with rare insight and thoroughness.
31. Cardozo, *The Nature of the Judicial Process*, 20.
32. This use of the term *ratio decidendi* is not the common use. It usually means the rule which the court has laid down for the case as the ground upon which the court rested its decision. It may be that Cardozo thinks there is no distinction between that use and his, but there seems to the author to be a crucial carry-over in which the judge's own judgment may significantly enter.
   For a discussion of technical refinements pertaining to the multipoint decision, see Llewellyn, *The Bramble Bush*, 40.
33. Term in parentheses author's.
34. Term in parentheses author's.
35. Cardozo, *The Nature of the Judicial Process*, 31.

a precedent which, accepted as a datum, contains implicitly within itself the germ of the conclusion.'[36] There are previous cases somewhat like the case to be decided. The principle underlying them is said (or made) to cover the case in question. The relation may vary from remote analogy to strict logical development.

Further analysis would have to distinguish sharply between precedents, rules, principles, *dicta*, and holdings. But this rough description suffices here. It will be apparent from the point of view we are here developing that 'symmetry' would be a more appropriate designation for this method than 'philosophy,' if philosophy is thought of as the 'love of wisdom.'

The *structural goal* of this method is an ordered legal system. That end is a desirable one for whatever continuity or definiteness it affords (much less, as we shall see, than is commonly supposed) but, in the last analysis, it is an aesthetic end. It reflects the concern of a legal craftsman to assemble his materials into a pattern. If this symmetry of the legal corpus were to be more widely recognized and avowed as the structural objective of this method, we should be in a better position to regard it in its proper, subordinated status. We should more easily be able to free ourselves from its tight hold, long-standing and inbred. Cardozo admits that the method has its inspiration in the 'yearning for consistency, for certainty, for uniformity of plan and structure'; its roots in 'the constant striving of the mind for a larger and more inclusive unity, in which differences will be reconciled, and abnormalities will vanish.'[37]

From the point of view of pure theory, in which lawyers have had all too little interest, an ideally unified and compre-

36. *Ibid.*49.
37. *Ibid.*50.

hensive pattern is an admirable goal. But even among philosophers of science there is much recent reservation as to whether the importance of a complete theoretical system has not been over-stressed. In a quasi-science like law, the need for attention to the social grounds and equities of the particular case and its consequences, even at the expense of consistency and internal order, is even more urgent. That modern trend which we have described as *individuality* has particular point. But there is a difficulty encountered in trying to attend to the idiosyncracies of the particular case, as in making treatment fit the criminal, not the crime. People expect equality from the law. Their feelings are violated if A receives one penalty and B another for the same illegal act. In the salutary effort increasingly to respect this phase of the trend of *individuality*, we must not lose sight of the 'principle of polarity' which applies here also.

Cardozo gladly concedes that this method of symmetry should yield to others when the situation demands it. He urges clearer recognition and wider adoption of other methods. The extent to which these various methods are to be preferred is a problem which runs through the centre of discussion of legal method, constituting the chief issue of current debate.[38] While no definitive or systematic solution can be given, we need not abandon in despair all consideration of the problem which might yield insight and direction.

When we look not at the structural goal, but at the *processes* of this method (this distinction is not made by Cardozo), we see that the method is indispensable as the means of transportation by which judges and lawyers know how to get around in the sprawling, but withal inter-related, legal 'sys-

38. *Cf.* Cardozo, Address, 55 *Report of New York State Bar Association* 277–8.

tem.' There is no thought of abandoning the method. The effort is only to erase its sillier, wooden, mechanical features; at the same time to become more aware of its elasticity; and, finally, more willing to subordinate to more vital considerations the conclusions to which it brings us.

Within the method itself, there is far more flexibility than is customarily supposed. It is regrettable that an innovator like Cardozo, in adhering to the traditional language and concepts of 'precedent' and *stare decisis* (which means 'standing on precedent'), should at the same time affirm: '*Stare decisis* is at least the everyday working rule of our law.'[39] Such a statement obscures the power for change present even in our orthodox procedure. A subsequent case is rarely *exactly* like a previous one. And any previous rule may be held to its naked meaning or extended to the extreme of its intimations. Before the judge has even abstracted a rule from a prior case, he may decide to limit the opinion in this prior case to its precise holding on its peculiar facts or he may go to the length of regarding a strong *obiter dictum* (remark about the law, not strictly relevant, made in passing) as a ground for the decision, and a principle on which to lean. We are dealing with several precedents none of which is commonly on all fours. Any precedent, in company with other related precedents, can be forced into a phalanx driving to one objective or another. We discern a *ratio decidendi* which may potentially move in any one of several varied directions. Is it not idle, in these circumstances, to suppose that the ancient 'analogical' procedure of the common law is hard and fast; that the processes of judge-made law do violence to that method; and that every change through judicial legislation is an aban-

39. Cardozo, *The Nature of the Judicial Process*, 20. *Cf*. Address, 55 *Report of New York State Bar Association* 274.

donment of precedent, a defiance of *stare decisis*, a torture of
'the' *ratio decidendi* involved?

To be sure, there are rare instances in the books, and doubtless in the service of *frankness* and directness they ought to
increase, when the court will find, especially in Constitutional
law where the court's authority is so final, that it wants to
make a clean sweep and depart from a previous trend as
sharply as Copernicus remade the view of an earth-centred
universe.

'I think that when a rule, after it has been duly tested by
experience, has been found to be inconsistent with the sense
of justice or with the social welfare, there should be less hesitation in frank avowal and full abandonment,'[40] says Cardozo.

In the case of *Klein* v. *Maravelas*, the constitutionality of a
state statute, the so-called sales in bulk law, was at issue. In
Wright v. *Hart*, ten years earlier, a substantially similar act
had been held to be unconstitutional. Said Cardozo bluntly:

'We think it is our duty to hold that the decision in *Wright*
v. *Hart* is wrong. The unanimous or all but unanimous voice
of the judges of the land, in federal and state courts alike, has
upheld the constitutionality of these laws. At the time of our
decision in *Wright* v. *Hart*, such laws were new and strange.
They were thought in the prevailing opinion to represent the
fitful prejudices of the hour. . . . The fact is that they have
come to stay, and like laws may be found on the statute books
of every state. . . . The one jurisdiction in which such
statutes remain invalid is Utah . . . , and there the adverse
judgment was rendered many years ago.

'In such circumstances we can no longer say, whatever past
views may have been, that the prohibitions of this statute are
arbitrary and purposeless restrictions upon liberty of con-

40. Cardozo, *The Nature of the Judicial Process*, 150.

tract. . . . The needs of successive generations may make restrictions imperative today which were vain and capricious to the vision of times past . . . Back of this legislation, which to a majority of the judges who decided *Wright* v. *Hart* seemed arbitrary and purposeless, there must have been a real need. We can see this now, even though it may have been obscure before. Our past decisions ought not to stand in opposition to the uniform convictions of the entire judiciary of the land. Least of all should it stand when rendered by a closely divided court against the earnest protest of distinguished judges. Indeed, in a later case . . . we stated with the concurrence of all the members of the court, that the authority of *Wright* v. *Hart* had been shaken, though the case did not call upon us to determine whether it was still the law. We cannot say today in the face of such overwhelming authority, that the presumption of validity which attaches to every act of legislation has been overcome. The present statute is similar in essentials to the one condemned in 1905. In details it may be distinguished from the earlier one, but the details are in reality trifling. We cannot without a sacrifice of candor rest our judgment upon them. We think we ought not to do so. We should adopt the argument and the conclusion of the dissenting judges in *Wright* v. *Hart*, and affirm the validity of the statute on which the plaintiff builds his rights.'[41]

Ordinarily, however, the traditional techniques, if we are adroit in their use, allow sufficient leeway within circumscribed bounds. In any case the judge must decide where he wants to come out, however much prestidigitation of precedents may tend to conceal that fact. The implications of failure to face this fact have been pointed out by no one more forcefully than by Llewellyn:

41. Klein v. Maravelas, 219 N.Y. 383, 385-7, 114 N.E. 809, 810 (1916).

'A decision on policy remains inescapable, because the precedents are multiform, ambiguous, *never* fixed; and because the tradition-hallowed techniques for dealing with them (*wholly within the "principle" of stare decisis*) permit you to squeeze out of the same set of precedents any one of a dozen *different* conclusions or rules. The only thing gained by pretending that to abide by precedent is to cut out questions of policy is, on occasion, the saving of effort and the evasion of responsibility as you make a blind decision on policy instead of an intelligent one. But the effort is effort which should not be saved, and the responsibility is responsibility which it is the judge's job to face. Wise choice of policy is his function.

'I do not of course mean that judges are free. I mean that the leeway which strict "adherence to precedent" has always allowed is infinitely greater than the current conscious ideology (in contradistinction to the standard going judicial practices) gives any inkling of. The result is that we profit by the leeway only some of the time, not all; we profit therefore by the judges' wisdom on whether to change or not and if so, in what direction, only some of the time, not all. But once the leeway is seen, once demonstrated from the *work* of respected courts with precedents to be *constantly* present, it may be hoped, sooner or later, to make the conscious facing of the policy questions difficult to escape. It may be hoped, even, to lessen word-juggling in the opinions by lessening the pretense that the precedents are firm and sure. Word-juggling becomes unnecessary when judges *know* what they have been doing.'[42]

In his latest thoughts on the doctrine of *stare decisis*, Car-

---

42. Llewellyn, 'Legal Tradition and Social Science Method—A Realist's Critique,' *Essays on Research in the Social Sciences* (Brookings, Washington, 1931) 108 f.n. Italics his.

dozo has distinguished between two limitations of the doctrine: present limitations and those limitations which seem imminent for the future in terms of bringing legal method into closer accord with scientific method. For the present limitations, Cardozo briefly suggests a distinction between the 'principle arguendo' and the 'principle sine qua non,'[43] the full and useful understanding of which must await further explanation and example at his hands. The limitations which Cardozo thinks will come in the future involve the recognition that the laws governing society, like the laws of nature, are hypotheses, some more deeply entrenched than others and unlikely to be dislodged, but all of them ultimately susceptible of realignment or burial as a wider experience brings the need for new theory.

It is not at all clear why we should have to wait any longer before fully. realizing and applying the force of this observation. After referring to the tentative and experimental character of the laws of nature as expounded by Dewey in *Experience and Nature*,[44] Cardozo has aptly added:

'Jurisprudence must accept something of this provisional quality for the deliverances of her judges, or avow her own failure to establish a due co-ordination between the precepts of the law and those of expediency and justice.'[45]

This does not mean that we are to abandon the effort to arrive at fundamental legal principles or generalizations. The point important to stress is that when these are formulated they do not become permanent and unchangeable. In this respect they have exactly the same standing as any (even well-established) scientific hypothesis.

43. Cardozo, Address, 55 *Report of New York State Bar Association* 293.
44. John Dewey, *Experience and Nature* (Open Court Publishing Company, Chicago, 1926).
45. Cardozo, Address, 55 *Report of New York State Bar Association* 290–1.

'Its [the law's] principles or rules or concepts are not always finalities. They may mark what is only a stage of progress, or at times a stage of retrogression. Even so, their implications are something more than vanities. They are to be heeded like the laws of nature till superseded by another formulation more truthful in its expression of the order of the juristic universe.'[46]

Just as Newton's partly corpuscular theory of light gave way to Huygen's wave theory, which is now in turn being modified by De Broglie,[47] so a relatively well-settled legal doctrine may serve its day well, providing a helpful working hypothesis for handling a certain array of data, and then, with changing conditions, it may be forced to yield.

The capacity of a principle to influence future law depends on the covering scope with which it is formulated. If it is narrow in its announced range, it may still, in the course of time, through its application in different situations, secure a potency at first unsuspected.[48]

Certain it is that in terms of the criticism we have ventured, Cardozo would seem to have only partially explored the implications of his own insight. He has made it clear that when the judge now sitting on the bench is confronted with a case, even *stare decisis* may afford much leeway for change. But judges have always so acted (regardless of what the theory has been) and will so act in the future. Does not discernment of this truth and a frank facing of its implications result in a loosening of the entire legal framework? If, in addition, the principles by which the judge is guided are themselves only hypotheses, does not the 'analogical' legal process become

46. *Ibid.*284.
47. See A.S.Eddington, *The Nature of the Physical World* (Macmillan, New York, 1928) 201, for a popular discussion.
48. Cardozo, Address, 55 *Report of New York State Bar Association* 280–1.

even more tentative, provisional, experimental, more supple, changeable, and free than his own description of it vouchsafes?

When the deductions or analogies lead to two or more conflicting lines, as may often happen, what is the judge to do if he is not to be content with arbitrary choice or purblind concept-tossing? 'History or custom or social utility or some compelling sentiment of justice or sometimes perhaps a semi-intuitive apprehension of the pervading spirit of our law, must come to the rescue of the anxious judge, and tell him where to go.'[49]

Function of the Past

THE initial method of symmetry, which reigns especially in the decision of cases in the fields of conflict of laws[50] and of bills and notes,[51] often comes into clash with modes of judicial reaction which find outlet in other methods. All of these methods are intertwined but it is necessary, for purposes of analysis, to discuss each of them as if it were separately insulated. We now turn to the method of *history*.

Instead of a principle being 'logically' extended, there may be a tendency to confine it within the bounds set by its history. In the law of real property, for example, to which Cardozo thinks the method of history may be even more appropriate than the first method, he insists that we must be mindful of origins, of the birth of a rule and its subsequent career, if we are to proceed meaningfully.[52]

49. Cardozo, *The Nature of the Judicial Process*, 43.
50. *Cf.* Dean v. Dean, 241 N.Y.240, 149 N.E.844 (1925); reprinted in full *infra* p.241.
51. *Cf.* Strang v. Westchester County National Bank, 235 N.Y.68, 138 N.E.739 (1923); reprinted in full *infra* p.231.
52. *Cf.* Roman v. Lobe, 243 N.Y.51, 152 N.E.461 (1926); reprinted in full *infra* p.267.

But when he says: 'The directive force of the precedent may be found either in the events that made it what it is, or in some principle which enables us to say of it that it is what it ought to be,'[53] we are led to wonder how the former, independently, can be a *directive* force at all. Our rules of land tenure may be intelligible only in the light of their medieval history, but why should they take from history the impetus of their future development? There is much of soundness in the past, of course, and there are abiding elements to which progressive tendencies should not blind us, but the past alone can scarcely be said to yield a sensible guide to the future. 'An appeal to origins,' Cardozo warns us in another book, 'will be futile, their significance perverted, unless tested and illumined by an appeal to ends.'[54]

The worthy belief that the experience of the past represents a fund of knowledge for our direction may degenerate into the idolatry of blindly following some particular embodiment of that past 'wisdom.' Let us look to the historical development of a rule, not in a spirit of obeisance but in one of critical inquiry, when we think that it may help us. Let us determine whether to follow its trend in the light of our analysis of what is at present socially desirable. Perhaps it will be expedient, in order to keep as much of symmetry as is necessary, to justify the conclusion to which our social analysis brings us by convenient reference to a tendency which the history of the rule discloses. It may even be that our deliberated judgment will exactly coincide with the historical trend of the rule. But let us be sure we are not victimized by making an object of worship of that which is valuable as pointing to a beaten pathway which may or may not be wisely followed.

53. Cardozo, *The Nature of the Judicial Process*, 52.
54. Cardozo, *The Growth of the Law*, 106–7.

Of course, the judge is not engaged mainly in steering a ship, even if he be conceded to be as responsible for the course of the ship of state as the executive and the legislature. But in this account, we are focusing, not on the judge's work in merely laying down one rule or another so that men can follow some guide, any guide; nor on his work in *merely* settling a wrangle between two litigants. We are looking principally at the judge who must make up his mind in what direction to move when the field is fairly open, and when the rule which he develops will be significant in its regulatory effects and policy implications. From this angle, he may still look to history, especially in certain bodies of law where that has been the special practice, but, in the last analysis, particularly in the hard case, history cannot suffice to tell him where he should go.

Vitalizing Law

IF history and symmetry leave the direction of a principle unfixed, *custom* may step in. Today we look to custom, the practices and usages in an industry or a locality, 'not so much for the creation of new rules, but for the tests and standards that are to determine how established rules shall be applied.'[55] Thus in *First National Bank* v. *Farson*, the New York Court of Appeals said:

'The power or authority of a partner in a commercial partnership is to be tested and measured, when the actual agreements between the partners are unknown, by the ordinary usages of and the methods customarily used in partnerships conducting a business like unto, or by the usages and methods of, his own partnership.'[56]

55. Cardozo, *The Nature of the Judicial Process*, 60.
56. 226 N.Y.218,222, 123 N.E.490,491 (1919).

Custom is invoked today even less than it was in an earlier stage of our law, and what we look for here is really animated revival. Law will be, in so far as the customs of groups in particular activities or places are increasingly respected, more in rapport with the doings of the men whose conduct the law is presuming to regulate. Especially is this true in the law of sales where the following view expressed by the United States Supreme Court in 1870 now sounds antiquated.

'If the doctrine of *caveat emptor* can be changed by a special usage of trade, in the manner proposed by the custom of dealers of wool in Boston, it is easy to see it can be changed in other particulars and in this way the whole doctrine frittered away.'[57]

Lord Mansfield in assimilating to the common law the long-established customs of merchants (known as the 'law merchant'), in order to create modern mercantile law, wrought havoc with symmetry. He earned the reputation of being dangerous to the Kingdom. But he imbued the common law with a vitality for which it has reason today to be grateful. While general rules are wisely established for attaining justice with ease, certainty, and dispatch, he pointed out, their great end is to 'do justice,' and the Court will see that it *is* really obtained. Though today the legislature will often make a direct response to the pressures of custom, that is no reason why the courts should not be more ready to yield to them also.[58]

Enforcing Ethics

THE passage from the method of custom to the method of *sociology (ethics)* is gradual. 'A slight extension of custom iden-

57. Barnard v. Kellogg, 77 U.S.383,394 (1870).
58. *Cf.* Cardozo, *The Nature of the Judicial Process*, 61.

tifies it with customary morality, the prevailing standard of right conduct, the *mores* of the time.'[59] Not business or local habits alone, such as are germane to set the standards of application of a rule in a particular dispute, but all forms of behaviour become influences in the development of law. Not alone customary behaviour in the community, but canons and norms of conduct, the teachings of political economy, social science, and philosophy, especially ethics, are relevant.[60] In our generation there can be no doubt about the growing importance of these latter factors and the supremacy of the method of 'social justice.'[61] 'Even when it does not seem to dominate, it is always in reserve.'[62] Once we see that the final end and purpose of law is the social good, we must concede that when social needs demand one settlement rather than another 'there are times when we must bend symmetry, ignore history and sacrifice custom in the pursuit of other and larger ends.'[63]

Because of the actual orientation and the inclusiveness of this method as well as its sovereign significance, it would seem better to describe it as the method of 'ethics,' rather than of 'sociology,' which is the name for a still embryonic discipline. Especially is this so if, as in our account, the stress be, more than it has been, on reflection and knowledge relating to morals and social objectives.

If we ask how to choose among these four methods, we cannot, of course, receive a pat answer. 'Which method will predominate in any case, may depend at times upon intui-

---

59. *Ibid.*63.
60. *Ibid.*31; Cardozo, *The Growth of the Law*, 126; see Jacob and Youngs v. Kent, 230 N.Y.239,242–3, 129 N.E.889,891 (1921); reprinted in full *infra* p.206.
61. Cardozo, *The Nature of the Judicial Process*, 65–6.
62. *Ibid.*98.
63. *Ibid.*65.

tions of convenience or fitness too subtle to be formulated, too imponderable to be valued, too volatile to be localized or even fully apprehended.'[64] A carefully hedged formula is suggested by Cardozo. It offers emphasis-help but little more; and we are still left to protest that justice should be more pointedly stressed.

'You shall not for some slight profit of convenience or utility depart from standards set by history or logic; the loss will be greater than the gain. You shall not drag in the dust the standards set by equity and justice to win some slight conformity to symmetry and order; the gain will be unequal to the loss.'[65]

The agony of thinking (and there *is* agony in thinking) cannot be avoided as we grope to meet each new situation, as we strive for continually vital readaptation.[66] There is danger indeed that even so much of a crystallizing of judicial method as Cardozo permits himself will be taken by the slothful or mechanical-minded to be applicable in some ritualistic way, not as a guide or suggestion, but as a stencil. There is danger that through its crystallization there may be added resistance to further constructive criticism.

We have seen that the method of symmetry is not so hidebound as is popularly supposed. Even so, it is submitted that the method of ethics—held to be the most vital and important—should have a greater sway, both in an ultimate value sense, and in a temporal sense with respect to what the judge considers first as he reflects on grounds for his opinion. The method of ethics will meet greater resistance in some fields, like real property, than in other fields—as in Constitutional

64. *Ibid.*58.
65. Cardozo, *The Growth of the Law*, 88.
66. *Cf. Ibid.*108.

law or in decisions traditionally determined by 'public policy' such as those affecting labour unions or contracts in restraint of trade—where it is more at home.[67] But our contention is that this method should increasingly filter through the whole judicial process far more readily than at present, though even today, in every department of law, 'the social value of a rule has become a test of growing power and importance,'[68] and there is 'no branch where the method is not fruitful.'[69]

Judicial Prestige

THERE remains a method, often quite potent, which Cardozo does not single out—a method which we may call *judicial prestige*. Perhaps it is just as well that in an account as definitive as his, Cardozo did not exalt this method as a separate one, for there is disproportionate appeal to such authority in the law as it is.

Still it remains true that often a judge seeking for guidance among the opinions of his predecessors is arrested by a name —Lord Scrutton or Lord Mansfield in commercial law, Marshall or Taney, or Holmes, Brandeis or Stone (even when dissenting) in Constitutional law, and so on. The judge gives more attention to their views in forming his own. The following is a typical avowal, taken at random from an inconspicuous case, of the persuasive influence exercised by a highly respected judge:

'It is true that this language is taken from a dissenting opinion, but it seems to announce the unanimous conclusion of the three judges upon the point here involved, and, be-

67. But *cf*. Berkey v. Third Avenue R.Co., 244 N.Y.84, 155 N.E.58 (1926); reprinted in full *infra* p.196.
68. Cardozo, *The Nature of the Judicial Process*, 73.
69. *Ibid.*98.

sides, these words come from the pen of one of the most distinguished jurists that ever adorned the bench of this state.'[70]

Another instance of it is found in Cardozo's use of Holmes's graphic language to support the difficult and unpopular position which he adopted in the *Doyle* case which we have described. Frequently we find eminent scholars like Wigmore and Williston similarly deferred to.[71]

Cardozo himself occupies a position uniquely influential in this sense—so much so that it has been said there is a B.C. period in New York common law: Before Cardozo. Indeed, because of the weighty effect of his opinions, his *dicta* (mere remarks in passing) no less than his holdings (actual decisions), and sometimes because of the writing of an opinion which is regarded as gratuitous, not a few veteran lawmen have complained that he 'upsets' the central direction of many a well-grooved channel of law.

Collateral Factors

AT this point it is well to pause to remember that there is more to the doing-of-justice than the brew of elements which make up the judge's opinion. For a complete picture we should have to examine the cognate activities of legislative, executive, and administrative officials and the coils in which the judge may find himself caught.

In addition to the legislature, there would also be the efforts of commissions on uniform state laws, law revision commissions, committees of bar and trade associations and chambers

70. Adams v. Mississippi State Bank, 75 Miss.701,720, 23 So.395,396 (1898).
71. See *The Growth of the Law*, 11.

of commerce, as well as personal and organization lobbying groups. Much depends on the executive arm in the enforcement of the law as, for example, when a governor refuses his aid in support of an injunction. The executive and legislative branches in conjunction may curtail or enlarge the power of the courts. The executive officer may also affect the complexion of the court by his appointments. On the administrative side, there is not only the work of official boards but that of various minor officials: clerks, wardens, sheriffs, policemen, *et al.*, all of whom may seriously advance or retard our rights. To cover even the judicial phases completely, we should need to do far more than merely consider the operations of the single judge. There are the social currents and surrounding institutions in which the judge himself, for all his insight and independence, finds himself engulfed.[72] There are the trial judges, especially those who preside over the lower courts with whom so many citizens have their only contacts. There is the very tissue of the law itself. If A walks in a green field, he may do so unhampered. If B walks in the same field, he may be ejected. Before the eye of heaven the field is free and A and B are equal; before the law A is a land-owner and B is a trespasser. This is not to say that the courts should not enforce property rights. It is only to indicate how, in standing behind those which are at the base of the common law, the courts may sometimes find themselves committing what, to a moralizing observer uncorrupted by the study of law, may seem to be an injustice. It is obvious also that the poor man is sometimes caught in the web of the law like the fly in the spider's web, while the wasp or beetle, with expensive counsel, may break through. The back-stage

72. See Max Lerner, 'The Supreme Court and American Capitalism' (1933) 42 *Yale L.J.*698–9.

manœuvering of politicians and the tactics of newspapers, radios, and movies in reporting a trial would also have to receive attention.

But coming back to the judge himself, we encounter many collateral factors acting upon him—factors which influence many a decision but never appear on the record. There are private matters like the state of the judge's digestion or temper. There are physical conditions like the temperature of the courtroom. There are personal relations and influences which, at one extreme, affect a judge's subconscious and, at the other, become conscious corruption. Even when a judge is relatively free of obligation and pressure, the limitations and frailties of ordinary human experience and judgment cannot be transcended. 'The important thing,' as Cardozo says for the judges, 'is to rid our prepossessions, so far as may be, of what is merely individual or personal, to detach them in a measure from ourselves, to build them, not upon instinctive or intuitive likes and dislikes, but upon an informed and liberal culture. . . . Of course, when our utmost efforts have been put forth, we shall be far from freeing ourselves from the empire of inarticulate emotion, of beliefs so ingrained and inveterate as to be a portion of our very nature.'[73]

In this strenuous effort toward self-emancipation, the best are none too successful. The promise of assistance offered by the embryonic techniques of psychoanalysis might deserve investigation. Such efficacy as they have, in clarifying to the conscious mind its subconscious weights and disturbances, possesses peculiar relevance for those whose professional proficiency depends on unclouded judgment. Through being psychoanalysed, if not through a less rigorous and less expensive use of psychoanalytic techniques, the judge might

73. Cardozo, *The Paradoxes of Legal Science*, 127.

become more aware of his motives and hence more impartial. If he had enjoyed their benefits at an earlier age, it would be still better. Consider the following incident. A judge in his chambers was considering the three possibilities open to him in deciding a pending case. He kept hesitating in recalling the third, which had also eluded him often before. Thereupon, being skilled in the free association of ideas, he proceeded to relax and report everything that crossed his mind. This resulted in producing a series of legal catch phrases, and presently the picture of a law classroom formed. Several incidents were recalled centring around a law professor whom this judge, when a student, had humiliatingly failed to impress. This professor had a habit of referring ironically to 'this freedom of contract.' In the case before the judge, the attorney arguing for the third possibility used the same phrase with customary unction. This aroused in the judge's mind the tone of the professor's voice and his own early failure, which led to his present tendency to repress everything associated with the episode, including the attorney's argument.[74] If a judge could learn more generally how specious are the rationalizations which he sometimes gives for an attitude rooted in hidden emotional drives, perhaps he would be in a position to try to free himself from their hold.

Our hope, then, of a deliverance from the routine following of dead doctrines (though, of course, live doctrines may happen to be embodied in prior opinions) lies in judges who are psychologically, politically, and economically free, who, in the course of settling disputes not only efficiently but fairly, are consecrated to the effort to serve the best interests of society as far as their light can carry them. The counsel of perfection

74. Related in Harold D.Lasswell, *Psychopathology and Politics* (University of Chicago Press, Chicago, 1931) 34.

is clearly a loosened judicial procedure, with an appellate judiciary emotionally liberated, ethically directed, and intellectually enlightened.

We must add to the following statement by Hobbes of the qualities of the good judge, an appreciation of scientific method and a mastery of the relevant results of scientific inquiry, as well as an informed concern for the social objectives which the law serves, if we are to have an adequate picture:

'First, *A right understanding* of . . . *Equity.* . . . Secondly, *Contempt of unnecessary Riches,* and Preferments. Thirdly, *To be able in judgement to devest himselfe of all feare, anger, hatred, love and compassion.* Fourthly, and lastly, *Patience to heare; diligent attention in hearing; and memory to retain, digest and apply what he hath heard.*'[75]

All too often the judges, especially in the lower courts, have not shaped their minds by varied human experiences and deep contemplation of human ways, by diligent studies of social activity, history, economics, philosophy, and psychology. So long as this remains true, it is probably better, as at present, to have lower court judges following the lead of their brethren on the higher courts, who, because of the different standards usually prevailing in their appointment or nomination, frequently do possess superior ability and training. In any event, no sound theory of judicial practice can be grounded on inadequacy in the practitioners.

The Content of Justice

IF we are to give greater weight to the method of ethics, as is here urged, we are compelled to arrive at a closer understand-

75. *Leviathan,* *146–7.

ing of justice. As we endeavour to do so, we must turn our minds toward social forces, agencies, and ideals, and must try to estimate their bearing on the case. We must accept as facts the flux of law and some goal toward which it ought to move. The determinations of judges, unlike those of scientists, are always characterized by this *ought* element.[76]

Cardozo rejects the Kantian approach to morality which is concerned with the purity of will with which an act is performed. He finds a sounder basis in the Utilitarian view which judges conduct by its effects.[77] Negligence, for example, does not pertain in the law, as it often does in common speech, to the mental phenomenon of a careless will—indifference, inadvertence, or whatever—accompanying a man's conduct. Viewed objectively, as the law views it, the state of his will has nothing to do with it, and negligence is, to follow Cardozo in quoting Edgerton, 'unreasonably dangerous conduct.' The corresponding legal requirement of 'due care,' or freedom from negligence, is only a duty of reasonably safe conduct—such conduct as is as little likely to cause harm as a 'normal' person's would be. We indulge in this fictitious criterion of normalcy or reasonableness in a manner expounded by Vaihinger in *The Philosophy of 'As If.'* 'The jural pattern of moral conduct is the conduct that is moral in any given situation when the actor is viewed "als ob," as if, endowed with normal powers of will and understanding.'[78] The common legal test of the goodness of conduct is thus an

---

76. *Cf.* C.J.Friedrich, 'Remarks on Llewellyn's View of Law, Official Behavior, and Political Science' (1935) 50 *Pol.Sci.Q.*419.
77. Cardozo, *The Paradoxes of Legal Science*, 35,36,43. Though Cardozo says he will leave it to students of ethics to choose between the conflicting schools of ethical thought (*Ibid.*32), the author believes that Cardozo's discussion, much qualified and studded with quotation as it is, will sustain the interpretation given here.
78. *Ibid.*35.

objective and utilitarian one. The conduct we require is that
which we may expect from an average prudent and reasonable
man.[79]

Of the community's morality, thus approached, the justice
of the law consists of just so much as is found to be enforcible
wisely and efficiently with the aid of legal sanctions.[80] Found
by what criterion? It is what 'the thought and practice of a
given epoch shall conceive to be' appropriate, 'the principle
and practice of the men and women of the community whom
the social mind would rank as intelligent and virtuous.'[81]
The judge is faced with a highly delicate job in seeking to
determine what these currents are without being seduced by
his own inclinations and convictions.

The judge decides when the power of society, through the
use or threat of its agencies of compulsion, should deter what
society's opinion has condemned. It behooves the judge
therefore to become a most careful student of public opinion.
Only in that way can he be really familiar with community
morality, instead of just surmising what it is or confusing it
with that of his own social stratum. He must penetrate
through the fogs of propaganda and special pleading, through
hastily formed attitudes and ephemeral vogues, through the
crowd's unconsidered impressions. He must seize that *critically thought-out judgment which is strong and preponderant and
long-lived enough* to be granted legal recognition. The judge's
method is 'pragmatic' and 'inductive,' after the fashion of
Hobhouse and Lévy-Bruhl, in determining such conduct at
the appointed time and place under the influence of tradi-

79. It is interesting to reflect whether the flavour of these words in which
    the test of negligence is put to the jury does not serve as a damper
    upon courageous or creative conduct.
80. Cardozo, *The Paradoxes of Legal Science,* 35.
81. *Ibid.*42,37.

tion, practice, and reason. In following this informed and disciplined procedure, he may feel some assurance that his values are objectively grounded, that they are not merely an exaltation of his own bias. After such objective tests fail him, Cardozo would permit the judge to look within himself. At this point, however, would it not still be advisable for the judge to turn, for whatever light can be found, to the relevant literature, especially ethical teachings on the subject? These are too intimately and vitally related to the judge's function, as Cardozo depicts it, for the judge any longer to be able to shift responsibility to the moralist. Is it not of the essence of Cardozo's view, when followed through, that insulation here should yield to cross-fertilization? The relation of morals to law, Von Jhering remarked, is the Cape Horn of jurisprudence. We have not braved shipwreck here, but no phase of our study more urgently demands further attention.

If a judge is dogmatic, opinionated, and arbitrary, or if he is untrained to gauge the expression of the genuine opinion of the community, he cannot but perform less than his job. Nor will it be easy to decide between the high standard of the punctilious and the degraded standard of the lowest, or, having decided, to resist espousing one or the other. The discerning judge may even be able in apt circumstances to utilize the lever of law to elevate prevailing practices. Law, instead of being the proverbial social laggard, might, through the courageous yet delicate efforts of the judge, hasten the attainment of cherished social ideals. Again we find the sharp stress emerging that the judge should never be merely a technical expert, his nose in cases and statutes, his mind on their prestidigitation. He must be also a student of the movements of society if he is to be the organ of a breathing and growing law.

But the complaint is heard: There is no time for so comprehensive and exhaustive an analysis. The answer is that if less time were spent seeking and distinguishing precedents, more time would be available for this redirected activity. And if we need more and better trained judges and better research and library facilities for the courts in order to do the job thoroughly, we might reconsider the claims which doing-justice has on the public budget. If a heavy burden is imposed upon the judge, it is no heavier than that imposed upon any craftsman of whom significant accomplishment is expected. 'All things excellent,' said Spinoza, 'are as difficult as they are rare.'

Mercy is not to be contrasted with justice, as we commonly find that it is, but is compounded into the very essence of justice, as Cardozo views it. Esau knows that by the terms of his bargain he can never expect to enjoy his inheritance. But the exchange was improvident and Jacob may be made by the law to display charity, in spite of himself, and to refrain from exploiting his brother's urgent needs. The law has in similar circumstances been so construed.[82] Justice is nothing less than justice-tempered-with-mercy.[83] Far from being a strict pound-of-flesh standard, it is rather what is altogether fair and equitable, consistent with good conscience.[84]

In *Graf* v. *Hope Building Corporation*, for example, there was an action to foreclose a mortgage because of a default in payment of an instalment of the interest. At the option of the mortgagee the whole of the principal was to become due after default for twenty days. Here are the undisputed facts.

82. Cardozo, *The Paradoxes of Legal Science*, 40, citing Pomeroy, *Equity Jurisprudence*, sec.953.
83. 'What doth the Lord require of thee but to do justice and to love mercy . . . ?' Micah, 6:8.
84. Cardozo, *The Paradoxes of Legal Science*, 39. See Mirizio v. Mirizio, 248 N.Y.175, 161 N.E.461 (1928); reprinted in full *infra* p.226.

The defendant corporation was owned and controlled by Mr.H., its president. On 2 June 1927, he left for Europe on a business trip. Before his departure, he signed a check for $4,219.69 to cover the interest payment due on 1 July. This amount was $401.87 short, owing to an error of the secretary-bookkeeper. Soon after, she discovered her error, but, since only Mr.H. could sign checks, she mailed the check to the plaintiff on 24 June, explaining the error and announcing that Mr.H. would return on about 5 July, at which time the balance would follow. She then forgot about the incident. The twenty days elapsed and on 22 July, without notice of any kind, the plaintiff commenced the action. The corporation tendered the overdue sum the same day, but it was rejected.

The majority of the Court refused to be moved by sympathy for the slight inadvertence, the smallness of the amount, or the fact that the plaintiff was obviously seizing his advantage. 'The secretary's forgetfulness during this time,' wrote Judge O'Brien for an unyielding majority, 'is not sufficient excuse for a court of equity to refuse to lend its aid to the prosecution of an action based upon an incontestably plain agreement. Such a refusal would set at nought the rules announced and enforced for a century. . . .'[85]

It was one of the rare cases in which the Chief Judge could not win the court to his view and he felt compelled to state his difference in a dissent in which Lehman and Kellogg concurred.

'There is no undeviating principle,' wrote Cardozo, 'that equity shall enforce the covenants of a mortgage, unmoved by an appeal *ad misericordiam,* however urgent or affecting. The development of the jurisdiction of the chancery is lined

85. 254 N.Y.1,5, 171 N.E.884,885 (1930).

with historic monuments that point another course. . . .
Equity follows the law, but not slavishly nor always. . . .
If it did, there could never be occasion for the enforcement of
equitable doctrine. . . .

   'When an advantage is unconscionable depends upon the
circumstances. It is not unconscionable generally to insist
that payment shall be made according to the letter of a contract. It may be unconscionable to insist upon adherence to
the letter where the default is limited to a trifling balance,
where the failure to pay the balance is the product of mistake,
and where the mortgagee indicates by his conduct that he
appreciates the mistake and has attempted by silence and
inaction to turn it to his own advantage. The holder of this
mortgage must have understood that he could have his money
for the asking. His silence, followed, as it was, by immediate
suit at the first available opportunity, brings conviction to
the mind that he was avoiding any act that would spur the
mortgagor to payment. What he did was almost as suggestive
of that purpose as if he had kept out of the way in order to
avoid a tender. . . .

   'In this case, the hardship is so flagrant, the misadventure
so undoubted, the oppression so apparent, as to justify a
holding that only through an acceptance of the tender will
equity be done. The omission to pay in full had its origin in
a clerical or arithmetical error that accompanied the act of
payment, the very act to be performed. The error was not
known to the debtor except in a constructive sense, for the
secretary, a subordinate clerk, omitted to do her duty and
report it to her principal. The deficiency, though not so small
as to be negligible within the doctrine of *de minimis*, was still
slight and unimportant when compared with the payment
duly made. The possibility of bad faith is overcome by many

circumstances, of which not the least is the one that instantly upon the discovery of the error, the deficiency was paid, and this only a single day after the term of grace was at an end. Finally, there is no pretence of damage or even inconvenience ensuing to the lender. On the contrary, and this is the vital point, the inference is inevitable that the lender appreciated the blunder and was unwilling to avert it. From his conduct on the day immediately succeeding the default, we can infer his state of mind as it existed the day before. When all these circumstances are viewed in their cumulative significance, the enforcement of the covenant according to its letter is seen to approach in hardship the oppression of a penalty. . . . Equity declines to intervene at the instance of a suitor who after fostering the default would make the court his ally in an endeavor to turn it to his benefit.'[86]

It is not, of course, that judges may, by a series of flank moves, tidy up the law as it now is, in order to conform to this ideal of justice. The ideal always looms above; 'a man's aim must exceed his grasp.'

'It [justice] remains to some extent, when all is said and done, the synonym of an aspiration, a mood of exaltation, a yearning for what is fine or high.'[87]

The fact is that the judges may move in the indicated direction, in their own piecemeal way, as case after case comes along, until a trend is launched, and before long the jural norm is identical with the moral norm. Justice can thus be said to be, in another phrasing, legally organizable morality. Let us consider some conspicuous instances of legal recognition of duties which were previously only moral.

86. 254 N.Y.1,5, 171 N.E.884,886–9; citations and much technical discussion omitted. For numerous other instances see Cardozo, *The Paradoxes of Legal Science*, 40–1.
87. Cardozo, *The Growth of the Law*, 87.

Suppose A exacts a promise in due legal form from B for the benefit of A's son, C. Formerly C could not sue B to enforce this contract. It was said that 'privity' existed between A and B, but not between C and B, so that only A could enforce the contract, despite C's having the vital interest in its enforcement. Today in such situations C may sue. 'Privity' is being sensibly worn away by the courts.[88]

'The general rule, both in law and equity . . . was that privity between a plaintiff and a defendant is necessary to the maintenance of an action on the contract. The consideration must be furnished by the party to whom the promise was made. The contract cannot be enforced against the third party and, therefore, it cannot be enforced by him. On the other hand, the right of the beneficiary to sue on a contract made expressly for his benefit has been fully recognized in many American jurisdictions, either by judicial decision or by legislation, and is said to be "the prevailing rule in this country." . . . It has been said that "the establishment of this doctrine has been gradual, and is a victory of practical utility over theory, of equity over technical subtlety." . . . The reasons for this view are that it is just and practical to permit the person for whose benefit the contract is made to enforce it against one whose duty it is to pay.'[89]

Suppose that A has entered into a contract with B but does so only because B has a gun to his head. The contract has been entered into under duress and may be voided at A's instance.[90]

88. See Seaver v. Ransom, 224 N.Y.233, 120 N.E.639 (1918); Buchanan v. Tilden, 158 N.Y.109, 52 N.E.724 (1899); Todd v. Weber, 95 N.Y. 181, 47 Am.R.20 (1884).
89. Pound, J., in Seaver v. Ransom, 224 N.Y.233,237, 120 N.E.639,640 (1918). See also Cardozo, *The Growth of the Law*, 77; *The Paradoxes of Legal Science*, 46–7.
90. See The Oregon Pacific Railroad Company v. Forrest, 128 N.Y.83, 28 N.E.137 (1891).

There are various forms of duress, less melodramatic but as effective.[91] The courts have been pleased to extend the scope of application of this concept.

Formerly one could harm one's neighbour with impunity under certain circumstances where now the motive will be inquired into and pure spite work, 'disinterested malevolence,' will be curbed. 'A growing altruism, or if not this, a growing sense of social interdependence, is at the bottom of the change. Power might be exercised with brutal indifference to the many when society was organized on a basis of special privilege for the few. Democracy has brought in its wake a new outlook, and with the new outlook a new law. The social forces contributing to the change did not write their message down into the set paragraphs of a statute. They left it in the air where the pressure was more effective because felt by all alike. At last, the message became law.'[92]

Many other examples from this and previous centuries could be given, but these will suffice to indicate the type of case where judicial law-making is particularly in point. Such cases are probably encountered most frequently in the fields of contracts and torts which cover so vastly the contacts most of us have with the law.

Up to this point we have no difficulty. A disturbing distinction is, however, now introduced by Cardozo.

'I have isolated the quality of justice,' says Cardozo, 'and viewed it as if the search to understand and declare it were something singular and special. In truth the search is but a phase of a wider effort . . . We read the quality of legal justice in the disclosures of the social mind. We read in the same

91. See a wide exploration of the implications of this key concept in Hale, 'Force and the State' (1935) 35 Col.L.Rev.149.
92. Cardozo, The Paradoxes of Legal Science, 19.

book the values of all the social interests, *moral*, economic, educational, scientific, or aesthetic.'[93]

We had thought that legal justice *was* as much of moral interests as the courts would stand behind. And indeed two pages further on, Cardozo reiterates just that: 'justice *or* moral value is only one value among many that must be appraised by the same method.'[94] We had thought moral values dealt with the totality of human conduct. But now we are told: 'Other values, not moral, values of expediency or of convenience or of economic or cultural advancement, a host of values that are not final, but merely means to others, are to be ascertained and assessed and equilibrated, the less sacrificed to the greater, all in subjection to like tests, the thought and the will and the desires of society as the judge perceives and interprets them supplying the measure and the scale.'[95] Apparently, from among the variety of interests discoverable in social conduct, certain ones are now to be regarded as separable from the rest as 'moral' and as final, not instrumental or subservient to other values. What these are we are not informed. From his examples below they would appear to centre mainly about the safety and preservation of human life. But does it not seem from the following extract that he means also to include medicine and knowledge among 'many other forms of worth'?[96] And is not medicine, surely, and is not knowledge, sometimes, a means to other ends?

'Thinkers have complained with justice of the lack of any formula whereby preference can be determined when values are conflicting. There is no common denominator to which it is possible to reduce them. In general we may say that

93. Cardozo, *The Paradoxes of Legal Science*, 52. Italics author's.
94. *Ibid.* 54. Italics author's.
95. *Ibid.* 54–5.
96. *Ibid.* 58.

where conflict exists, moral values are to be preferred to economic, and economic to aesthetic. Yet casuistry will discover overlappings and exceptions. We build skyscrapers, though smaller dwellings might be safer for the builders. We run railroads, though lives might be saved if we were satisfied to travel slowly. We experiment with airplanes, though pilots run the risk of death. Yet even in these cases, indifference to moral values is not as clear as it may seem upon the surface. Moral or cultural gains, cultural in a large sense, are often indirectly served, or will be in the years to come. The skyscraper gives economic opportunity to many who without it might feel the pinch of want. The railroad brings foods and medicine and knowledge and many other forms of worth when worth would evaporate with delay. The airplane has possibilities so many that fancy cannot limit them.'[97]

The difficulty seems to be caused by using 'moral' to refer, first, to every phase of prevailing human conduct plus standards of behaviour, and second, to certain supremely prized values or interests, whatever they may be discerned to be. Cardozo's scale of preferences, if taken in an absolute sense, would be difficult to defend, and there is even some doubt about a relative priority of moral over economic, and economic over aesthetic interests. Says Morris R.Cohen:

'Justice Cardozo has suggested a rather simple hierarchy of social values, to wit: moral, economic and aesthetic, which the law should protect in the order named. Does this mean that no amount of economic interest can outweigh a moral duty? That would logically follow from the absolutistic conception of morality. No community however, no matter how enlightened, ever takes that position. Thus there can be no higher moral obligation for a community than to prevent

97. *Ibid.*56–8.

whenever possible the killing of human beings. Yet, measures
for the protection of life can not be free from economic
scrutiny, and certain costs will always be regarded as pro-
hibitive. . . .

'Similarly, we may well question whether economic interests should prevail over aesthetic ones, and many today condemn the extent to which our American courts have carried
this doctrine. Recent thought has come to realize that the
traditional Anglo-American view dictated by our business
men is based on a very superficial conception of life and social
needs. Aesthetic needs are basic and grow out of our fundamental instincts which are often of greater vital urge than
ordinary economic ones. Certainly a major part of humanity
thinks cosmetics and beautiful clothes worthy of economic
sacrifice, even at the expense of adequate food. If we were to
accept categorically the superiority of the economic over the
aesthetic, we should allow the progressive uglification of our
roads as well as city streets and the subordination of the
scenic beauty of Niagara to the interests of electric power. But
that is hardly a self-evident requirement of justice.'[98]

In such complicated situations, the function of the judge,
as Cardozo says he sees it, is not to transform civilization, but
to regulate and order it.[99] As he pursues his task, however, the
judge is ultimately forced, as we have already seen, to make
a choice among multifarious values and interests. In doing
so, is he not really engaged, as we shall presently find, in the
process of reconstructing society?

98. M.R.Cohen, 'On Absolutes in Legal Thought' (1936) 84 *U.of Pa.L.
    Rev.*709.
99. *The Paradoxes of Legal Science*, 59.

III
THE JUDGE AS ARTIST

If the birds in building nests felt the utility of what they do, they would be practising an art; and for the instinct to become rational it would even suffice that their traditional purpose and method should become conscious occasionally.

George Santayana,
Reason in Art (1905).

III

THE JUDGE AS ARTIST

'OF course,' said Holmes, 'the law is not the place for the artist or poet. The law is the calling of thinkers.'[1]

Despite this disclaimer from high authority, there are open to the judge, when he rises to his full height, the privileges and burdens of any artist. For 'art has a far wider signification than is, in the hands of aestheticians, commonly assigned to it. It has not to do exclusively with the composition of symphonies, the painting of pictures, the chiseling of statues. It is the name for that process of intelligent direction by which the natural tendencies of events, implicit and unrealized meanings of objects are furthered and secured. It is that conscious technique by which, out of some uncertainty and crisis, desired goods, first foreseen as ideal possibilities, the self-suggesting hopes of an imperfect present, are achieved and stabilized. It is the technique by which what is problematic, harassing, and confused becomes clear, satisfying, and sustained.'[2]

We shall undertake to show that, in this broad sense, the judge is an artist in three distinct ways: in the construction of

1. Holmes, 'The Profession of the Law,' *Collected Legal Papers,* 29–30; originally in Holmes, *Speeches* (Little, Brown, & Co., Boston).
2. Irwin Edman, 'A Philosophy of Experience as a Philosophy of Art,' *Essays in Honor of John Dewey* (edited by John J.Coss, Holt, New York, 1929) 123–4. See George Santayana, *Reason in Art* (Scribner's, New York, 1905); John Dewey, *Art as Experience* (Minton Balch, New York, 1934); Edman, *The World, the Arts, and the Artist* (Norton, New York, 1928) 15.

his opinions; in the realignment of the legal corpus; in the moulding of society.

Constructing the Opinion

LET us suppose a judge to have decided, in a case offering some leeway, that a particular result, from his point of view, is just. He does not reach this conclusion in a void. His decision is not merely a 'hunch,' a guess, a sentiment.[3] He has doubtless pondered the whole situation, not only the rights of the parties involved but the broader social implications, not only the equities which occur to him but the arguments of opposing counsel, the cases, articles, and books cited, et cetera. He is working in an atmosphere of common sense or rationality and with some stability of values and technique. He now sits down to compose his opinion. Its function is to make his conclusion plausible, to justify it to the legal world and to society's conscience. He has before him a mass of precedents, concepts, principles, analogies, rules, presumptions, fictions, theories, *dicta*, customs, maxims, policies, economic and sociological knowledge, philosophic doctrines, moral standards. He picks and chooses and combines as one would in weaving a rug, in painting a picture from colours on a palette, or in composing a symphony out of myriad possible notes.

He must do the same with the facts so that they tell their story his way. The case of *Graf* v. *Hope Building Corporation*, which we have already described, aptly illustrates how the decision may revolve on the facts, even where the facts are 'undisputed' and in a court which is supposed to consider questions of law only.

3. *Cf.* Joseph C. Hutcheson, Jr., 'The Judgment Intuitive: The Function of the "Hunch" in Judicial Decisions' (1929) 14 *Corn.L.Q.*274.

He must create lights and shadows in the legal writings or statutes to be construed.[4]

When he is through he has created out of this plethora of data a literary document. But it is different from other literary documents. It contains commands which will be enforced. 'I know a very wise man,' wrote Fletcher of Saltoun, 'that believed that if a man were permitted to make all the ballads, he need not care who should make the laws of a nation.' There may be a deep justification for the confidence of his boast. But the judge, nonetheless, has the quiet satisfaction of knowing that his literary compositions have the backing of society's organized force—its policemen and executioners, its jails and its devices for exacting money penalties.

We have earlier described the conventional view of the formation of an opinion. Here is a precedent which *must* be followed; there an analogy from which there is *no* escape; here a public policy from which it would be *unthinkable* to depart.

We have seen that, to a certain extent, there is such compulsion in the legal materials. Especially is this so in cases where the social situation has not changed much in recent years, the readiest and most obvious technical result is fair to the litigants, and the trend of law is one on which people have come to rely. But suppose, for example, that the judge is convinced that a change in the law is, for some reason, advisable. The legal materials brought to his attention do not seem to head up the way he wants to go. What then?

'Repeatedly, when one is hard beset,' says Cardozo of such a dilemma, 'there are principles and precedents and analogies

4. See Fosmire v. National Surety Co., 229 N.Y.44, 127 N.E.472 (1920); reprinted in full *infra* p.212, and Matter of Fowles, 222 N.Y.222, 118 N.E.611 (1918); reprinted in full *infra* p.219.

which may be pressed into the service of justice if one has the perceiving eye to use them.'[5]

The rugged realism of this observation is startling. Here is a judge frankly admitting that in constructing an opinion he does not so much *follow* precedents as *use* them. When once justice has manifested its form to his mind, the task of clothing the decision in legal matter is a challenge to the law craftsman to justify his conclusion to other lawmen and the public mind. He must do the job in a workmanlike fashion. In doing so, there is not *deference* to legal principles so much as *reference* to them. There is not reasoning *from* analogy so much as *by* analogy. It is said that when Lord Coke encountered difficulty in finding precedents for the decision he wished to reach, he went so far as to pen 'as the old Latin maxim saith'—and then to invent the maxim.[6] A technical theory for the decision in the case simply must be fashioned. An opinion, unless copied from a brief, is never found ready to hand. Its process of creation is not unlike that of any other artistic enterprise.

'The law has its piercing intuitions, its tense, apocalyptic moments. We gather together our principles and precedents and analogies, even at times our fictions, and summon them to yield the energy that will best attain the jural end. If our wand has the divining touch, it will seldom knock in vain.'[7]

5. *The Paradoxes of Legal Science*, 59.
6. T.R.Powell, 'The Logic and Rhetoric of Constitutional Law' (1918) 15 *Journal of Philosophy, Psychology and Scientific Method* 653.
7. Cardozo, *The Paradoxes of Legal Science*, 60; see 59,286. *Cf.* 'Should there not go along with the plain and severely logical study of jural relations study and reflection upon, and an endeavor to discover and develop, those processes of the mind by which such decisions are reached, those processes and faculties which, lifting the mind above the mass of constricting matter whether of confused fact or precedent that stands in the way of just decision enable it by a kind of apocalyptic vision to " trace the hidden equities . . ." ' Hutcheson, 'The Judgment Intuitive: The Function of the "Hunch" in Judicial Decisions' (1929) 14 *Corn.L.Q.*288.

There may be some doubt as to whether Cardozo really wishes to suggest that the reasoning process is quite so belated an event, once the decision has been reached, as has here been indicated. It is likely, of course, that a certain amount of reasoning is done before the decision is reached and that other reasons occur to the judge as he is formulating the vindication for his view in the opinion. The extent to which the reasoning follows the decision or the decision follows the reasoning is naturally indeterminate. It depends on the familiarity of the individual judge with the particular legal materials and on his personal habits of thinking. This matter of how a man thinks in order to arrive at a result is most elusive. How many persons are aware, each time, of going through the several stages expounded in Dewey's *How We Think*:[8] from recognition of a general problematic situation, to the narrowing of it into a specific problem, to the summoning of various hypotheses or suggestions, and the disposing by logic and experiment of all but those which provide a solution? The mind does not march with the regularity of a Prussian goose-step. No amount of discipline can insure against the fitful dart, the capricious turn, the mercurial sliding.

As the judge struggles with the task of constructing a coherent and convincing opinion, the very traditions which bind him often suggest, as in other arts, the unexpected avenue of advance. From two sonnets of Wordsworth in praise of the constrictions of the sonnet form, we take these lines:

> 'Scorn not the sonnet; Critic, you have frown'd,
> Mindless of its just honours; with this key
> Shakespeare unlock'd his heart . . .'

* * *

8. John Dewey, *How We Think* (Heath, Boston, 1910).

'Nuns fret not at their convent's narrow room,
And hermits are contented with their cells,
And students with their pensive citadels; . . .
In truth the prison unto which we doom
Ourselves no prison is: and hence for me,
In sundry moods, 'twas pastime to be bound
Within the Sonnet's scanty plot of ground . . .'

In a similar vein is Cardozo's observation:

'The restraints of rhyme or metre, the exigencies of period or balance, liberate at times the thought which they confine, and in imprisoning release.'[9]

Apply this insight to law:

'Logic and history, the countless analogies suggested by the recorded wisdom of the past, will in turn inspire new expedients for the attainment of equity and justice.'[10]

The composer who has not resorted to raucous atonality, the poet who has not run amuck in free verse, the painter who has not carried innovation to meaningless abstraction—each of these, if he is solidly grounded in the cumulative achievements of his art and if he strives for an edge of original individual expression, knows the experience of which Cardozo writes. In the case of the judge the task is dictated, not by a solitary ambition to be original, but by the poignant pressure of changing social forces or the uniqueness of some case before him.

When the task has been done, the oracle whose word became law, if he is as frank with himself as is Cardozo, will have many an inner qualm and reservation:

'I go over the old opinions, and wonder whether they are

9. Cardozo, *The Growth of the Law*, 89.
10. *Ibid.*89.

right, and then I say to myself that if I had written the other way, I should be just as doubtful as before.'[11]

The sweeping suggestion has been urged that the judge abandon the traditional, ceremonial, and artificial language of the courts altogether and, more and more, seek to state in plain king's English the reasons and rationalizations which compose his opinion. An analogy, which is more than whimsical, has been drawn between our present-day judicial procedure and that of the Middle Ages. In both instances, the judicial practice is presumably to decide the case partly, if not entirely, on the basis of non-technical considerations. In both instances 'torture' is employed to produce a legally acceptable form for the decision. In the Middle Ages, the instruments of hypocrisy were the rack and the wheel which forced the 'confession' required in that period. Today they are fiction, analogies, theories.[12]

There is much to be said for a rejection of such indirection and the adoption of a more forthright and honest approach. It is well to purge a legal opinion as much as possible of its artificial elements. It is well in a democracy to make an opinion as understandable as possible to all who run and read; and the courts of New Jersey even have laymen sitting on the appellate bench. Still, it must be remembered that, after all, the technical language of law, like the technical vocabulary of a science, is meant to serve a function. It is meant as an armoury of tools to render analysis more precise and effective. In the hands of an analytic scholar like Hohfeld[13] the tools be-

11. Cardozo, *The Paradoxes of Legal Science,* 79.
12. L.L.Fuller, 'American Legal Realism' (1934) 82 *U. of Pa.L.Rev.*435, referring to Gnaeus Flavius (H.U.Kantorowicz), *Der Kampf um Die Rechtswissenschaft* (1906) 49.
13. See Wesley Newcomb Hohfeld, *Fundamental Legal Conceptions as Applied in Judicial Reasoning and Other Legal Essays* (edited by Walter Wheeler Cook, Yale, New Haven, 1919).

come even more sharp and serviceable. In the hands of the non-thinking, it is true, they become a substitute for thought; but there is no help for them in any case. So long as a useful function is served, no functionalist would advise abandonment. The remedy is not to discard altogether a helpful, though often clumsy and archaic, instrument. Rather should we seek to refine the instrument and at the same time improve the ability and standards of those who wield it. Thus, though the medieval evil was eliminated by allowing the judge more freedom in passing on the sufficiency of the evidence, it would not be wise to ask the present-day judge to compound his opinion out of every single consideration, non-technical as well as technical, which goes into the construction of his decision. This would be carrying the current tendency toward *frankness* to an extreme approaching absurdity. Even Felix S. Cohen, whose juristic criticism is so thoroughgoing, does not wish absolutely to discard the apparatus of traditional rationalization. He wishes only to make sure that counters are not mistaken for coins, that the legally acceptable justifications or after-thoughts given for a decision are not supposed to be, and are not allowed to be, the full and adequate grounds of that decision.

'Of course,' writes Cohen, 'it would be captious to criticize courts for delivering their opinion in the language of transcendental nonsense. Logicians sometimes talk as if the only function of language were to convey ideas. But anthropologists know better and assure us that "language is primarily a pre-rational function." Certain words and phrases are useful for the purpose of releasing pent-up emotions, or putting babies to sleep, or inducing certain emotions and attitudes in political or judicial audience. . . .

'When the vivid fictions and metaphors of traditional jurisprudence are thought of as reasons for decisions, rather than poetical or mnemonic devices for formulating decisions reached on other grounds, then the author, as well as the reader, of the opinion or argument, is apt to forget the social forces which mold the law and the social ideals by which the law is to be judged.'[14]

Even though a court be regarded as engaged in an essentially legislative function, it cannot be expected to make all the inquiries and consider all the grounds which a legislature would. We cannot escape recognition of the fact that the court and the legislature are two separate and differently functioning institutions. They have different jobs. They operate under different time-pressures. They may each be legislating, but their facilities and capacity for inquiry, and the scope of their commands, differ.

While the appellate court is not adequately equipped for a complete survey, it may, however, become more hospitably inclined to consult the social data than it usually is. In effectuating such a tendency it could follow the procedure of the United States Supreme Court in *Chastleton Corporation* v. *Sinclair*.[15] Cardozo's explanatory comment reveals his approval of this course:

'The decision of the Supreme Court in the Chastleton case,' he writes, 'may prove to be the entering wedge that will open up a new technique. The question was whether in the District of Columbia there had come an end to the emergency that had been thought to justify a statute limiting the rents of dwellings. The court said that if its own judicial knowledge were to be the sole basis of its action, it would hold that the

14. F.S.Cohen, 'Transcendental Nonsense and the Functional Approach' (1935) 35 *Col.L.Rev.*812.
15. 264 U.S.543 (1924).

emergency had passed. It refused, however, to be so limited, but remitted the case to the trial court to investigate and report. There is little doubt that according to the practice in vogue in many jurisdictions, the court would have dealt with the case upon the footing of judicial notice. We have here the germ of a method capable of expansion. Courts should feel freer than they have hitherto felt to inform their judgment by inquiry.'[16]

Things being as they are, the judge who is adroit in the intricacies of his craft is often tempted to employ his ingenuity n reaching the desired result. He is reluctant to make a clean break, but prefers, as we have indicated, to torture the legal data, by splitting—not an arm or a leg, like his medieval brother, but a hair. The charge is frequently made even against Cardozo that his technique is over-subtle, that he stretches legal doctrine not wisely but too well. This criticism is made from two sources for different reasons. On the one hand, out of a recognition of recent drastic shifts in our social order, many alert lawyers and many more non-lawyers prefer a readiness *wholly* to depart from past common law doctrine. On the other hand, seasoned conservative lawyers are impatient with Cardozo's artfully spun and, as they allege, sometimes superfluous opinions because, in the business of daily law work, these complicate the problem of definitely advising clients. Though there be merit in this point, one is reminded of Samuel Johnson, who thought it was easy to refute Bishop Berkeley, and show that 'matter' really existed, simply by kicking a stone.

One such example of Cardozo's craftsmanship should suffice. In the case of *De Cicco* v. *Schweizer*,[17] Mr. Schweizer

16. Cardozo, *The Paradoxes of Legal Science*, 125.
17. 221 N.Y.431, 117 N.E.807 (1917).

entered into 'articles of agreement' with Count Gulinelli, who was affianced to his daughter. The wording was: 'Whereas, Miss Blanche Josephine Schweizer, daughter of said Mr. Joseph Schweizer . . . is now affianced to and is to be married to the above said Count Oberto Giacomo Giovanni Francesco Maria Gulinelli, Now in consideration of all that is herein set forth the said Mr. Joseph Schweizer promises and expressly agrees by the present contract to pay annually to his said daughter Blanche, during his own life and to send her, during her lifetime, the sum of Two Thousand Five Hundred dollars. . . .'[18]

Later the father-in-law renegued. The plaintiff (who holds an assignment executed by the daughter in which her husband joined) is suing for an annual instalment. The question is whether there is any consideration, *i.e.*, something done or given in exchange for the promise, to bind it, according to the formal requirements of the law of contracts.

The argument for the defendant is that, since the Count was already affianced to Miss Schweizer, the marriage was merely the fulfilment of an existing legal duty and hence nothing additional was done, and thus consideration was lacking. In view of the well-settled law of the state this is, on its face, a sound argument. 'The courts of this state,' Cardozo had to admit, 'are committed to the view that a promise by A to B to induce him not to *break* his contract with C is void . . .'[19] Then comes the canniness. 'We have never held, however, that a like infirmity attaches to a promise by A, not merely to B, but to B and C jointly, to induce them not to *rescind* or *modify* a contract which they are free to abandon.'[20]

18. 221 N.Y.431,432–3, 117 N.E.807,808.
19. 221 N.Y.435, 117 N.E.807,808. Italics Court's.
20. 221 N.Y.431, 117 N.E.808–9. Italics Court's.

This promise, Cardozo argues, was intended to affect the conduct of both the daughter and her husband. Though it runs to the Count, it was for the benefit of the daughter. As a natural consequence of the defendant's promise, they had put aside the thought of rescission or delay. Consideration had been provided.

Later on in the opinion, however, Cardozo's real concern comes to the fore.

'The law favors marriage settlements, and seeks to uphold them. It puts them for many purposes in a class by themselves. . . . It has enforced them at times where consideration, if present at all, has been dependent upon doubtful inference. . . . It strains, if need be, to the uttermost the interpretation of equivocal words and conduct in the effort to hold men to the honorable fulfilment of engagements designed to influence in their deepest relations the lives of others.' [21]

There is no direct assault in his opinion on the doctrine of 'consideration,' which many lawyers acknowledge today to be often superfluous. There is no dismissal of the recitals in the instrument and a direct acceptance of the marriage as consideration, if consideration be retained. Nor is there a welcome and extension of the doctrine of 'moral obligation' to supply the consideration whereby to make valid a subsequent express promise from one who is under such obligation. There is not a direct disposition, such as Judge Crane's in his concurrence, to put promises affecting entrance into marriage into an exceptional category as far as consideration is concerned. But there is instead a great *tour de force* of the method of symmetry, the lawyering skill at its sharpest.

21. 221 N.Y.439, 117 N.E.810–11. *Cf.* Wood v. Lucy, Lady Duff-Gordon, 222 N.Y.88, 118 N.E.214 (1917); reprinted in full *infra* p.142.

In the creation of his opinions, a judge is an artist in still another and more obvious sense, and one in which Cardozo is transcendent. The opinion, when completed, may need no further excuse for being than its own literary beauty. It may be itself a work of art, as an essay of Bacon or a sonnet of Shakespeare is a work of art. Too few of our judges have a literary gift.[22] Holmes had. Cardozo has, but in a different way. Cardozo's style is more metaphorical, musical, and lyric, less incisive and economical. Those who prefer a simpler style criticize the long periods, the inverted expressions, the negative constructions, the sinuous turns and the genteel phrases.[23] But many a weary lawyer, researching into the cases, will attest his gratitude for refreshing pauses at a Cardozan oasis. Single epigrams do not stand out as often as one might expect. But certain paragraphs are themselves prose poems. We may draw from *Wagner* v. *International Railway Company*. There had been a lurch of the train and the plaintiff's cousin was thrown off. Though it was night, the plaintiff retraversed the trestle, lost his footing, fell, and was hurt. He sued the railroad company. Said Cardozo:

'Danger invites rescue. The cry of distress is the summons to relief. The law does not ignore these reactions of the mind in tracing conduct to its consequences. It recognizes them as normal. It places their effects within the range of the natural and probable. The wrong that imperils life is a wrong to the imperilled victim; it is a wrong also to his rescuer. . . .

'The risk of rescue, if only it be not wanton, is born of the occasion. The emergency begets the man. The wrongdoer

22. See Cardozo's own analysis of judicial styles: 'Law and Literature,' *Law and Literature*, 3; originally in the *Yale Review*, July 1925.
23. See his description of the facts in People v. Zackowitz, 254 N.Y.192, 172 N.E.466 (1930); reprinted in full *infra* p.145, and Mirizio v. Mirizio, 248 N.Y.175, 161 N.E.461 (1928); reprinted in full *infra* p.226.

may not have foreseen the coming of a deliverer. He is accountable as if he had. . . .'[24]

By deftly employing the devices of rhetoric, by stating a conclusion eloquently and persuasively, the judge also finds that it *is* more persuasive. The judge who writes seductively is producing an aesthetic object. He is also giving a more effective and influential expression to his labours.

Reshaping the Legal Corpus

BESIDES resolving the issues in the case before him, the judge has the second and correlative duty of clearly setting out the law of the place. Though professors of law threaten more and more to pre-empt this function,[25] the judge is, as yet, the chief and most authoritative expositor of law. Taking advantage of the opportunity afforded by a particular dispute in the case before him, the judge may decide to illumine the entire law surrounding it, especially if there has been cloudiness. The same literary effort serves two functions. While justifying his decision, it also brings to bear the judge's knowledge and capacity for systematic clarification. The judge writes a little treatise on the law,[26] as a result of which the face of the legal map changes.

Two reforms, heartily supported by Cardozo, have already been launched and now assist the courts in this task of reshaping the legal corpus. The task is clearly one not best done in

24. Wagner v. International Ry.Co., 232 N.Y.176,180, 133 N.E.437,437–8 (1921). If Cardozo had decided that the railroad should not be liable, he might have coined an equally apt epigram: 'Rescue invites danger.'

25. 'More and more we are looking to the scholar in his study, to the jurist rather than to the judge or lawyer, for inspiration and for guidance.' Cardozo, *The Growth of the Law*, 11. *Cf.* A.A.Berle, Jr., 'The Legal Profession,' 9 *Encyclopedia of the Social Sciences* 340.

26. See Matter of Rouss, 221 N.Y.81, 116 N.E.782 (1917); reprinted in full *infra* p.187.

patchwork fashion. It requires, first, basic analysis, for which a judge does not usually possess the time; nor does he too often have the analytic inclination or capacity. It frequently requires, second, basic change beyond the judge's power to accomplish.

To provide basic analysis, the American Law Institute, organized in 1923, has launched a series of 'restatements' of the law, to which Cardozo, as vice-president of the Institute, has given active sponsorship. 'I have great faith in the power of such a restatement to unify our law,'[27] he asserts.

To provide basic change, Cardozo has proposed a 'ministry of justice' to mediate between the courts and the legislature,[28] a suggestion now embodied in the New York Law Revision Commission.[29]

Respecting *basic analysis*, we have already seen that Cardozo, for all his advocacy of legal change to accord with changed social tendencies, does believe that the fundamental legal principles may be worked out. Precisely because of the unwieldy mass of precedents it is imperative that we should be clear as to our principles, not that we are to adhere to any principle blindly, but that we must critically examine and formulate those we employ.

'The very strength of our common law, its cautious advance and retreat a few steps at a time is turned into a weakness unless bearings are taken at frequent intervals, so that we may know the relation of the step to the movement as a whole. One line is run here; another there. We have a filigree of threads and cross-threads, radiating from the center, and dividing one another into sections and cross-sections. We

27. Cardozo, *The Growth of the Law*, 9.
28. Cardozo, 'A Ministry of Justice,' *Law and Literature*, 41; originally in 35 *Harv.L.Rev.*113 and in *Lectures on Legal Topics 1921–2.*
29. See note to Re Horner's Will *infra* p.245.

shall be caught in the tentacles of the web, unless some super-intending mind imparts the secret of the structure, lifting us to a height where the unity of the circle will be visible as it lies below. The perplexity of the judge becomes the scholar's opportunity.'[30]

The Institute has appointed distinguished scholars to work under its auspices in their respective fields of specialization to produce such restatements which should be 'something less than a code and something more than a treatise.'[31]

In an address before the Institute, at its third annual meeting in 1925, Cardozo drew two lessons from the progress of the work: a lesson for 'legal science,' to wit, that accurate analysis of fundamental conceptions is imperative to provide a sound foundation; and a lesson for 'legal philosophy,' to wit, that the deductive implications of fundamental conceptions may be forced to yield to other pressing considerations.[32]

The law, like the method of symmetry, may be viewed from the aspect of its *structure*, in which case the systematic clarification of principles and conceptions looms, or it may be seen from the point of view of its *processes* of change. Different temperaments will warm either to the classifying, systematizing, or to the vitalizing, adaptive activity. That temperaments differ radically in some such way as this has been often recognized. Thus Coleridge remarked that every one is either a Platonist or Aristotelian; James spoke of the tough-minded and the tender-minded; we frequently contrast rationalist and empiricist. It is tragic that in the world of scholarship where, if anywhere, rivalry and hostility could yield to co-operative pursuit of a common cause, there should be ex-

30. Cardozo, *The Growth of the Law*, 5–6.
31. *Ibid.*9.
32. Cardozo, 'The American Law Institute,' *Law and Literature*, 131–2. *Cf. The Growth of the Law*, 1.

pressed so much intolerance, misunderstanding, and disdain by those whose talents and activity lie in the one direction toward those who favour the other. It is only a rare spirit like Cardozo who can lend his sympathy and intelligence to both.

It may be noted that in the very midst of discussing this project for the fixed assemblage of legal principles, doubts arise as to how fixed it can be. The doubt expressed even by Cardozo has been taken up much more vigorously by more drastic realists of the younger school who deplore the entire venture of restating the law as simply a conspiracy to aid and abet the old scholastic, concept-juggling mode of legal analysis, which is inattentive to pressing realities.[33]

Respecting *basic change*, we have seen that *stare decisis* cannot be infinitely relaxed or wholly left behind, else there would be no judicial ordering, no navigable lanes within the legal system. The time comes, however, when a change is imperative and still the court does not feel justified in overruling some archaic case. It is then, as we have seen, that the courts abdicate and expect the legislature to act. Unfortunately the courts are grotesquely islanded from the more official lawmakers; nor is there any traditional channel for communication of the need for drastic alteration. Often a need exists though no case has been litigated to attract attention. Thus it is that Cardozo has urged, following the lead of others, a 'ministry of justice.'

The major medium of legal change, as Maine has pointed

33. 'The age of the classical jurists is over, I think. The "Restatement of the Law" by the American Law Institute is the last long-drawn-out gasp of a dying tradition. The more intelligent of our younger law teachers and students are not interested in "restating" the dogmas of legal theology.' F.S.Cohen, 'Transcendental Nonsense and the Functional Approach' (1935) 35 *Col.L.Rev.*833. *Cf.* Arnold, Book Review (1936) 36 *Col.L.Rev.*687.

out,[34] was originally through fiction; later through equity. But now legislation is clearly the aptest and most utilized vehicle. If there is a sore spot requiring legislative action, but no agency—in the form of a lobbyist or a designated official— is present to press its importance, the legislature is not likely to act.

'We must have a courier who will carry the tidings of distress to those who are there to save when signals reach their ears. Today courts and legislature work in separation and aloofness. The penalty is paid both in the wasted effort of production and the lowered quality of the product. On the one side, the judges, left to fight against anachronism and injustice by the methods of judge-made law, are distracted by the conflicting promptings of justice and logic, of consistency and mercy, and the output of their labors bears the token of the strain. On the other side, the legislature, informed only casually and intermittently of the needs and problems of the courts, without expert or responsible or disinterested or systematic advice as to the workings of one rule or another, patches the fabric here and there, and mars often when it would mend. Legislature and courts move on in proud and silent isolation. Some agency must be found to mediate between them.'[35]

Since philosophic and scholarly ability must be combined with knowledge of life and affairs, Cardozo has suggested that a committee should be constituted, consisting of two or three representatives of faculties of law or political science, a representative of the bench and one of the bar. Besides observing the workings of the law as the courts daily administer it, such

34. Henry Sumner Maine, *Ancient Law* (Pollock's 4th American from the 10th London edition, Holt, New York, 1906) 24.
35. Cardozo, 'A Ministry of Justice,' *Law and Literature,* 42.

a board would seek every available source of instruction from journals and scholars and through comparative law investigations. Their conclusions would be recommendations only, to be debated by bar and public. Perhaps the legislature would reject them. But at least the lines of communication would have been established.

Moulding Society

THE judge is an artist, last and most important, with material less pliant, with results more momentous. The conditions of society are his subject matter. His decision once made, the conduct of the people affected by it will no longer be the same. Those wholesomely influenced by sociology in their theories of jurisprudence sometimes jump to the conclusion that while society affects law, law does not also affect society. But the lawmaker works upon the social stuff that is there and brings it 'nearer to his heart's desire.' There is a re-making of the institutions and the lives which are touched by a rule newly enunciated. In his own delimited way, the judge, like the more official legislator, is moulding society, as a sculptor moulds clay.

The judiciary, as much as the executive and the legislature, holds the power, in many crucial instances, to re-assemble whole sections of our society. While the exercise of power of executive and legislative branches of the government is subject to judicial restraint, the only check upon the judicial exercise of power, as Stone pointed out for the minority in his notable A.A.A. dissent, is its 'own sense of self-restraint.'[36] Stone was talking of Constitutional cases, but the decisions of the courts also determine ways of dealing in a

36. United States v. Butler, 297 U.S.1,79 (1935).

business,[37] the extent of one's care or diligence in ordinary conduct,[38] standards of honour in a profession or position of trust,[39] and countless other social conditions.[40]

Cases affecting various aspects of conduct, so that some corner of social life is now different, will come flocking to the mind of any lawyer. Let us take one simple instance. In the first year that Cardozo was on the Court of Appeals, a case arose evoking the rule that a patient cannot sue a public hospital for the wrongful act of its doctors.[41] The doctor is to be regarded, not as a servant, but as a professional man responsible for the details of his own behaviour, over which the hospital has no control. The hospital has discharged its obligation when due care has been exercised in the selection of the doctor.

'A ruling would, indeed, be an unfortunate one,' wrote Cardozo, 'that might constrain charitable institutions, as a measure of self-protection, to limit their activities. A hospital opens its doors without discrimination to all who seek its aid. It gathers in its wards a company of skilled physicians and trained nurses, and places their services at the call of the

37. See Henry Glass & Co. v. Misroch, 239 N.Y.475, 147 N.E.71 (1925); reprinted in full *infra* p.258; Wood v. Lucy, Lady Duff-Gordon, 222 N.Y.339, 162 N.E.99 (1928); reprinted in full *infra* p.142; Strang v. Westchester County Nat. Bank, 235 N.Y.68, 138 N.E.739 (1923); reprinted in full *infra* p.231.
38. See Palsgraf v. Long Island R.Co., 248 N.Y.339, 162 N.E.99 (1928); reprinted in full *infra* p.124.
39. See Meinhard v. Salmon, 249 N.Y.458, 164 N.E.545 (1928); reprinted in full *infra* p.168; Roman v. Lobe, 243 N.Y.51, 152 N.E.461 (1926); reprinted in full *infra* p.267; Globe Woolen Co. v. Utica Gas & Electric Co., 224 N.Y.483, 121 N.E.378 (1918); reprinted in full *infra* p.180; Matter of Rouss, 221 N.Y.81, 116 N.E.782 (1917); reprinted in full *infra* p.187.
40. See Helvering v. Davis, 301 U.S.619 (1937); reprinted in full *infra* p.300.
41. Schloendorff v. New York Hospital, 211 N.Y.125, 105 N.E.92 (1914); reprinted in full *infra* p.159.

afflicted, without scrutiny of the character or the worth of those who appeal to it, looking at nothing and caring for nothing beyond the fact of their affliction. In this beneficent work, it does not subject itself to liability to damages though the ministers of healing whom it has selected have proved unfaithful to their trust.'[42]

The same rule was held by Cardozo to apply by analogy to instructors at a university.

'We think a hospital's immunity from liability for the errors of surgeons and physicians is matched in the case of a university by a like immunity from liability for the errors of professors or instructors or other members of its staff of teachers. . . . There is indeed a duty to select them with due care. That duty fulfilled, there is none to supervise day by day the details of their teaching. The governing body of a university makes no attempt to control its professors and instructors as if they were its servants. By practice and tradition, the members of the faculty are masters, and not servants, in the conduct of the classroom. They have the independence appropriate to a company of scholars.'[43]

It is evident that this rule relieves such institutions of a grave responsibility and a budgetary item which otherwise they would have had to assume. In these area-ways society is remade.

It becomes transparent that a choice is being made among diverse social interests, some of which are being promoted at the expense of others, if we contrast the theory by which Cardozo reached his conclusion in these cases with the so-

42. Schloendorff v. New York Hospital, 211 N.Y.125,135, 105 N.E.92,95 (1914). To correct our over-brief condensation, read the case in full.
43. Hamburger v. Cornell University, 240 N.Y.328,336-7, 148 N.E.539, 541 (1925).

called 'entrepreneur' theory of agency.[44] By the latter theory,
the institution, which can best spread the risk, through making small charges to its many patients and taking out insurance,
would be held liable (*i.e.*, legally responsible), especially since
the individual doctor is not so likely to be in a financial position to repair the damage. To decide rather to leave a hospital
as free as possible from such additional burdens, however
slight, is to play a favourite among competing social forces.
Thus we see that tort law—which in relation to the problem
we have been considering overlaps the law of agency—
becomes, in the last analysis, a phase of social philosophy.
No one sees this more clearly than Cardozo, who has been
a pathfinder especially in tort law.[45]

'In problems such as these, the need is fairly obvious for a
balancing of social interests and a choice proportioned to the
value. One is surprised at every turn to find that the same
need is present, lurking beneath the surface, when other processes and methods, at least upon a hasty view, might seem
predominant or perhaps exclusive. Take such a legal concept
as the familiar one of negligence. Involved at every turn is the
equilibration of social interests, moral and economic. Negligence as a term of legal art is, strictly speaking, a misnomer,
for negligence connotes to the ordinary man the notion of
lack of care, and yet one can be negligent in the view of the
law though one has taken what one has supposed to be ex-

44. William O.Douglas, 'Vicarious Liability and Administration of Risk'
    (1929) 38 *Yale L.J.*584,586; Young B.Smith, 'Frolic and Detour'
    (1923) 23 *Col.L.Rev.*444,456ff.
45. Bohlen pointed out in 1930 that 'during the last five years American
    courts have made great strides in the development and analysis of the
    law of Torts. This is particularly true of the New York Court of
    Appeals. Its opinions under the able guidance of Chief Judge Car-
    dozo have done much to clarify many of the most obscure and dif-
    ficult parts of the subject.' *Cases on the Law of Torts* (Bobbs-Merrill,
    Indianapolis, 1930) Preface iii.

traordinary care, and not negligent though one has taken no care at all. Moreover, one can deliberately choose to be indifferent to the greatest peril, and yet avoid the charge of negligence for all one's scorn of prudence.

'Two factors, both social, contribute to the paradox. The first is the conception of the "reasonable man," the man who conforms in conduct to the common standards of society. If the individual falls short of the standards of the group, he does so at his peril. He must then answer for his negligence though his attention never flagged. Enough that a reasonable man would have appreciated the peril which because of stupidity or ignorance may have been hidden to the actor. The standard may be different for infants. It may be different also for those whose ignorance or stupidity is carried to such a point as to put them in the class of the abnormal—the insane or the defective—though as to this the law is still unsettled. On the other hand, if one acts at one's peril when one falls below the common standard, one may have protection at the other extreme; one may not need to go beyond it. There may be occasions when an individual charged with negligence has taken no care at all or at all events very little, and yet by luck has conformed in overt act to the standard of conduct exacted of the diligent. In such a case, his mere subjective delinquency, the mere negligence of his thought, will not avail without more to put liability upon him. Very likely the law has not been wholly consistent in this field any more than it has been in others. The standard of common care as measured by the conduct of a reasonable man is at times the expression of a minimum of duty rather than a maximum. If the individual has special skill or opportunities for knowledge, he may be required to do whatever a reasonable man would do if equally favored by nature and occasion. By and large, however, with whatever allowance may be made for deviation or exception, the test of liability is external and objective.

'There is, however, a second factor that contributes to the paradox. I may call it the calculus of interests. The measure of care imputed to that standardized being, the reasonable man, is one dependent upon the value of the interests involved. As to this I have learned much from Professor Bohlen, a great master of the law of Torts. The law measures the risks that a man may legitimately take by measuring the value of the interests furthered by his conduct. I may accumulate explosives for the purpose of doing some work of construction that is important for mankind when I should be culpably reckless in accumulating them for pleasure or caprice. I may risk my life by plunging into a turbulent ocean to save a drowning man when I should be culpably reckless if I were to make the plunge for sport or mere bravado. Inquiries that seem at the first glance the most simple and unitary—was this or that conduct negligent or the opposite?—turn out in the end to be multiple and complex. Back of the answers is a measurement of interests, a balancing of values, an appeal to the experience and sentiments and moral and economic judgments of the community, the group, the trade. Of course, some of these valuations have become standardized with the lapse of years, and thus instantaneous or, as it were, intuitive. We know at once that it is negligence to drive at breakneck pace through a crowded street, with children playing in the centre, at least where the motive of the drive is the mere pleasure of the race. On the other hand, a judgment even so obvious as this yields quickly to the pressure of new facts with new social implications. We assign a different value to the movement of the fire engine or the ambulance. Constant and inevitable, even when half concealed, is the relation between the legality of the act and its value to society. We are balancing and compromising and adjusting every moment that we judge.'[46]

So far we have talked of the balancing of these forces as if society had stopped for an instant in its nervous movement through time, and as though the entire problem were solved once the interest or interests to be protected by the law had been chosen. But society moves. The rule of today sometimes becomes the crutch for the step of tomorrow. Let the courts remove that crutch after tomorrow's move has been made and those who have leaned upon it may have a grievance. Bewilderment is supposed to ensue. We are confronted with the hobgoblin of legal reformers—certainty: how and how much.

At the outset we must make a distinction between certainty from the standpoint of the lawyer and certainty from the point of view of the layman.

'Often we confuse the two. If a choice is necessary between them, we may find it wise to prefer the kind known to the layman, for it is his conduct that is to be regulated, it is from him, not from the lawyer, for the most part, that conformity is due. If the law as declared in a judgment is made to accord with established custom or with the plain and unquestioned dictates of morality it will seldom fail that certainty is promoted, not hindered, though lawyers may espy a flaw in the symmetry of the legal sphere, a break in the *elegantia juris* so precious to their hearts. The layman cares little about *elegantia* and has never had occasion to make a survey of the legal sphere. What is important for him is that the law be made to conform to his reasonable expectations, and this it will seldom

46. Cardozo, *The Paradoxes of Legal Science*, 72–5. See Hynes v. N.Y.C. R.R.Co., 231 N.Y.229, 131 N.E.898 (1921); Wagner v. International Ry.Co., 232 N.Y.176, 133 N.E.437 (1921); Palsgraf v. Long Island R.Co., 248 N.Y.88, 118 N.E.214 (1917); reprinted in full *infra* p.124.

do if its precepts are in glaring opposition to the *mores* of the times. Genuine certainty will very often be better attained, the ideal of the legal order more fully realized, by causing these expectations to prevail, than by developing the formula of an ancient dictum to the limit of its logic. Once more it is a question of degree, a matter of more or less, an adjustment of the weights and a reading of the scales.'[47]

To the extent that, in a particular business or transaction lawyers are consulted all the way down the line, these two certainties coincide. That is the relatively rare situation, however. In the common run, few persons know the law or normally bother, in advance of controversy, to find it out. 'My impression is,' says Cardozo, 'that the instances of honest reliance [on the law] and genuine disappointment are rarer than they are commonly supposed to be by those who exalt the virtues of stability and certainty.'[48] Even where the rule is known, however, and the change foreseen, we have it also on Cardozo's authority that in 'the rarest instances, if ever, would conduct have been different.'[49] We saw in discussing the method of custom that the law is vitalized for the better, and it serves its purpose more adequately, when brought more and more into accord with the actual doings of men in their diverse activities. It is usually thought that this gain is won at the cost of certainty. That reservation disappears when it is realized that, if any certainty, only that of the lawyer suffers. When the court steps outside an artificial legal groove, the honour of the lawyer as a prophet is clearly jeopardized. That lawyers should be unable to predict the decisions of a court is not very important, however, if these

47. Cardozo, Address, 55 *Report of New York State Bar Association* 288–9.
48. *Ibid.*295.
49. Cardozo, *The Growth of the Law*, 122. See also Cardozo, *The Nature of the Judicial Process*, 146.

decisions confirm the hopes and expectations of honest men who have acted rightly in their routine affairs.

But even if there were to be less of the certainty which is generally acclaimed as a cardinal legal value (usually to the oblivion of the 'principle of polarity' to which we again return), would not men be better off to accustom themselves to the same relative certainty or lack of certainty in law, as in every other phase of life?[50] How high a degree of certainty do we have in trade and commerce, on the stock market, in matters of health, in the efficacy of educational methods? We have come to recognize how infantile and illusory are the ideal and absolute objectives generated in other fields by the desire for a refuge from the trials and hazards of day-to-day living. The battle which, to some extent, has already been won in religion and philosophy has only just begun in law.

It is said that certainty in law encourages accumulations and investments because it permits reliance on contracts. 'But,' as Max Lerner has pointed out, 'it is to be conjectured that a speculative period in capitalist development thrives equally or better on uncertainty in the law. And in periods of economic collapse the crystallized certainty of capitalist law acts as an element of inflexibility in delaying adjustments to new conditions.'[51]

Lacking a mind capable of appreciating new legal mechanisms, one would have to be content to leave the situation

---

50. 'As the years have gone by, and as I have reflected more and more upon the nature of the judicial process, I have become reconciled to the uncertainty, because I have grown to see it as inevitable. I have grown to see that the process in its highest reaches is not discovery but creation; and that the doubts and misgivings, the hopes and fears, are part of the travail of mind, the pangs of death and the pangs of birth, in which principles that have served their day expire and new principles are born.' Cardozo, *The Nature of the Judicial Process*, 166.

51. Lerner, 'The Supreme Court and American Capitalism' (1933) 42 *Yale L.J.* 672 f.n.8.

there. Cardozo is not content. He has embraced a fresh proposal. At first he urged the suggestion somewhat timidly.
Doubts concerning its constitutionality, if put into a statute,
gave some pause. Then a state legislature adopted it. And by
one of those incredible turns of fate, it fell to Cardozo, as a
member of the United States Supreme Court, to pass upon
the constitutionality of the very device he had urged. Where a
retroactive holding should be regarded as gravely inadvisable,
where it would upset the justifiable expectations of well-mean-
ing men who have conducted themselves properly, Cardozo
endorses a judicial practice which was originally proposed by
Wigmore: apply the archaic rule to the instant case but serve
warning that the court will feel free to adopt a new rule for
future transactions.

'I am not persuaded altogether,' he said in 1932, 'that competence to proceed along these lines does not belong to the
judges even now without the aid of statute. If the competence
does not exist, it should be conferred by legislation, reinforced
if need be by constitutional amendment. . . . Much of the
evasion, the pretense, the shallow and disingenuous distinctions too often manifest in opinions—distinctions made in the
laudable endeavor to attain a just result while preserving a
semblance of consistency—would disappear from our law
forever if there were such a statute on the books.'[52]

In *The Great Northern Railroad Company* v. *Sunburst Oil
and Refining Company*,[53] Cardozo stated in emphatic terms
that a State may define by statute the limits of its adherence
to precedent, that it may make its own choice as to the forward operation of a rule and its retrospective reference. The
adherence to precedent, coupled with the declaration of an

52. Cardozo, Address, 55 *Report of New York State Bar Association* 297–8.
53. 287 U.S.358 (1932).

intention to refuse to adhere to it in adjudicating any con-
troversies growing out of the transactions of the future, was
held not to deprive a person of liberty or property in violation
of the 'due process of law' clause of the Constitution.

SUMMARY CONCLUSION

IN so far as our discussion has centred in Cardozo's own judicial opinions and juristic writings, it reflects the work of the appellate judge concerned primarily with private law questions. Concentration has been on the techniques of realistic and rational decision, especially in the making of common law, rather than on more routine activities.

So influential is the New York Court of Appeals, and so influential was Cardozo in that court, that many regretted his advance to the United States Supreme Court. Because of the partisan and political controversy raging around the Supreme Court and Constitutional questions at this time, and also because our interest has been in more pervasive judicial method, we have not dwelt on the implications of Cardozo's position as they bear directly on these public issues. He has already indicated that the method of 'free decision' is appropriately dominant in Constitutional law,[54] and perhaps his experience in the Supreme Court will result in some change in his general views.

Much of the value of an analysis of this kind resides in the statement of the problems, the perspective in which they are placed, and their integration with respect to other spheres of human knowledge and social needs. Nonetheless, by way of sharpening critical points emerging from our study, we briefly summarize.

Cardozo's approach to law is that of the philosophic-minded and scholarly judge. To practical men who scoff at

54. Cardozo, *The Nature of the Judicial Process*, 17,76.

'mere' theorizing his mastery is a rebuke and a caution.

'The theorist,' he tells us, 'has a hard time to make his way in an ungrateful world. He is supposed to be indifferent to realities; yet his life is spent in the exposure of realities which, till illumined by his searchlight, were hidden and unknown. He is contrasted, and to his great disfavour, with the strenuous man of action, who ploughs or builds or navigates or trades, yet, in moments of meditation he takes the consoling knowledge to his heart that the action of his favoured brothers would be futile unless informed and inspired by thoughts that came from him.'[55]

To be sure, Cardozo had not been lacking in experience at the bar when he ascended the bench, but he rose to the Court of Appeals without training as an appellate judge and his achievements have been written mainly in terms of philosophic breadth and acuteness combined with deep legal and general learning. His success has not hinged on acquaintance with law office routine or business or financial mechanics. Not that these, together with other knowledge bearing on human activities and conflicts, are to be neglected or belittled. But only that central and controlling in this mode of approach is intellectual facility and perspective, to which all else is auxiliary.

A new type of lawyer is arising in a new generation which has had more exposure to a university law school training by teachers devoting themselves to that task solely. We have some reason to hope that this generation, which has been educated so differently from the law office apprentice of yesterday, will deeply leaven the ways of lawyers.[56] If and as

55. Cardozo, *The Growth of the Law*, 21–2.
56. 'If there are an intellectual tradition and an intellectual inheritance in the law . . . law schools must see to it that they are transmitted to law students even if law students are more interested in the latest devices

it does so, the great tradition of American law, the Holmes-Cardozo philosophic approach, will grow more normal. Law practice will become less of a trade and more of a learned profession.

We have seen that few judges have been as aware as Cardozo of the extent to which judges legislate. But we have seen also that Cardozo is still enough of a traditionalist and apt technician to prefer, commonly, to make changes not openly but through a skilful manipulation of precedents. The capacity of our legal system to permit growth in this way has implications for its flexibility which Cardozo has explored, but not to the fullest extent. The utilization of this technique of judicial decision sometimes eventuates in a strained and devious opinion. This result is regrettable in so far as it complicates the lawyer's task and undermines the litigant's respect for the courts. Candour and directness demand a more open and more frequent use of the method of ethics. A consistent *functionalism* requires the forthright abandonment of those common law rules which were born under a different social order and are now obsolete.

The methods of history and custom have not been treated so extensively because they are more limited in their scope, and the basic issue—so far as these various methods can be separated from one another—is between the other two. The method of history must be qualified by the purposes to be

---

for evading the Sherman Antitrust Act.' Robert Maynard Hutchins, *The Higher Learning in America* (Yale University Press, New Haven, 1936) 71–2. See *Ibid.*42–3. *Cf.* Hutchins, 'The Bar and Legal Education' (1937) 23 *American Bar Association Journal* 923. Despite the scholastic atmosphere surrounding the insistence of President Hutchins and Professor Mortimer J.Adler at Chicago University that law and legal education must have a philosophic, especially ethical, foundation, an appreciation of its essentially sound elements ought not to be impaired.

effected. The method of custom should be invoked wherever possible to close the gap between men's doings and law's sayings. The method of judicial prestige, which we have added to Cardozo's four methods, as one frequently encountered, should be followed only in proportion as the authority of the prominent judge is solidly grounded.

As the method of sociology comes into more frequent use, it should more habitually embrace not only community opinion but political science, economics, psychology, psychiatry, sociology, moral theory, religious and social reform ideals —all the knowledge, insight, and aspiration which bear on men's relations to one another. That is why we have preferred to call it the method of 'ethics.' Perhaps, indeed, we might be said to have here two distinct methods: one concerned with an analysis of prevailing social opinions—which might unexceptionally be called the method of sociology, and another with an appraisal of various ethical views which have been advanced and are being promoted or which are found to be sound even though not widely held.

As the judge who is emancipated turns his mind out upon society and upon sources of human wisdom other than the accumulated cases, he is faced with a difficult task in trying to do justice. He cannot institute the same sort of investigation as a legislature can and he must be sensitive to moral factors without falling prey to his own prejudices. How much importance he should attach to this or that social, economic, or political theory or trend is a grave and urgent problem, but outside the scope of our present discussion. The effectiveness of psychoanalytic techniques in removing prejudice and blind spots also awaits further exploration.

Once the judge becomes more consciously an artist, and is generally so regarded, we should have a wholesome reorientation of approach to law. Instead of starting with precedents—learning them, assembling them, sorting them—we should consider a vast variety of data from diverse sources. From this material the judge would study how to reach—and the lawyer how to predict—a sound decision. Since both the lawyer and the judge would have the same bodies of wisdom to draw on for a judgment which representative men of perspective, responsibility, and good sense would applaud as just, there need be, in contrast with the treacherous method of symmetry, no diminution of certainty. From these same materials the judge would also fuse his opinion. The opinion would reflect, not wholly, but as nearly as is consistent with retention of the method of symmetry, the actual grounds for the decision.

When we stress also the artistic character of the other phases of the judge's doings, they take on a greater sense of purpose and dignity. The making of law by judges (and by the lawyers who contribute their briefs and oral argument) becomes as consciously creative as any of the fine arts, though weighted with more obvious practical consequences.

The neo-realists have stressed the necessity for respecting the social facts, but insufficient attention has been directed toward the ends to be achieved, not superimposed ends but ends soundly arrived at. If judges realized fully what their opportunities for reconstruction are, they would approach the social consequences of their decisions with opened eyes. Their results would not only be grounded in the social facts but informed by our social needs and accepted ideals. Such conscious and deliberative procedure is surely preferable to a blind and mechanical, repetitious, slot-machine procedure. 'I think,' said Holmes, 'that the judges themselves have failed adequately to recognize their duty of weighing considerations of social advantage. The duty is inevitable, and the result of the often proclaimed judicial aversion to deal with such considerations is simply to leave the very ground and foundation of judgments inarticulate and often unconscious.'[57]

Because the legislature is more expressive of the wishes of the people, a judge in a democracy, faced with a Constitutional law question, will follow the rule which the high court has repeatedly laid down, and indulge every presumption in favour of the constitutionality of a statute which has been passed.[58] In moulding common law doctrine, which he *must* do *willy-nilly*, the judge will explicitly formulate new law based on careful analysis when occasion arises. If his rule of law is approved it will abide. If it is disapproved, because it is the product of obtuseness, politics, or for any other reason, the legislature will be called upon to change it. In either case, the problem will at least have been faced. Only good can result.

Extremists of the younger school of militant neo-realists may join with old guard legalists in taking exception to the gentle, catholic hospitality of a mind like Cardozo's. Yet his juristic counsel remains persuasive and illuminating precisely because he is neither iconoclastic nor quagmired in the past but, firmly rooted in the traditions of his profession and steadily expanding his horizon, 'marches breast forward.'

57. Holmes, 'The Path of the Law,' *Collected Legal Papers*, 184.
58. See Helvering v. Davis, 301 U.S.619 (1937), reprinted in full *infra* p.300.

SELECTED CASES IN
WHICH THE OPINION OF
THE COURT WAS WRITTEN
BY CARDOZO

INTRODUCTION TO OPINIONS

THE opinions which follow are all but one from the New York Court of Appeals, the highest state court to which disputed questions of law ultimately come. Partly because of Cardozo's leading and unifying influence on the court (as well as the intrinsic eminence of other members) and partly because of the grave importance of the financial and industrial disputes of the Empire State, the opinions of this court are viewed with great respect by other jurisdictions. It has been said that its opinions are cited more frequently than those of any other tribunal except the United States Supreme Court.

One case is included from the United States Supreme Court: the opinion upholding the constitutionality of the Social Security Act as it affects old age pensions. To the non-lawyer who will pierce through its technicalities it is an admirable illustration of Cardozo's humane and informed social understanding. To the lawyer it is a model 'liberal' opinion in its fidelity to the presumption of constitutionality which Cardozo is determined to allow fully to a statute which the legislature has enacted, and in its protest that the court should confine itself to the precise legal issue arising.

The opinions have been printed in full as they appear in the New York Reports, with the same spelling and punctuation. The reporter's headnotes for the guidance of legal researchers are omitted, however, except in the case of *Palsgraf* v. *Long Island Railroad Company*, which provides a single complete illustration of the way a case looks in the books. Citation of authorities, usually deleted in a compilation of this kind, is advisedly allowed to remain, so as to exhibit how authorities may be used to make various points along the lines indicated in our analysis of 'standing on' precedent. In the *Palsgraf* case and in *People* v. *Zackowitz* we have included also the dissenting opinions, not only or primarily to set off Cardozo's views but to make it plain how learned and fair judges may politely but fundamentally differ. It will be apparent from the concluding words at the end of each case (which indicate how the judges of the court voted) when there have been concurring or dissenting opinions which we have not reprinted.

It has been remarked that it was easy for Cardozo to write such vivid and fascinating opinions since the most interesting cases fell to him. The truth, however, is that Cardozo's imagination and deftness frequently transform the dullest legal dispute into a clash of gripping intensity. It is the approach which he makes to a case rather than the nature of the issue in the case which is usually responsible for both its illumination and verve. In the Court of Appeals, unlike the United States Supreme Court, the cases are distributed to members of the court not by the Chief but in rotation. This system makes for well-rounded judges rather than specialists in particular subjects on whom the others may come to rely too much. It explains how it was possible to find a significant opinion by Cardozo in each major field of law listed by the New York Board of Law Examiners. In some fields an embarrassment of riches made choice difficult and many a favourite and notable opinion is missing. In other fields it was difficult to find even one opinion appropriate for a collection of this kind. Sometimes opinions which appear under one heading might equally well appear under another (*People* v. *Zackowitz*, *e.g.*, might have been classified under Evidence and *Roman* v. *Lobe* under Constitutional Law). Sometimes there is more than one facet to the case. But on the whole it was thought better not to excise or abridge but to let the opinions stand intact and speak for themselves. The facts of each case are usually stated clearly by Cardozo at the beginning of the case with considerable narrative skill. The main outlines of the legal argument can, in almost every instance, be understood even by those without legal training.

TORTS

HELEN PALSGRAF, Respondent, *v.* THE LONG ISLAND RAILROAD COMPANY, Appellant.

Negligence—railroads—passengers—package carried by passenger, dislodged while guards were helping him board train, and which falling to track exploded—plaintiff, an intending passenger standing on platform many feet away, injured as result of explosion—complaint in action against railroad to recover for injuries dismissed.

A man carrying a package jumped aboard a car of a moving train and, seeming unsteady as if about to fall, a guard on the car reached forward to help him in and another guard on the platform pushed him from behind, during which the package was dislodged and falling upon the rails exploded, causing injuries to plaintiff, an intending passenger, who stood on the platform many feet away. There was nothing in the appearance of the package to give notice that it contained explosives. In an action by the intending passenger against the railroad company to recover for such injuries, the complaint should be dismissed. Negligence is not actionable unless it involves the invasion of a legally protected interest, the violation of a right, and the conduct of the defendant's guards, if a wrong in relation to the holder of the package, was not a wrong in its relation to the plaintiff standing many feet away.

Palsgraf v. *Long Island R.R.Co.*, 222 App.Div.166, reversed.

(Argued February 24, 1928; decided May 29, 1928.)

APPEAL from a judgment of the Appellate Division of the Supreme Court in the second judicial department, entered December 16, 1927, affirming a judgment in favor of plaintiff entered upon a verdict.

William McNamara and *Joseph F.Keany* for appellant. Plaintiff failed to establish that her injuries were caused by negligence of the defendant and it was error for the court to deny the defendant's motion to dismiss the complaint. (*Paul* v. *Cons. Fireworks Co.*, 212 N.Y.117; *Hall* v. *N.Y.Tel. Co.*, 214 N.Y.49; *Perry* v. *Rochester Lime Co.*, 219 N.Y.60; *Pyne* v. *Cazenozia Canning Co.*, 220 N.Y.126; *Adams* v. *Bullock*, 227

N.Y.208; *McKinney* v. *N.Y.Cons.R.R.Co.*, 230 N.Y.194; *Palsey* v. *Waldorf Astoria, Inc.*, 220 App.Div.613; *Parrott* v. *Wells Fargo & Co.*, 15 Wall.524; *A., T. & S. Fe Ry.Co.* v. *Calhoun*, 213 U.S.1; *Prudential Society, Inc.*, v. *Ray*, 207 App.Div.496; 239 N.Y.600.)

Matthew W.Wood for respondent. The judgment of affirmance was amply sustained by the law and the facts. (*Saugerties Bank* v. *Delaware & Hudson Co.*, 236 N.Y.425; *Milwaukee & St. Paul Ry.Co.* v. *Kellogg*, 94 U.S.469; *Lowery* v. *Western Union Tel.Co.*, 60 N.Y.198; *Insurance Co.* v. *Tweed*, 7 Wall. 44; *Trapp* v. *McClellan*, 68 App.Div.362; *Ring* v. *City of Cohoes*, 77 N.Y.83; *McKenzie* v. *Waddell Coal Co.*, 89 App. Div.415; *Slater* v. *Barnes*, 241 N.Y.284; *King* v. *Interborough R.T.Co.*, 233 N.Y.330.)

CARDOZO, Ch.J. Plaintiff was standing on a platform of defendant's railroad after buying a ticket to go to Rockaway Beach. A train stopped at the station, bound for another place. Two men ran forward to catch it. One of the men reached the platform of the car without mishap, though the train was already moving. The other man, carrying a package, jumped aboard the car, but seemed unsteady as if about to fall. A guard on the car, who had held the door open, reached forward to help him in, and another guard on the platform pushed him from behind. In this act, the package was dislodged, and fell upon the rails. It was a package of small size, about fifteen inches long, and was covered by a newspaper. In fact it contained fireworks, but there was nothing in its appearance to give notice of its contents. The fireworks when they fell exploded. The shock of the explosion threw down some scales at the other end of the platform, many feet away.

The scales struck the plaintiff, causing injuries for which she sues.

The conduct of the defendant's guard, if a wrong in its relation to the holder of the package, was not a wrong in its relation to the plaintiff, standing far away. Relatively to her it was not negligence at all. Nothing in the situation gave notice that the falling package had in it the potency of peril to persons thus removed. Negligence is not actionable unless it involves the invasion of a legally protected interest, the violation of a right. "Proof of negligence in the air, so to speak, will not do" (Pollock, Torts [11th ed.], p.455; *Martin v. Herzog*, 228 N.Y.164,170; cf. Salmond, Torts [6th ed.], p.24). "Negligence is the absence of care, according to the circumstances" (WILLES, J., in *Vaughan v. Taff Vale Ry.Co.*, 5 H. & N.679,688; 1 Beven, Negligence [4th ed.], 7; *Paul v. Consol. Fireworks Co.*, 212 N.Y.117; *Adams v. Bullock*, 277 N.Y.208,211; *Parrott v. Wells-Fargo Co.*, 15 Wall.[U.S.] 524). The plaintiff as she stood upon the platform of the station might claim to be protected against intentional invasion of her bodily security. Such invasion is not charged. She might claim to be protected against unintentional invasion by conduct involving in the thought of reasonable men an unreasonable hazard that such invasion would ensue. These, from the point of view of the law, were the bounds of her immunity, with perhaps some rare exceptions, survivals for the most part of ancient forms of liability, where conduct is held to be at the peril of the actor (*Sullivan v. Dunham*, 161 N.Y.290). If no hazard was apparent to the eye of ordinary vigilance, an act innocent and harmless, at least to outward seeming, with reference to her, did not take to itself the quality of a tort because it happened to be a wrong, though apparently not one involving the risk of bodily insecurity, with reference to some one else. "In every instance, before negligence can be predicated of a given act, back of the act must be sought and found a duty to the individual complaining, the observance of which would have averted or avoided the injury" (McSHERRY, C.J., in *W.Va. Central R.Co.* v. *State*, 96 Md.652,666; cf. *Norfolk & Western Ry.Co.* v. *Wood*, 99 Va.156,158,159; *Hughes* v. *Boston & Maine R.R.Co.*, 71 N.H. 279,284; *U.S. Express Co.* v. *Everest*, 72 Kan.517; *Emry* v. *Roanoke Nav.Co.*, 111 N.C.94,95; *Vaughan* v. *Transit Dev. Co.*, 222 N.Y.79; *Losee* v. *Clute*, 51 N.Y.494; *DiCaprio* v. *N.Y.C.R.R.Co.*, 231 N.Y.94; 1 Shearman & Redfield on Negligence, §8, and cases cited; Cooley on Torts [3d ed.], p.1411; Jaggard on Torts, vol.2, p.826; Wharton, Negligence, §24; Bohlen, Studies in the Law of Torts, p.601). "The ideas of negligence and duty are strictly correlative" (BOWEN, L.J., in *Thomas* v. *Quartermaine*, 18 Q.B.D.685,694). The plaintiff sues in her own right for a wrong personal to her, and not as the vicarious beneficiary of a breach of duty to another.

A different conclusion will involve us, and swiftly too, in a maze of contradictions. A guard stumbles over a package which has been left upon a platform. It seems to be a bundle of newspapers. It turns out to be a can of dynamite. To the eye of ordinary vigilance, the bundle is abandoned waste, which may be kicked or trod on with impunity. Is a passenger at the other end of the platform protected by the law against the unsuspected hazard concealed beneath the waste? If not, is the result to be any different, so far as the distant passenger is concerned, when the guard stumbles over a valise which a truckman or a porter has left upon the walk? The passenger far away, if the victim of a wrong at all, has a cause of action, not derivative, but original and primary. His claim to be protected against invasion of his bodily security is neither greater nor less because the act resulting in the invasion is a wrong to another far removed. In this case, the rights that are said to have been violated, the interests said to have been invaded, are not even of the same order. The man was not injured in his person nor even put in danger. The purpose of the act, as well as its effect, was to make his person safe. If there was a wrong to him at all, which may very well be doubted, it was a wrong to a property interest only, the safety of his package. Out of this wrong to property, which threatened injury to nothing else, there has passed, we are told, to the plaintiff by derivation or succession a right of action for the invasion of an interest of another order, the right to bodily security. The diversity of interests emphasizes the futility of the effort to build the plaintiff's right upon the basis of a wrong to some one else. The gain is one of emphasis, for a like result would follow if the interests were the same. Even then, the orbit of the danger as disclosed to the eye of reasonable vigilance would be the orbit of the duty. One who jostles one's neighbor in a crowd does not invade the rights of others standing at the outer fringe when the unintended contact casts a bomb upon the ground. The wrongdoer as to them is the man who carries the bomb, not the one who explodes it without suspicion of the danger. Life will have to be made over, and human nature transformed, before prevision so extravagant can be accepted as the norm of conduct, the customary standard to which behavior must conform.

The argument for the plaintiff is built upon the shifting meanings of such words as "wrong" and "wrongful," and shares their instability. What the plaintiff must show is "a wrong" to herself, *i.e.*, a violation of her own right, and not merely a wrong to some one else, nor conduct "wrongful" because unsocial, but not "a wrong" to any one. We are told that one who drives at reckless speed through a crowded city street is guilty of a negligent act and, therefore, of a wrongful one irrespective of the consequences. Negligent the act is, and wrongful in the sense that it is unsocial, but wrongful and unsocial in relation to other travelers, only because the eye of vigilance perceives the risk of damage. If the same act were to be committed on a speedway or a race course, it would lose its wrongful quality. The risk reasonably to be perceived defines the duty to be obeyed, and risk imports relation; it is risk to another or to others within the range of apprehension (Seavey, Negligence, Subjective or Objective, 41 H.L.Rv.6; *Boronkay* v. *Robinson & Carpenter*, 247 N.Y.365). This does not mean, of course, that one who launches a destructive force is always relieved of liability if the force, though known to be destructive, pursues an unexpected path. "It was not necessary that the defendant should have had notice of the particular method in which an accident would occur, if the possibility of an accident was clear to the ordinarily prudent eye" (*Munsey* v. *Webb*, 231 U.S.150,156; *Condran* v. *Park & Tilford*, 213 N.Y.341,345; *Robert* v. *U.S.E.F.Corp.*, 240 N.Y. 474,477). Some acts, such as shooting, are so imminently dangerous to any one who may come within reach of the missile, however unexpectedly, as to impose a duty of prevision not far from that of an insurer. Even today, and much oftener in earlier stages of the law, one acts sometimes at one's peril (Jeremiah Smith, Tort and Absolute Liability, 30 H.L.Rv. 328; Street, Foundations of Legal Liability, vol.1, pp.77,78). Under this head, it may be, fall certain cases of what is known as transferred intent, an act willfully dangerous to A resulting by misadventure in injury to B (*Talmage* v. *Smith*, 101 Mich. 370,374). These cases aside, wrong is defined in terms of the natural or probable, at least when unintentional (*Parrot* v.

Wells-Fargo Co. [*The Nitro-Glycerine Case*], 15 Wall.[U.S.] 524). The range of reasonable apprehension is at times a question for the court, and at times, if varying inferences are possible, a question for the jury. Here by concession, there was nothing in the situation to suggest to the most cautious mind that the parcel wrapped in newspaper would spread wreckage through the station. If the guard had thrown it down knowingly and willfully, he would not have threatened the plaintiff's safety, so far as appearances could warn him. His conduct would not have involved, even then, an unreasonable probability of invasion of her bodily security. Liability can be no greater where the act is inadvertent.

Negligence, like risk, is thus a term of relation. Negligence in the abstract, apart from things related, is surely not a tort, if indeed it is understandable at all (BOWEN, L.J., in *Thomas* v. *Quartermaine*, 18 Q.B.D.685,694). Negligence is not a tort unless it results in the commission of a wrong, and the commission of a wrong imports the violation of a right, in this case, we are told, the right to be protected against interference with one's bodily security. But bodily security is protected, not against all forms of interference or aggression, but only against some. One who seeks redress at law does not make out a cause of action by showing without more that there has been damage to his person. If the harm was not willful, he must show that the act as to him had possibilities of danger so many and apparent as to entitle him to be protected against the doing of it though the harm was unintended. Affront to personality is still the keynote of the wrong. Confirmation of this view will be found in the history and development of the action on the case. Negligence as a basis of civil liability was unknown to medieval law (8 Holdsworth, History of English Law, p.449; Street, Foundations of Legal Liability, vol.1, pp.189,190). For damage to the person, the sole remedy was trespass, and trespass did not lie in the absence of aggression, and that direct and personal (Holdsworth, op.cit. p.453; Street, op.cit. vol.3, pp.258,260, vol.1, pp.71,74). Liability for other damage, as where a servant without orders from the master does or omits something to the damage of another, is a plant of later growth (Holdsworth, op.cit. 450,457; Wigmore, Responsibility for Tortious Acts, vol.3, Essays in Anglo-American Legal History, 520,523,526,533). When it emerged out of the legal soil, it was thought of as a variant of trespass, an offshoot of the parent stock. This appears in the form of action, which was known as trespass on the case (Holdsworth, op.cit. p.449; cf. *Scott* v. *Shepard*, 2 Wm.Black. 892; Green, Rationale of Proximate Cause, p.19). The victim does not sue derivatively, or by right of subrogation, to vindicate an interest invaded in the person of another. Thus to view his cause of action is to ignore the fundamental difference between tort and crime (Holland, Jurisprudence [12th ed.], p.328). He sues for breach of a duty owing to himself.

The law of causation, remote or proximate, is thus foreign to the case before us. The question of liability is always anterior to the question of the measure of the consequences that go with liability. If there is no tort to be redressed, there is no occasion to consider what damage might be recovered if there were a finding of a tort. We may assume, without deciding, that negligence, not at large or in the abstract, but in relation to the plaintiff, would entail liability for any and all consequences, however novel or extraordinary (*Bird* v. *St. Paul F. & M.Ins.Co.*, 224 N.Y.47,54; *Ehrgott* v. *Mayor, etc., of N.Y.*, 96 N.Y.264; *Smith* v. *London & S.W.Ry.Co.*, L.R.6 C.P.14; 1 Beven, Negligence, 106; Street, op.cit. vol.1, p.90; Green, Rationale of Proximate Cause, pp.88,118; cf.

Matter of Polemis, L.R.1921, 3 K.B.560; 44 Law Quarterly
Review, 142). There is room for argument that a distinction is
to be drawn according to the diversity of interests invaded by
the act, as where conduct negligent in that it threatens an insignificant invasion of an interest in property results in an unforseeable invasion of an interest of another order, as, *e.g.*,
one of bodily security. Perhaps other distinctions may be
necessary. We do not go into the question now. The consequences to be followed must first be rooted in a wrong.

The judgment of the Appellate Division and that of the
Trial Term should be reversed, and the complaint dismissed,
with costs in all courts.

ANDREWS, J. (dissenting). Assisting a passenger to board a
train, the defendant's servant negligently knocked a package
from his arms. It fell between the platform and the cars. Of
its contents the servant knew and could know nothing. A
violent explosion followed. The concussion broke some scales
standing a considerable distance away. In falling they injured
the plaintiff, an intending passenger.

Upon these facts may she recover the damages she has
suffered in an action brought against the master? The result
we shall reach depends upon our theory as to the nature of
negligence. Is it a relative concept—the breach of some duty
owing to a particular person or to particular persons? Or
where there is an act which unreasonably threatens the safety
of others, is the doer liable for all its proximate consequences,
even where they result in injury to one who would generally
be thought to be outside the radius of danger? This is not a
mere dispute as to words. We might not believe that to the
average mind the dropping of the bundle would seem to
involve the probability of harm to the plaintiff standing many

feet away whatever might be the case as to the owner or to one so near as to be likely to be struck by its fall. If, however, we adopt the second hypothesis we have to inquire only as to the relation between cause and effect. We deal in terms of proximate cause, not of negligence.

Negligence may be defined roughly as an act or omission which unreasonably does or may affect the rights of others, or which unreasonably fails to protect oneself from the dangers resulting from such acts. Here I confine myself to the first branch of the definition. Nor do I comment on the word "unreasonable." For present purposes it sufficiently describes that average of conduct that society requires of its members.

There must be both the act or the omission, and the right. It is the act itself, not the intent of the actor, that is important. (*Hover* v. *Barkhoof*, 44 N.Y.113; *Mertz* v. *Connecticut Co.*, 217 N.Y.475.) In criminal law both the intent and the result are to be considered. Intent again is material in tort actions, where punitive damages are sought, dependent on actual malice—not on merely reckless conduct. But here neither insanity nor infancy lessens responsibility. (*Williams* v. *Hays*, 143 N.Y.442.)

As has been said, except in cases of contributory negligence, there must be rights which are or may be affected. Often though injury has occurred, no rights of him who suffers have been touched. A licensee or trespasser upon my land has no claim to affirmative care on my part that the land be made safe. (*Meiers* v. *Koch Brewery*, 229 N.Y.10.) Where a railroad is required to fence its tracks against cattle, no man's rights are injured should he wander upon the road because such fence is absent. (*Di Caprio* v. *N.Y.C.R.R.*, 231 N.Y.94.) An unborn child may not demand immunity from personal harm. (*Drobner* v. *Peters*, 232 N.Y.220.)

But we are told that "there is no negligence unless there is in the particular case a legal duty to take care, and this duty must be one which is owed to the plaintiff himself and not merely to others." (Salmond Torts [6th ed.], 24.) This, I think too narrow a conception. Where there is the unreasonable act, and some right that may be affected there is negligence whether damage does or does not result. That is immaterial. Should we drive down Broadway at a reckless speed, we are negligent whether we strike an approaching car or miss it by an inch. The act itself is wrongful. It is a wrong not only to those who happen to be within the radius of danger but to all who might have been there—a wrong to the public at large. Such is the language of the street. Such the language of the courts when speaking of contributory negligence. Such again and again their language in speaking of the duty of some defendant and discussing proximate cause in cases where such a discussion is wholly irrelevant on any other theory. (*Perry* v. *Rochester Line Co.*, 219 N.Y.60.) As was said by Mr. Justice HOLMES many years ago, "the measure of the defendant's duty in determining whether a wrong has been committed is one thing, the measure of liability when a wrong has been committed is another." (*Spade* v. *Lynn & Boston R.R.Co.*, 172 Mass.488.) Due care is a duty imposed on each one of us to protect society from unnecessary danger, not to protect A, B or C alone.

It may well be that there is no such thing as negligence in the abstract. "Proof of negligence in the air, so to speak, will not do." In an empty world negligence would not exist. It does involve a relationship between man and his fellows. But not merely a relationship between man and those whom he might reasonably expect his act would injure. Rather, a relationship between him and those whom he does in fact injure.

If his act has a tendency to harm some one, it harms him a mile away as surely as it does those on the scene. We now permit children to recover for the negligent killing of the father. It was never prevented on the theory that no duty was owing to them. A husband may be compensated for the loss of his wife's services. To say that the wrongdoer was negligent as to the husband as well as to the wife is merely an attempt to fit facts to theory. An insurance company paying a fire loss recovers its payment of the negligent incendiary. We speak of subrogation—of suing in the right of the insured. Behind the cloud of words is the fact they hide, that the act, wrongful as to the insured, has also injured the company. Even if it be true that the fault of father, wife or insured will prevent recovery, it is because we consider the original negligence not the proximate cause of the injury. (Pollock, Torts [12th ed.], 463.)

In the well-known *Polemis Case* (1921, 3 K.B.560), SCRUTTON, L.J., said that the dropping of a plank was negligent for it might injure "workman or cargo or ship." Because of either possibility the owner of the vessel was to be made good for his loss. The act being wrongful the doer was liable for its proximate results. Criticized and explained as this statement may have been, I think it states the law as it should be and as it is. (*Smith* v. *London & Southwestern Ry.Co.*, [1870–71] 6 C.P.14; *Anthony* v. *Slaid*, 52 Mass.290; *Wood* v. *Penn.R.R.Co.*, 177 Penn.St.306; *Trashansky* v. *Hershkovitz*, 239 N.Y.452.)

The proposition is this: Every one owes to the world at large the duty of refraining from those acts that may unreasonably threaten the safety of others. Such an act occurs. Not only is he wronged to whom harm might reasonably be expected to result, but he also who is in fact injured, even if he be outside what would generally be thought the danger zone. There needs be duty due the one complaining but this is not a duty to a particular individual because as to him harm might be expected. Harm to some one being the natural result of the act, not only that one alone, but all those in fact injured may complain. We have never, I think, held otherwise. Indeed in the *Di Caprio* case we said that a breach of a general ordinance defining the degree of care to be exercised in one's calling is evidence of negligence as to every one. We did not limit this statement to those who might be expected to be exposed to danger. Unreasonable risk being taken, its consequences are not confined to those who might probably be hurt.

If this be so, we do not have a plaintiff suing by "derivation or succession." Her action is original and primary. Her claim is for a breach of duty to herself—not that she is subrogated to any right of action of the owner of the parcel or of a passenger standing at the scene of the explosion.

The right to recover damages rests on additional considerations. The plaintiff's rights must be injured, and this injury must be caused by the negligence. We build a dam, but are negligent as to its foundations. Breaking, it injures property down stream. We are not liable if all this happened because of some reason other than the insecure foundation. But when injuries do result from our unlawful act we are liable for the consequences. It does not matter that they are unusual, unexpected, unforeseen and unforseeable. But there is one limitation. The damages must be so connected with the negligence that the latter may be said to be the proximate cause of the former.

These two words have never been given an inclusive definition. What is a cause in a legal sense, still more what is a proximate cause, depend in each case upon many considerations, as does the existence of negligence itself. Any philosophical doctrine of causation does not help us. A boy throws a stone into a pond. The ripples spread. The water level rises. The history of that pond is altered to all eternity. It will be altered by other causes also. Yet it will be forever the resultant of all causes combined. Each one will have an influence. How great only omniscience can say. You may speak of a chain, or if your please, a net. An analogy is of little aid. Each cause brings about future events. Without each ʰhe future would not be the same. Each is proximate in the sense it is essential. But that is not what we mean by the word. Nor on the other hand do we mean sole cause. There is no such thing.

Should analogy be thought helpful, however, I prefer that of a stream. The spring, starting on its journey, is joined by tributary after tributary. The river, reaching the ocean, comes from a hundred sources. No man may say whence any drop of water is derived. Yet for a time distinction may be possible. Into the clear creek, brown swamp water flows from the left. Later, from the right comes water stained by its clay bed. The three may remain for a space, sharply divided. But at last, inevitably no trace of separation remains. They are so commingled that all distinction is lost.

As we have said, we cannot trace the effect of an act to the end, if end there is. Again, however, we may trace it part of the way. A murder at Serajevo may be the necessary antecedent to an assassination in London twenty years hence. An overturned lantern may burn all Chicago. We may follow the fire from the shed to the last building. We rightly say the fire started by the lantern caused its destruction.

A cause, but not the proximate cause. What we do mean by the word "proximate" is, that because of convenience, of public policy, of a rough sense of justice, the law arbitrarily declines to trace a series of events beyond a certain point. This is not logic. It is practical politics. Take our rule as to fires. Sparks from my burning haystack set on fire my house and my neighbor's. I may recover from a negligent railroad. He may not. Yet the wrongful act as directly harmed the one as the other. We may regret that the line was drawn just where it was, but drawn somewhere it had to be. We said the act of the railroad was not the proximate cause of our neighbor's fire. Cause it surely was. The words we used were simply indicative of our notions of public policy. Other courts think differently. But somewhere they reach the point where they cannot say the stream comes from any one source.

Take the illustration given in an unpublished manuscript by a distinguished and helpful writer on the law of torts. A chauffeur negligently collides with another car which is filled with dynamite, although he could not know it. An explosion follows. A, walking on the sidewalk nearby, is killed. B, sitting in a window of a building opposite, is cut by flying glass. C, likewise sitting in a window a block away, is similarly injured. And a further illustration. A nursemaid, ten blocks away, startled by the noise, involuntarily drops a baby from her arms to the walk. We are told that C may not recover while A may. As to B it is a question for court or jury. We will all agree that the baby might not. Because, we are again told, the chauffeur had no reason to believe his conduct involved any risk of injuring either C or the baby. As to them he was not negligent.

But the chauffeur, being negligent in risking the collision, his belief that the scope of the harm he might do would be limited is immaterial. His act unreasonably jeopardized the safety of any one who might be affected by it. C's injury and that of the baby were directly traceable to the collision. Without that, the injury would not have happened. C had the right to sit in his office, secure from such dangers. The baby was entitled to use the sidewalk with reasonable safety.

The true theory is, it seems to me, that the injury to C, if in truth he is to be denied recovery, and the injury to the baby is that their several injuries were not the proximate result of the negligence. And here not what the chauffeur had reason to believe would be the result of his conduct, but what the prudent would foresee, may have a bearing. May have some bearing, for the problem of proximate cause is not to be solved by any one consideration.

It is all a question of expediency. There are no fixed rules to govern our judgment. There are simply matters of which we may take account. We have in a somewhat different connection spoken of "the stream of events." We have asked whether that stream was deflected—whether it was forced into new and unexpected channels. (*Donnelly* v. *Piercy Contracting Co.*, 222 N.Y.210.) This is rather rhetoric than law. There is in truth little to guide us other than common sense.

There are some hints that may help us. The proximate cause, involved as it may be with many other causes, must be, at the least, something without which the event would not happen. The court must ask itself whether there was a natural and continuous sequence between cause and effect. Was the one a substantial factor in producing the other? Was there a direct connection between them, without too many intervening causes? Is the effect of cause on result not too attenuated? Is the cause likely, in the usual judgment of mankind, to produce the result? Or by the exercise of prudent foresight could the result be foreseen? Is the result too remote from the cause, and here we consider remoteness in time and space.

(*Bird* v. *St. Paul F. & M.Ins.Co.*, 224 N.Y.47, where we passed upon the construction of a contract—but something was also said on this subject.) Clearly we must so consider, for the greater the distance either in time or space, the more surely do other causes intervene to affect the result. When a lantern is overturned the firing of a shed is a fairly direct consequence. Many things contribute to the spread of the conflagration—the force of the wind, the direction and width of streets, the character of intervening structures, other factors. We draw an uncertain and wavering line, but draw it we must as best we can.

Once again; it is all a question of fair judgment, always keeping in mind the fact that we endeavor to make a rule in each case that will be practical and in keeping with the general understanding of mankind.

Here another question must be answered. In the case supposed it is said, and said correctly, that the chauffeur is liable for the direct effect of the explosion although he had no reason to suppose it would follow a collision. "The fact that the injury occurred in a different manner than that which might have been expected does not prevent the chauffeur's negligence from being in law the cause of the injury." But the natural results of a negligent act—the results which a prudent man would or should foresee—do have a bearing upon the decision as to proximate cause. We have said so repeatedly. What should be foreseen? No human foresight would suggest that a collision itself might injure one a block away. On the contrary, given an explosion, such a possibility might be reasonably expected. I think the direct connection, the foresight of which the courts speak, assumes prevision of the explosion, for the immediate results of which, at least, the chauffeur is responsible.

It may be said this is unjust. Why? In fairness he should make good every injury flowing from his negligence. Not because of tenderness toward him we say he need not answer for all that follows his wrong. We look back to the catastrophe, the fire kindled by the spark, or the explosion. We trace the consequences—not indefinitely, but to a certain point. And to aid us in fixing that point we ask what might ordinarily be expected to follow the fire or the explosion.

This last suggestion is the factor which must determine the case before us. The act upon which defendant's liability rests is knocking an apparently harmless package onto the platform. The act was negligent. For its proximate consequences the defendant is liable. If its contents were broken, to the owner; if it fell upon and crushed a passenger's foot, then to him. If it exploded and injured one in the immediate vicinity, to him also as to A in the illustration. Mrs. Palsgraf was standing some distance away. How far cannot be told from the record—apparently twenty-five or thirty feet. Perhaps less. Except for the explosion, she would not have been injured. We are told by the appellant in his brief "it cannot be denied that the explosion was the direct cause of the plaintiff's injuries." So it was a substantial factor in producing the result—there was here a natural and continuous sequence—direct connection. The only intervening cause was that instead of blowing her to the ground the concussion smashed the weighing machine which in turn fell upon her. There was no remoteness in time, little in space. And surely, given such an explosion as here it needed no great foresight to predict that the natural result would be to injure one on the platform at no greater distance from its scene than was the plaintiff. Just how no one might be able to predict. Whether by flying fragments, by broken glass, by wreckage of machines or structures no one could say. But injury in some form was most probable.

Under these circumstances I cannot say as a matter of law that the plaintiff's injuries were not the proximate result of the negligence. That is all we have before us. The court refused to so charge. No request was made to submit the matter to the jury as a question of fact, even would that have been proper upon the record before us.

The judgment appealed from should be affirmed, with costs.

POUND, LEHMAN and KELLOGG, JJ., concur with CARDOZO, Ch.J.; ANDREWS, J., dissents in opinion in which CRANE and O'BRIEN, JJ., concur.

Judgment reversed, etc.

CONTRACTS

OTIS F.WOOD, Appellant, *v.* LUCY, LADY DUFF–GORDON, Respondent.

CARDOZO, J. The defendant styles herself "a creator of fashions." Her favor helps a sale. Manufacturers of dresses, millinery and like articles are glad to pay for a certificate of her approval. The things which she designs, fabrics, parasols and what not, have a new value in the public mind when issued in her name. She employed the plaintiff to help her to turn this vogue into money. He was to have the exclusive right, subject always to her approval, to place her indorsements on the designs of others. He was also to have the exclusive right to place her own designs on sale, or to license others to market them. In return, she was to have one-half of "all profits and revenues" derived from any contracts he might make. The exclusive right was to last at least one year from

April 1, 1915, and thereafter from year to year unless terminated by notice of ninety days. The plaintiff says that he kept the contract on his part, and that the defendant broke it. She placed her indorsement on fabrics, dresses and millinery without his knowledge, and withheld the profits. He sues her for the damages, and the case comes here on demurrer.

The agreement of employment is signed by both parties. It has a wealth of recitals. The defendant insists, however, that it lacks the elements of a contract. She says that the plaintiff does not bind himself to anything. It is true that he does not promise in so many words that he will use reasonable efforts to place the defendant's indorsements and market her designs. We think, however, that such a promise is fairly to be implied. The law has outgrown its primitive stage of formalism when the precise word was the sovereign talisman, and every slip was fatal. It takes a broader view to-day. A promise may be lacking, and yet the whole writing may be "instinct with an obligation," imperfectly expressed (SCOTT, J., in *McCall Co.* v. *Wright*, 133 App.Div.62; *Moran* v. *Standard Oil Co.*, 211 N.Y.187,198). If that is so, there is a contract.

The implication of a promise here finds support in many circumstances. The defendant gave an *exclusive* privilege. She was to have no right for at least a year to place her own indorsements or market her own designs except through the agency of the plaintiff. The acceptance of the exclusive agency was an assumption of its duties (*Phœnix Hermetic Co.* v. *Filtrine Mfg.Co.*, 164 App.Div.424; *W.G.Taylor Co.* v. *Bannerman*, 120 Wis.189; *Mueller* v. *Bethesda Mineral Spring Co.*, 88 Mich.390). We are not to suppose that one party was to be placed at the mercy of the other (*Hearn* v. *Stevens & Bro.*, 111 App.Div.101,106; *Russell* v. *Allerton*, 108 N.Y.288). Many other terms of the agreement point the same way. We are told at the outset by way of recital that "the said Otis F. Wood possesses a business organization adapted to the placing of such indorsements as the said Lucy, Lady Duff-Gordon has approved." The implication is that the plaintiff's business organization will be used for the purpose for which it is adapted. But the terms of the defendant's compensation are even more significant. Her sole compensation for the grant of an exclusive agency is to be one-half of all the profits resulting from the plaintiff's efforts. Unless he gave his efforts, she could never get anything. Without an implied promise, the transaction cannot have such business "efficacy as both parties must have intended that at all events it should have" (BOWEN, L.J., in *The Moorcock*, 14 P.D.64,68). But the contract does not stop there. The plaintiff goes on to promise that he will account monthly for all moneys received by him, and that he will take out all such patents and copyrights and trademarks as may in his judgment be necessary to protect the rights and articles affected by the agreement. It is true, of course, as the Appellate Division has said, that if he was under no duty to try to market designs or to place certificates of indorsement, his promise to account for profits or take out copyrights would be valueless. But in determining the intention of the parties, the promise *has* a value. It helps to enforce the conclusion that the plaintiff *had* some duties. His promise to pay the defendant one-half of the profits and revenues resulting from the exclusive agency and to render accounts monthly, was a promise to use reasonable efforts to bring profits and revenues into existence. For this conclusion, the authorities are ample (*Wilson* v. *Mechanical Orguinette Co.*, 170 N.Y.542; *Phœnix Hermetic Co.* v. *Filtrine Mfg.Co.*, *supra*; *Jacquin* v. *Boutard*, 89 Hun, 437; 157 N.Y.686; *Moran* v. *Standard Oil Co.*, *supra*; *City of N.Y.* v. *Paoli*, 202 N.Y.

CRIMINAL LAW

18; *M'Intyre* v. *Belcher*, 14 C.B. [N.S.] 654; *Devonald* v. *Rosser & Sons*, 1906, 2 K.B.728; *W.G.Taylor Co.* v. *Bannerman*, *supra*; *Mueller* v. *Bethesda Mineral Spring Co.*, *supra*; *Baker Transfer Co.* v. *Merchants' R. & I.Mfg.Co.*, 1 App. Div.507).

The judgment of the Appellate Division should be reversed, and the order of the Special Term affirmed, with costs in the Appellate Division and in this court.

CUDDEBACK, MCLAUGHLIN and ANDREWS, JJ., concur; HISCOCK, Ch.J., CHASE and CRANE, JJ., dissent.

Judgment reversed, etc.

CRIMINAL LAW

THE PEOPLE OF THE STATE OF NEW YORK, Respondent, *v.* JOSEPH ZACKOWITZ, Appellant.

CARDOZO, Ch.J. On November 10, 1929, shortly after midnight, the defendant in Kings county shot Frank Coppola and killed him without justification or excuse. A crime is admitted. What is doubtful is the degree only.

Four young men, of whom Coppola was one, were at work repairing an automobile in a Brooklyn street. A woman, the defendant's wife, walked by on the opposite side. One of the men spoke to her insultingly, or so at least she understood him. The defendant, who had dropped behind to buy a newspaper, came up to find his wife in tears. He was told she had been insulted, though she did not then repeat the words. Enraged, he stepped across the street and upbraided the offenders with words of coarse profanity. He informed them, so the survivors testify, that "if they did not get out of there in five minutes, he would come back and bump them all off." Rejoining his wife, he walked with her to their apartment house located close at hand. He was heated with liquor which he had been drinking at a dance. Within the apartment he induced her to tell him what the insulting words had been. A youth had asked her to lie with him, and had offered her two dollars. With rage aroused again, the defendant went back to the scene of the insult and found the four young men still working at the car. In a statement to the police, he said that he had armed himself at the apartment with a twenty-five calibre automatic pistol. In his testimony at the trial he said that this pistol had been in his pocket all the evening. Words and blows followed, and then a shot. The defendant kicked Coppola in the stomach. There is evidence that Coppola went for him with a wrench. The pistol came from the pocket, and from the pistol a single shot, which did its deadly work. The defendant walked away and at the corner met his wife who had followed him from the home. The two took a taxicab to Manhattan where they spent the rest of the night at the dwelling of a friend. On the way the defendant threw his pistol into the river. He was arrested on January 7, 1930, about two months following the crime.

At the trial the vital question was the defendant's state of mind at the moment of the homicide. Did he shoot with a deliberate and premeditated design to kill? Was he so inflamed by drink or by anger or by both combined that, though he knew the nature of his act, he was the prey to sudden impulse, the fury of the fleeting moment? (*People* v. *Caruso*, 246 N.Y.437,446). If he went forth from his apartment with a preconceived design to kill, how is it that he failed to shoot at once? How reconcile such a design with the drawing of the pistol later in the heat and rage of an affray? These and like questions the jurors were to ask themselves and answer before measuring the defendant's guilt. Answers consistent with guilt in its highest grade can reasonably be made. Even so, the line between impulse and deliberation is too narrow and elusive to make the answers wholly clear. The sphygmograph records with graphic certainty the fluctuations of the pulse. There is no instrument yet invented that records with equal certainty the fluctuations of the mind. At least, if such an instrument exists, it was not working at midnight in the Brooklyn street when Coppola and the defendant came together in a chance affray. With only the rough and ready tests supplied by their experience of life, the jurors were to look into the workings of another's mind, and discover its capacities and disabilities, its urges and inhibitions, in moments of intense excitement. Delicate enough and subtle is the inquiry, even in the most favorable conditions, with every warping influence excluded. There must be no blurring of the issues by evidence illegally admitted and carrying with it in its admission an appeal to prejudice and passion.

Evidence charged with that appeal was, we think, admitted here. Not only was it admitted, and this under objection and exception, but the changes were rung upon it by prosecutor and judge. Almost at the opening of the trial the People began the endeavor to load the defendant down with the burden of an evil character. He was to be put before the jury as a man of murderous disposition. To that end they were allowed to prove that at the time of the encounter and at that of his arrest he had in his apartment, kept there in a radio box, three pistols and a tear-gas gun. There was no claim that he had brought these weapons out at the time of the affray, no claim that with any of them he had discharged the fatal shot. He could not have done so, for they were all of different calibre. The end to be served by laying the weapons before the jury was something very different. The end was to bring persuasion that here was a man of vicious and dangerous propensities, who because of those propensities was more likely to kill with deliberate and premeditated design than a man of irreproachable life and amiable manners. Indeed, this is the very ground on which the introduction of the evidence is now explained and defended. The District Attorney tells us in his brief that the possession of the weapons characterized the defendant as "a desperate type of criminal," a "person criminally inclined." The dissenting opinion, if it puts the argument less bluntly, leaves the substance of the thought unchanged. "Defendant was presented to the jury as a man having dangerous weapons in his possession, making a selection therefrom and going forth to put into execution his threats to kill." The weapons were not brought by the defendant to the scene of the encounter. They were left in his apartment where they were incapable of harm. In such circumstances, ownership of the weapons, if it has any relevance at all, has relevance only as indicating a general disposition to make use of them thereafter, and a general disposition to make use of them thereafter is without relevance except as indicating a "desperate type of criminal," a criminal affected with a murderous propensity.

We are asked to extenuate the error by calling it an incident: what was proved may have an air of innocence if it is styled the history of the crime. The virus of the ruling is not so easily extracted. Here was no passing reference to something casually brought out in the narrative of the killing, as if an admission had been proved against the defendant that he had picked one weapon out of several. Here in the forefront of the trial, immediately following the statement of the medical examiner, testimony was admitted that weapons, not the instruments of the killing, had been discovered by the police in the apartment of the killer; and the weapons with great display were laid before the jury, marked as exhibits, and thereafter made the subject of animated argument. Room for doubt there is none that in the thought of the jury, as in that of the District Attorney, the tendency of the whole performance was to characterize the defendant as a man murderously inclined. The purpose was not disguised. From the opening to the verdict, it was flaunted and avowed.

If a murderous propensity may be proved against a defendant as one of the tokens of his guilt, a rule of criminal evidence, long believed to be of fundamental importance for the protection of the innocent, must be first declared away. Fundamental hitherto has been the rule that character is never an issue in a criminal prosecution unless the defendant chooses to make it one (Wigmore, Evidence, vol.1, §§55,192). In a very real sense a defendant starts his life afresh when he stands before a jury, a prisoner at the bar. There has been a homicide in a public place. The killer admits the killing, but urges self-defense and sudden impulse. Inflexibly the law has set its face against the endeavor to fasten guilt upon him by proof of character or experience predisposing to an act of crime (Wigmore, Evidence, vol.1, §§57,192; *People* v. *Molineux*, 168 N.Y.264). The endeavor has been often made, but always it has failed. At times, when the issue has been self-defense, testimony has been admitted as to the murderous propensity of the deceased, the victim of the homicide (*People* v. *Druse*, 103 N.Y.655; *People* v. *Rodawald*, 177 N.Y.408; Wigmore, Evidence, vol. 1, §§63,246), but never of such a propensity on the part of the killer. The principle back of the exclusion is one, not of logic, but of policy (Wigmore, vol.1, §§57,194;

People v. *Richardson*, 222 N.Y.103,109,110). There may be cogency in the argument that a quarrelsome defendant is more likely to start a quarrel than one of milder type, a man of dangerous mode of life more likely than a shy recluse. The law is not blind to this, but equally it is not blind to the peril to the innocent if character is accepted as probative of crime. "The natural and inevitable tendency of the tribunal— whether judge or jury—is to give excessive weight to the vicious record of crime thus exhibited, and either to allow it to bear too strongly on the present charge, or to take the proof of it as justifying a condemnation irrespective of guilt of the present charge" (Wigmore, Evidence, vol.1, §194, and cases cited).

A different question would be here if the pistols had been bought in expectation of this particular encounter. They would then have been admissible as evidence of preparation and design (Wigmore, Evidence, vol.1, §238; *People* v. *Scott*, 153 N.Y.40). A different question would be here if they were so connected with the crime as to identify the perpetrator, if he had dropped them, for example, at the scene of the affray (*People* v. *Hill*, 198 N.Y.64). They would have been then admissible as tending to implicate the possessor (if identity was disputed), no matter what the opprobrium attached to his possession. Different, also, would be the question if the defendant had been shown to have gone forth from the apartment with all the weapons on his person. To be armed from head to foot at the very moment of an encounter may be a circumstance worthy to be considered, like acts of preparation generally, as a proof of preconceived design. There can be no such implication from the ownership of weapons which one leaves behind at home.

The endeavor was to generate an atmosphere of professional criminality. It was an endeavor the more unfair in that, apart from the suspicion attaching to the possession of these weapons, there is nothing to mark the defendant as a man of evil life. He was not in crime as a business. He did not shoot as a bandit shoots in the hope of wrongful gain. He was engaged in a decent calling, an optician regularly employed, without criminal record, or criminal associates. If his own testimony be true, he had gathered these weapons together as curios, a collection that interested and amused him. Perhaps his explanation of their ownership is false. There is nothing stronger than mere suspicion to guide us to an answer. Whether the explanation be false or true, he should not have been driven by the People to the necessity of offering it. Brought to answer a specific charge, and to defend himself against it, he was placed in a position where he had to defend himself against another, more general and sweeping. He was made to answer to the charge, pervasive and poisonous even if insidious and covert, that he was a man of murderous heart, of criminal disposition.

The argument is made that the evidence, if incompetent when admitted, became competent thereafter when the defendant took the stand. By taking the stand he subjected himself like any other witness to cross-examination designed to shake belief in his veracity by exhibiting his ways of life (*People* v. *Webster*, 139 N.Y.73,84; *People* v. *Hinksman*, 192 N.Y.421,433). Cross-examination brought out the fact that he had no license for a pistol. That fact disclosed, the prosecution was at liberty to prove the possession of the weapons in an attempt to impeach his credibility, since possession was a felony. All this may be true, but the evidence was not offered or admitted with such an end in view. It was received at a time when there was nothing to show that the defendant was without a license, and without suggestion that any such evidence would be brought into the case thereafter. The jury were not told that the possession of the weapons had significance only in so far as possession without a license had a tendency to cast a shadow on the defendant's character and so to impair the faith to be given to his word (cf. Wigmore, Evidence, vol.2, §981, *et seq.*; *People* v. *De Garmo*, 179 N.Y.130,134,135). They were told in effect through the whole course and tenor of the trial that irrespective of any license, the mere possession of the weapons was evidence of murderous disposition, which, apart from any bearing upon the defendant's credibility as a witness, was evidence of guilt. Here is no case of a mere technical departure from the approved order of proof. If the evidence had been received for the purpose of impeachment merely, the People would have been bound by the answer of the witness as to the time and purpose of the purchase, and would not have been permitted to contradict him (*Stokes* v. *People*, 53 N.Y.164,176; *People* v. *De Garmo*, *supra*). Here is a case where evidence offered and received as probative of an essential element of the crime, used for that purpose, and for no other, repeatedly throughout the trial, is now about to be viewed as if accepted at a later stage and accepted for a purpose unmentioned and unthought of. This is not justice in accordance with the forms of law. "The practice of calling out evidence for one purpose, apparently innocent, and using it for another, which is illegal, is improper; and, if it is clear and manifest that the avowed object is colorable merely, its admission is error" (*Coleman* v. *People*, 55 N.Y.81,88). Even more plainly is it a perversion to call out evidence for an avowed object manifestly illegal, and use it later on appeal as if admitted at another stage in aid of another purpose innocent and lawful.

The judgment of conviction should be reversed, and a new trial ordered.

POUND, J. (dissenting). The indictment herein accuses defendant of the crime of murder in the first degree committed in Kings county on November 10, 1929, by shooting Frank Coppola with a revolver. That defendant did shoot and kill Coppola is admitted. The jury was justified on the evidence in finding that he did so from a deliberate and premeditated design to effect death. The proofs tend to establish that defendant, aged twenty-four, and his seventeen-year-old wife "Fluff" had attended a dance at a dance hall; that they left for their home at 105 Devoe street about midnight; that defendant dropped behind his wife to buy some newspapers; that she went on a block ahead of him when she arrived at Devoe street; that on the opposite side of the street in the middle of the block four young men, including Coppola, were at work repairing an automobile; that Mrs. Zackowitz was either "insulted" by some remarks of one of them or thought she was; that she upbraided them; that when defendant came up to his wife she told him that she had been "insulted" and they crossed the street and defendant with much profanity threatened them that "if they did not get out of there in five minutes he would come back and bump them all off;" that defendant returned to the scene armed with a twenty-five calibre automatic pistol; that he kicked Coppola who bent over; that as Coppola got up defendant drew his pistol and fired one shot; that Coppola was struck in the lung and heart and, as a result of the shot, died soon afterwards; that defendant then met his wife on the street and they took a taxi to Manhattan; that defendant was arrested on or about January 7, 1930; that he made a confession in which he sought to defend the act of killing by saying that Coppola threatened him with a monkey wrench and that he did not realize that he had shot him; that he got the gun at his home and went back to ask them to apologize; that he took the gun to protect himself "because they were four guys;" that he had been drinking, was a little excited but not drunk; that he knew what he was doing.

On the trial, defendant and his wife testified. Defendant said in substance that he had carried the .25 automatic to the dance and had it with him on the occasion of the first encounter; that he talked with the men; that they denied that they had insulted his wife; that he thought it was not worth quarreling about and left them; that he did not threaten to bump them off; that when they went home his wife in tears and evident distress reluctantly told him that they had made a proposition to her which was understood as an offer of two dollars for sexual intercourse; that he went back to demand an apology; that he kicked at Coppola but did not hit him; that Coppola threatened him with a monkey wrench; that he was frightened; that he did not intend to kill Coppola but drew the pistol to frighten him; that the discharge of the gun was an accident; that he was partly intoxicated; that he had no permit to carry a gun.

The court submitted to the jury the various degrees of felonious homicide, and the law as to justifiable and excusable homicide and instructed them particularly as to the law of killing in self-defense. On the theory that defendant repudiated intoxication as a partial defense, tending to reduce the degree of the crime, the court did not instruct the jury on the question of intoxication. (Penal Law, §1220.) In the circumstances, the judgment should not be reversed on this ground as the defendant did not make the question a serious one.

(*People* v. *Van Zandt*, 224 N.Y.354; *People* v. *Koerber*, 244 N.Y.147,150.) At the conclusion of the charge defendant's counsel said:

"Mr. Rubenstein: The defendant excepts to the entire charge, and specifies as his ground the manner in which the charge was delivered, the inflection of your Honor's voice, the use of your hands, your eyebrows—the pauses and other mannerisms. No requests."

Unfortunately, perhaps, we have no record of the judge's manner of delivery. The point is not pressed on the appeal.

The questions of intent and deliberation and premeditation were for the jury. Their verdict is amply sustained by the evidence and the conviction should be affirmed "without regard to technical errors or defects which have not prejudiced the substantial rights of the defendants." (Code Crim.Pro. §764.) "But the question of substantial right is not the abstract question of guilt or innocence. A guilty man is entitled to a fair trial. * * * Error is substantial when we can say that it tended to influence the verdict." (*People* v. *Sobieskoda*, 235 N.Y.411.) We must, therefore, give careful heed to one matter which is brought to our attention on this appeal without regard to the convincing character of the People's evidence.

Nearly two months after the killing of Coppola, the police entered defendant's home in connection with his arrest and found there concealed in a box in the radio three revolvers and a tear-gas bomb, together with a supply of cartridges suitable for use both in the revolvers and the bomb. Defendant had in his confession, which was received without objection, admitted that he had these weapons in his possession at the time of the killing. The twenty-five calibre automatic was not among them. Defendant says that he threw it away after he shot Coppola. The People, as a part of their principal case, introduced these articles in evidence over defendant's objection and exception. This is the only ruling by which the question of error in law is presented on this appeal. No objection was made to the summation by the District Attorney nor to any specific instructions by the court. The possession of these dangerous weapons was a separate crime. (Penal Law, §1897.) The broad question is whether it had any connection with the crime charged. The substantial rights of the defendant must be protected. Where the penalty is death, we may grant a new trial if justice requires it, even though no exception was taken in the court below. (Code Crim.Pro. §528.)

The People may not prove against a defendant crimes not alleged in the indictment committed on other occasions than the crime charged as aiding the proofs that he is guilty of the crime charged unless such proof tends to establish (1) motive; (2) intent; (3) absence of mistake or accident; (4) a common scheme or plan embracing the commission of two or more crimes so related to each other that proof of the one tends to establish the other; (5) the identity of the person charged with the commission of the crime on trial. These exceptions are stated generally and not with categorical precision and may not be all-inclusive. (*People* v. *Molineux,* 168 N.Y.264; *People* v. *Pettanza,* 207 N.Y.560; *People* v. *Moran,* 246 N.Y. 100,106.) None of them apply here nor were the weapons offered under an exception to the general rule. They were offered as a part of the transaction itself. The accused was tried only for the crime charged. The real question is whether the matter relied on has such a connection with the crime charged as to be admissible on any ground. If so, the fact that it constitutes another distinct crime does not render it inadmissible. (*Commonwealth* v. *Snell,* 189 Mass.12,

21.) The rule laid down in the *Molineux* case has never been applied to prevent the People from proving all the elements of the offense charged, although separate crimes are included in such proof. Thus in this case no question is made as to the separate crime of illegal possession of the weapon with which the killing was done. It was "a part of the history of the case" having a distinct relation to and bearing upon the facts connected with the killing. (*People* v. *Governale*, 193 N.Y.581; *People* v. *Rogers*, 192 N.Y.331; *People* v. *Hill*, 198 N.Y.64; *People* v. *Rodawald*, 177 N.Y.408.)

As the District Attorney argues in his brief, if defendant had been arrested at the time of the killing and these weapons had been found on his person, the People would not have been barred from proving the fact, and the further fact that they were nearby in his apartment should not preclude the proof as bearing on the entire deed of which the act charged forms a part. Defendant was presented to the jury as a man having dangerous weapons in his possession, making a selection therefrom and going forth to put into execution his threats to kill; not as a man of a dangerous disposition in general, but as one who, having an opportunity to select a weapon to carry out his threats, proceeded to do so.

If the confession was admissible on this point, the weapons themselves were admissible in evidence. If the evidence corroborates the confession and several crimes having "an obvious relation to the crime charged in the indictment" are referred to in the same confession, both the entire confession and the corroborative evidence are admissible. (*People* v. *Rogers*, *supra*, p.352.) The relation between the possession of the weapons and the crime charged tended to corroborate the confession as a whole. The sequence of events made the chain incomplete without this important link.

The case would have been quite different if the weapons came into defendant's possession after the killing. The proof would then be of separate crimes unconnected with the killing and its admission reversible error under the *Molineux Case* (*supra*).

It is urged that defendant may have been half-drunk, infuriated, frightened, impulsive and measurably irresponsible; that he should not have been convicted of murder in the first degree; that the proof of possession of the weapons prejudiced the jury against him. If, as we have held, the proof was competent, the jury was free to give it such weight as it deserved. On the other hand, if it was incompetent, was the error substantial enough to call for the reversal of his conviction? Defendant presented his side of the case to the jury. He gave his account of the weapons and how he came by them, which was consistent with innocent purpose on his part. Admittedly he did have an argument with Coppola and his fellows, did go home, did return armed and did quarrel and kill. His answer is that the killing was accidental. How can we say with confidence in the circumstances of this case that the evidence, even if technically objectionable, so tended to influence the jury against him that "justice requires a new trial?" (Code Crim. Pro. §528.) While it is not inconceivable that the result might have been otherwise without this evidence (*People* v. *Slover*, 232 N.Y.264,267), it is unlikely that it turned the minds of the jury from a lesser degree of crime to the disadvantage of accused. In the circumstances of this case, whether he had one weapon or a dozen would not materially change the nature of his offense. The proof merely darkened that which was black enough when painted by his own brush.

The judgment of conviction should be affirmed.

LEHMAN, KELLOGG and O'BRIEN, JJ., concur with CAR-

DOZO, Ch.J.; POUND, J., dissents in opinion in which CRANE and HUBBS, JJ., concur.

Judgment reversed, etc.[1]

AGENCY

MARY E.SCHLOENDORFF, Appellant, *v.* THE SOCIETY OF THE NEW YORK HOSPITAL, Respondent.

CARDOZO, J. In the year 1771, by royal charter of George III., the Society of the New York Hospital was organized for the care and healing of the sick. During the century and more which has since passed, it has devoted itself to that high task. It has no capital stock; it does not distribute profits; and its physicians and surgeons, both the visiting and the resident staff, serve it without pay. Those who seek it in search of health, are charged nothing, if they are needy, either for board or for treatment. The well-to-do are required by its by-laws to pay $7 a week for board, an amount insufficient to cover the per capita cost of maintenance. Whatever income is thus received, is added to the income derived from the hospital's foundation, and helps to make it possible for the work to go on. The purpose is not profit, but charity, and the incidental revenue does not change the defendant's standing as a charitable institution. (*People ex rel. Society of N.Y. Hospital* v. *Purdy*, 58 Hun, 386; 126 N.Y.679.)

To this hospital the plaintiff came in January, 1908. She was suffering from some disorder of the stomach. She asked the superintendent or one of his assistants what the charge would be and was told that it would be $7 a week. She be-

---

1. For a critical discussion of the law of homicide, especially dealing with the distinctions in this case, see Cardozo, Address before the New York Academy of Medicine, 'What Medicine Can Do for Law,' 1 November 1928, *Law and Literature*, 96–101.

came an inmate of the hospital, and after some weeks of treatment the house physician, Dr. Bartlett, discovered a lump, which proved to be a fibroid tumor. He consulted the visiting surgeon, Dr. Stimson, who advised an operation. The plaintiff's testimony is that the character of the lump could not, so the physicians informed her, be determined without an ether examination. She consented to such an examination, but notified Dr. Bartlett, as she says, that there must be no operation. She was taken at night from the medical to the surgical ward and prepared for an operation by a nurse. On the following day ether was administered, and while she was unconscious a tumor was removed. Her testimony is that this was done without her consent or knowledge. She is contradicted both by Dr. Stimson and by Dr. Bartlett, as well as by many of the attendant nurses. For the purpose of this appeal, however, since a verdict was directed in favor of the defendant, her narrative, even if improbable, must be taken as true. Following the operation, and, according to the testimony of her witnesses, because of it, gangrene developed in her left arm; some of her fingers had to be amputated; and her sufferings were intense. She now seeks to charge the hospital with liability for the wrong.

Certain principles of law governing the rights and duties of hospitals when maintained as charitable institutions have, after much discussion, become no longer doubtful. It is the settled rule that such a hospital is not liable for the negligence of its physicians and nurses in the treatment of patients. (*Hordern* v. *Salvation Army,* 199 N.Y.233; *Collins* v. *N.Y. Post Graduate Med. School & Hospital,* 59 App.Div.63, and cases there cited; *Wilson* v. *Brooklyn Homeopathic Hospital,* 97 App.Div.37; *Cunningham* v. *Sheltering Arms,* 135 App.Div. 178; *Bruce* v. *Central M.E. Church,* 147 Mich.230; *U.P.R.Co.*

v. *Artist*, 60 Fed.Rep.365; *Hearns* v. *Waterbury Hospital*, 66 Conn.98; *Hillyer* v. *St. Bartholomew's Hospital*, L.R. [2 K.B. 1909] 820.) This exemption has been placed upon two grounds. The first is that of implied waiver. It is said that one who accepts the benefit of a charity enters into a relation which exempts one's benefactor from liability for the negligence of his servants in administering the charity. (*Hordern* v. *Salvation Army, supra.*) The hospital remains exempt though the patient makes some payment to help defray the cost of board. (*Collins* v. *N.Y. Post Graduate Med. School & Hospital, supra*; *Wilson* v. *Brooklyn Homeopathic Hospital, supra*; *Cunningham* v. *Sheltering Arms, supra*; *McDonald* v. *Mass.Gen. Hospital*, 120 Mass.432; *Downes* v. *Harper Hospital*, 101 Mich.555; *Powers* v. *Mass. Homeopathic Hospital*, 109 Fed.Rep.294.) Such a payment is regarded as a contribution to the income of the hospital to be devoted, like its other funds, to the maintenance of the charity. The second ground of the exemption is the relation subsisting between a hospital and the physicians who serve it. It is said that this relation is not one of master and servant, but that the physician occupies the position, so to speak, of an independent contractor, following a separate calling, liable, of course, for his own wrongs to the patient whom he undertakes to serve, but involving the hospital in no liability if due care has been taken in his selection. On one or the other, and often on both of these grounds, a hospital has been held immune from liability to patients for the malpractice of its physicians. The reasons that have led to the adoption of this rule are, of course, inapplicable where the wrong is committed by a servant of the hospital and the sufferer is not a patient. It is, therefore, also a settled rule that a hospital is liable to strangers, *i.e.*, to persons other than patients, for the torts of its employees committed within the line of their employment. (*Kellogg* v. *Church Charity Foundation*, 203 N.Y.191; *Hordern* v. *Salvation Army, supra*.)

In the case at hand, the wrong complained of is not merely negligence. It is trespass. Every human being of adult years and sound mind has a right to determine what shall be done with his own body; and a surgeon who performs an operation without his patient's consent, commits an assault, for which he is liable in damages. (*Pratt* v. *Davis*, 224 Ill.300; *Mohr* v. *Williams*, 95 Minn.261.) This is true except in cases of emergency where the patient is unconscious and where it is necessary to operate before consent can be obtained. The fact that the wrong complained of here is trespass rather than negligence, distinguishes this case from most of the cases that have preceded it. In such circumstances the hospital's exemption from liability can hardly rest upon implied waiver. Relatively to this transaction, the plaintiff was a stranger. She had never consented to become a patient for any purpose other than an examination under ether. She had never waived the right to recover damages for any wrong resulting from this operation, for she had forbidden the operation. In this situation, the true ground for the defendant's exemption from liability is that the relation between a hospital and its physicians is not that of master and servant. The hospital does not undertake to act through them, but merely to procure them to act upon their own responsibility. That view of the relation has the support of high authority. The governing principle was well stated by Durfee, Ch.J., speaking for the Supreme Court of Rhode Island in *Glavin* v. *Rhode Island Hospital* (12 R.I.411, 424): "If A. out of charity employs a physician to attend B., his sick neighbor, the physician does not become A.'s servant, and A., if he has been duly careful in selecting him, will not be answerable to B. for his malpractice. The reason is, that A. does not undertake to treat B. through the agency of the physician, but only to procure for B. the services of the physician. The relation of master and servant is not established between A. and the physician. And so there is no such relation between the corporation and the physicians and surgeons who give their services at the hospital. It is true the corporation has power to dismiss them; but it has this power not because they are its servants, but because of its control of the hospital where their services are rendered. They would not recognize the right of the corporation, while retaining them, to direct them in their treatment of patients." This language was quoted and adopted in a recent case in England, where the subject of a hospital's liability was much considered. (*Hillyer* v. *St. Bartholomew's Hosp.*, L.R. [2 K.B.1909] 820.) In the Court of Appeal it was said by FARWELL, L.J.: "It is, in my opinion, impossible to contend that Mr. Lockwood, the surgeon, or the acting assistant surgeon, or the acting house surgeon, or the administrator of anæsthetics, or any of them, were servants in the proper sense of the word; they are all professional men, employed by the defendants to exercise their profession to the best of their abilities according to their own discretion; but in exercising it they are in no way under the orders or bound to obey the directions of the defendants." (See also: *Hall* v. *Lees*, L.R. [2 K.B.1904] 602; *Evans* v. *Liverpool Corporation*, L.R. [1 K.B.1906] 160; *Kellogg* v. *Church Charity Foundation*, 128 App.Div.214,216; *Hearne* v. *Waterbury Hospital*, 66 Conn.98; *Laubheim* v. *De K.N.S.Co.*, 107 N.Y.228.)

The defendant undertook to procure for this plaintiff the services of a physician. It did procure them. It procured the services of Dr. Bartlett and Dr. Stimson. One or both of those physicians (if we are to credit the plaintiff's narrative) ordered that an operation be performed on her in disregard of her instructions. The administrative staff of the hospital believing in good faith that the order was a proper one, and without notice to the contrary, gave to the operating surgeons the facilities of the surgical ward. The operation was then performed. The wrong was not that of the hospital; it was that of physicians, who were not the defendant's servants, but were pursuing an independent calling, a profession sanctioned by a solemn oath, and safeguarded by stringent penalties. If, in serving their patient, they violated her commands, the responsibility is not the defendant's; it is theirs. There is no distinction in that respect between the visiting and the resident physicians. (*Hillyer* v. *St.Barth.Hosp.*, *supra*.) Whether the hospital undertakes to procure a physician from afar, or to have one on the spot, its liability remains the same.

I have said that the hospital supplied its facilities to the surgeons without notice that they contemplated a wrong. I think this is clearly true. The suggestion is made that notice may be gathered from two circumstances: from the plaintiff's statement to one or more of the nurses, and from her statement to the assistant administering the gas. To that suggestion I cannot yield my assent.

It is true, I think, of nurses as of physicians, that in treating a patient they are not acting as the servants of the hospital. The superintendent is a servant of the hospital; the assistant superintendents, the orderlies, and the other members of the administrative staff are servants of the hospital. But nurses are employed to carry out the orders of the physicians, to whose authority they are subject. The hospital undertakes to procure for the patient the services of a nurse. It does not undertake through the agency of nurses to render those services itself. The reported cases make no distinction in that respect between the position of a nurse and that of a physician (*Powers*

v. *Mass. Hospital, supra; Ward* v. *St. Vincent's Hospital,* 78 App.Div.317; *Cunningham* v. *Sheltering Arms, supra; Hillyer* v. *St. Bartholomew's Hospital, supra,* at p.827); and none is justified in principle. If there are duties performed by nurses foreign to their duties in carrying out the physician's orders, and having relation to the administrative conduct of the hospital, the fact is not established by this record, nor was it in the discharge of such duties that the defendant's nurses were then serving. The acts of preparation immediately preceding the operation are necessary to its successful performance, and are really part of the operation itself. They are not different in that respect from the administration of the ether. Whatever the nurse does in those preliminary stages is done, not as the servant of the hospital, but in the course of the treatment of the patient, as the delegate of the surgeon to whose orders she is subject. The hospital is not chargeable with her knowledge that the operation is improper any more than with the surgeon's.

If, however, it could be assumed that a nurse is a servant of the hospital, I do not think that anything said by the plaintiff to any of the defendant's nurses fairly gave notice to them that the purpose was to cut open the plaintiff's body without her consent. The visiting surgeon in charge of the case was one of the most eminent in the city of New York. The assistant physicians and surgeons were men of tested merit. The plaintiff was prepared for the operation at night. She said to the night nurse, according to her statement, that she was not going to be operated on, that she was merely going to be examined under the influence of ether, and the nurse professed to understand that this was so. "Every now and then I asked, 'Do you understand that I am not to be operated on?' 'Yes, I understand; ether examination.' 'But,' I asked, 'I understand that this preparation is for operation.' She said, 'It is just the same in ether examination as in operation—the same preparation.' " The nurse with whom this conversation is said to have occurred left the ward early in the morning, and the operation was performed in her absence the following afternoon. Was she to infer from the plaintiff's words that a distinguished surgeon intended to mutilate the plaintiff's body in defiance of the plaintiff's orders? Was it her duty, as a result of this talk, to report to the superintendent of the hospital that the ward was about to be utilized for the commission of an assault? I think that no such interpretation of the facts would have suggested itself to any reasonable mind. The preparation for an ether examination is to some extent the same as for an operation. The hour was midnight, and the plaintiff was nervous and excited. The nurse soothed her by acquiescing in the statement that an ether examination was all that was then intended. An ether examination *was* intended, and how soon the operation was to follow, if at all, the nurse had no means of knowing. Still less had she reason to suspect that it would follow against the plaintiff's orders. If, when the following afternoon came, the plaintiff persisted in being unwilling to submit to an operation, the presumption was that the distinguished surgeon in charge of the case would perform none. There may be cases where a patient ought not to be advised of a contemplated operation until shortly before the appointed hour. To discuss such a subject at midnight might cause needless and even harmful agitation. About such matters a nurse is not qualified to judge. She is drilled to habits of strict obedience. She is accustomed to rely unquestioningly upon the judgment of her superiors. No woman occupying such a position would reasonably infer from the plaintiff's words that it was the purpose of the surgeons to operate whether the plaintiff forbade it or not. I conclude, therefore, that the plaintiff's statements to the nurse on the night before the operation are insufficient to charge the hospital with notice of a contemplated wrong. I can conceive of cases where a patient's struggles or outcries in the effort to avoid an operation might be such as to give notice to the administrative staff that the surgeons were acting in disregard of their patient's commands. In such circumstances, it may well be that by permitting its facilities to be utilized for such a purpose without resistance or at least protest, the hospital would make itself a party to the trespass, and become liable as a joint tort feasor. (*Sharp* v. *Erie R.R.Co.*, 184 N.Y.100.) I do not find in this record the elements necessary to call that principle into play.

Still more clearly, the defendant is not chargeable with notice because of the plaintiff's statements to the physician who administered the gas and ether. She says she asked him whether an operation was to be performed, and that he told her he did not know; that his duty was to give the gas, and nothing more. She answered that she wished to tell some one that there must be no operation; that she had come merely for an ether examination, and he told her that if she had come only for examination, nothing else would be done. There is nothing in the record to suggest that he believed anything to the contrary. He took no part in the operation, and had no knowledge of it. After the gas was administered she was taken into another room. It does not appear, therefore, that this physician was a party to any wrong. In any event, he was not the servant of the hospital. His position in that respect does not differ from that of the operating surgeon. If he was a party to the trespass, he did not subject the defendant to liability.

The conclusion, therefore, follows that the trial judge did not err in his direction of a verdict. A ruling would indeed, be an unfortunate one that might constrain charitable institutions, as a measure of self-protection, to limit their activities. A hospital opens its doors without discrimination to all who seek its aid. It gathers in its wards a company of skilled physicians and trained nurses, and places their services at the call of the afflicted, without scrutiny of the character or the worth of those who appeal to it, looking at nothing and caring for nothing beyond the fact of their affliction. In this beneficent work, it does not subject itself to liability for damages though the ministers of healing whom it has selected have proved unfaithful to their trust.

The judgment should be affirmed, with costs.

HISCOCK, CHASE, COLLIN and CUDDEBACK, JJ., concur; WILLARD BARTLETT, Ch.J., absent; MILLER, J., not sitting.

Judgment affirmed.

PARTNERSHIP

MORTON H.MEINHARD, Respondent, *v.* WALTER J. SALMON et al., Appellants.[1]

CARDOZO, Ch.J. On April 10, 1902, Louisa M.Gerry leased to the defendant Walter J.Salmon the premises known as the Hotel Bristol at the northwest corner of Forty-second street and Fifth avenue in the city of New York. The lease was for a term of twenty years, commencing May 1, 1902, and ending April 30, 1922. The lessee undertook to change the hotel building for use as shops and offices at a cost of $200,000. Alterations and additions were to be accretions to the land.

Salmon, while in the course of treaty with the lessor as to the execution of the lease, was in course of treaty with Mein-

---

1. Though this is not strictly a 'partnership' case, it deals with a fundamental concept in the law of partnership.

hard, the plaintiff, for the necessary funds. The result was a joint venture with terms embodied in a writing. Meinhard was to pay to Salmon half of the moneys requisite to reconstruct, alter, manage and operate the property. Salmon was to pay to Meinhard 40 per cent of the net profits for the first five years of the lease and 50 per cent for the years thereafter. If there were losses, each party was to bear them equally. Salmon, however, was to have sole power to "manage, lease, underlet and operate" the building. There were to be certain preemptive rights for each in the contingency of death.

The two were coadventurers, subject to fiduciary duties akin to those of partners (*King* v. *Barnes*, 109 N.Y.267). As to this we are all agreed. The heavier weight of duty rested, however, upon Salmon. He was a coadventurer with Meinhard, but he was manager as well. During the early years of the enterprise, the building, reconstructed, was operated at a loss. If the relation had then ended, Meinhard as well as Salmon would have carried a heavy burden. Later the profits became large with the result that for each of the investors there came a rich return. For each, the venture had its phases of fair weather and of foul. The two were in it jointly, for better or for worse.

When the lease was near its end, Elbridge T.Gerry had become the owner of the reversion. He owned much other property in the neighborhood, one lot adjoining the Bristol Building on Fifth avenue and four lots on Forty-second street. He had a plan to lease the entire tract for a long term to some one who would destroy the buildings then existing, and put up another in their place. In the latter part of 1921, he submitted such a project to several capitalists and dealers. He was unable to carry it through with any of them. Then, in January, 1922, with less than four months of the lease to run, he approached the defendant Salmon. The result was a new lease to the Midpoint Realty Company, which is owned and controlled by Salmon, a lease covering the whole tract, and involving a huge outlay. The term is to be twenty years, but successive covenants for renewal will extend it to a maximum of eighty years at the will of either party. The existing buildings may remain unchanged for seven years. They are then to be torn down, and a new building to cost $3,000,000 is to be placed upon the site. The rental, which under the Bristol lease was only $55,000, is to be from $350,000 to $475,000 for the properties so combined. Salmon personally guaranteed the performance by the lessee of the covenants of the new lease until such time as the new building had been completed and fully paid for.

The lease between Gerry and the Midpoint Realty Company was signed and delivered on January 25, 1922. Salmon had not told Meinhard anything about it. Whatever his motive may have been, he had kept the negotiations to himself. Meinhard was not informed even of the bare existence of a project. The first that he knew of it was in February when the lease was an accomplished fact. He then made demand on the defendants that the lease be held in trust as an asset of the venture, making offer upon the trial to share the personal obligations incidental to the guaranty. The demand was followed by refusal, and later by this suit. A referee gave judgment for the plaintiff, limiting the plaintiff's interest in the lease, however, to 25 per cent. The limitation was on the theory that the plaintiff's equity was to be restricted to one-half of so much of the value of the lease as was contributed or represented by the occupation of the Bristol site. Upon cross-appeals to the Appellate Division, the judgment was modified so as to enlarge the equitable interest to one-half of the whole lease.

With this enlargement of plaintiff's interest, there went, of course, a corresponding enlargement of his attendant obligations. The case is now here on an appeal by the defendants.

Joint adventurers, like copartners, owe to one another, while the enterprise continues, the duty of the finest loyalty. Many forms of conduct permissible in a workaday world for those acting at arm's length, are forbidden to those bound by fiduciary ties. A trustee is held to something stricter than the morals of the market place. Not honesty alone, but the punctilio of an honor the most sensitive, is then the standard of behavior. As to this there has developed a tradition that is unbending and inveterate. Uncompromising rigidity has been the attitude of courts of equity when petitioned to undermine the rule of undivided loyalty by the "disintegrating erosion" of particular exceptions (*Wendt* v. *Fisher*, 243 N.Y.439,444). Only thus has the level of conduct for fiduciaries been kept at a level higher than that trodden by the crowd. It will not consciously be lowered by any judgment of this court.

The owner of the reversion, Mr. Gerry, had vainly striven to find a tenant who would favor his ambitious scheme of demolition and construction. Baffled in the search, he turned to the defendant Salmon in possession of the Bristol, the keystone of the project. He figured to himself beyond a doubt that the man in possession would prove a likely customer. To the eye of an observer, Salmon held the lease as owner in his own right, for himself and no one else. In fact, he held it as a fiduciary, for himself and another, sharers in a common venture. If this fact had been proclaimed, if the lease by its terms had run in favor of a partnership, Mr. Gerry, we may fairly assume, would have laid before the partners, and not merely before one of them, his plan of reconstruction. The pre-emptive privilege, or, better, the pre-emptive opportunity, that was thus an incident of the enterprise, Salmon appropriated to himself in secrecy and silence. He might have warned Meinhard that the plan had been submitted, and that either would be free to compete for the award. If he had done this, we do not need to say whether he would have been under a duty, if successful in the competition, to hold the lease so acquired for the benefit of a venture then about to end, and thus prolong by indirection its responsibilities and duties. The trouble about his conduct is that he excluded his coadventurer from any chance to compete, from any chance to enjoy the opportunity for benefit that had come to him alone by virtue of his agency. This chance, if nothing more, he was under a duty to concede. The price of its denial is an extension of the trust at the option and for the benefit of the one whom he excluded.

No answer is it to say that the chance would have been of little value even if seasonably offered. Such a calculus of probabilities is beyond the science of the chancery. Salmon, the real estate operator, might have been preferred to Meinhard, the woolen merchant. On the other hand, Meinhard might have offered better terms, or reinforced his offer by alliance with the wealth of others. Perhaps he might even have persuaded the lessor to renew the Bristol lease alone, postponing for a time, in return for higher rentals, the improvement of adjoining lots. We know that even under the lease as made the time for the enlargement of the building was delayed for seven years. All these opportunities were cut away from him through another's intervention. He knew that Salmon was the manager. As the time drew near for the expiration of the lease, he would naturally assume from silence, if from nothing else, that the lessor was willing to extend it for a term of years, or at least to let it stand as a lease from year to year. Not impossibly the lessor would have done so, whatever his protestations of unwillingness, if Salmon had not given assent to a project more attractive. At all events, notice of termination, even if not necessary, might seem, not unreasonably, to be something to be looked for, if the business was over and another tenant was to enter. In the absence of such notice, the matter of extension was one that would naturally be attended to by the manager of the enterprise, and not neglected altogether. At least, there was nothing in the situation to give warning to any one that while the lease was still in being, there had come to the manager an offer of extension which he had locked within his breast to be utilized by himself alone. The very fact that Salmon was in control with exclusive powers of direction charged him the more obviously with the duty of disclosure, since only through disclosure could opportunity be equalized. If he might cut off renewal by a purchase for his own benefit when four months were to pass before the lease would have an end, he might do so with equal right while there remained as many years (cf. *Mitchell* v. *Reed*, 61 N.Y. 123,127). He might steal a march on his comrade under cover of the darkness, and then hold the captured ground. Loyalty and comradeship are not so easily abjured.

Little profit will come from a dissection of the precedents. None precisely similar is cited in the briefs of counsel. What is similar in many, or so it seems to us, is the animating principle. Authority is, of course, abundant that one partner may not appropriate to his own use a renewal of a lease, though its term is to begin at the expiration of the partnership (*Mitchell* v. *Reed*, 61 N.Y.123; 84 N.Y.556). The lease at hand with its many changes is not strictly a renewal. Even so, the standard of loyalty for those in trust relations is without the fixed divisions of a graduated scale. There is indeed a dictum in one of our decisions that a partner, though he may not renew a lease, may purchase the reversion if he acts openly and fairly (*Anderson* v. *Lemon*, 8 N.Y.236; cf. White & Tudor, Leading Cases in Equity [9th ed.], vol.2, p.642; *Bevan* v. *Webb*, 1905, 1 Ch.620; *Griffith* v. *Owen*, 1907, 1 Ch.195,204,205). It is a dictum, and no more, for on the ground that he had acted slyly he was charged as a trustee. The holding is thus in favor of the conclusion that a purchase as well as a lease will succumb to the infection of secrecy and silence. Against the dictum in that case, moreover, may be set the opinion of DWIGHT, C., in *Mitchell* v. *Reed*, where there is a dictum to the contrary (61 N.Y. at p.143). To say that a partner is free without restriction to buy in the reversion of the property where the business is conducted is to say in effect that he may strip the good will of its chief element of value, since good will is largely dependent upon continuity of possession (*Matter of Brown*, 242 N.Y.1, 7). Equity refuses to confine within the bounds of classified transactions its precept of a loyalty that is undivided and unselfish. Certain at least it is that a "man obtaining his *locus standi*, and his opportunity for making such arrangements, by the position he occupies as a partner, is bound by his obligation to his copartners in such dealings not to separate his interest from theirs, but, if he acquires any benefit, to communicate it to them" (*Cassels* v. *Stewart*, 6 App.Cas.64,73). Certain it is also that there may be no abuse of special opportunities growing out of a special trust as manager or agent (*Matter of Biss*, 1903, 2 Ch.40; *Clegg* v. *Edmondson*, 8 D.M. & G.787, 807). If conflicting inferences are possible as to abuse or opportunity, the trier of the facts must make the choice between them. There can be no revision in this court unless the choice is clearly wrong. It is no answer for the fiduciary to say "that he was not bound to risk his money as he did, or to go into the enterprise at all" (*Beatty* v. *Guggenheim Exploration Co.*, 225 N.Y.380,385). "He might have kept out of it altogether, but if he went in, he could not withhold from his employer the benefit of the bargain" (*Beatty* v. *Guggenheim Exploration Co.*, *supra*). A constructive trust is then the remedial device through which preference of self is made subordinate to loyalty to others (*Beatty* v. *Guggenheim Exploration Co.*, *supra*). Many and varied are its phases and occasions (*Selwyn & Co.* v. *Waller*, 212 N.Y.507,512; *Robinson* v. *Jewett*, 116 N.Y.40; cf. *Tournier* v. *Nat.Prov. & Union Bank*, 1924, 1 K.B.461).

We have no thought to hold that Salmon was guilty of a conscious purpose to defraud. Very likely he assumed in all good faith that with the approaching end of the venture he might ignore his coadventurer and take the extension for himself. He had given to the enterprise time and labor as well as money. He had made it a success. Meinhard, who had given money, but neither time nor labor, had already been richly paid. There might seem to be something grasping in his insistence upon more. Such recriminations are not unusual when coadventurers fall out. They are not without their force if conduct is to be judged by the common standards of competitors. That is not to say that they have pertinency here. Salmon had put himself in a position in which thought of self was to be renounced, however hard the abnegation. He was much more than a coadventurer. He was a managing coadventurer (*Clegg* v. *Edmondson*, 8 D.M. & G.787,807). For him and for those like him, the rule of undivided loyalty is relentless and supreme (*Wendt* v. *Fischer*, *supra*; *Munson* v. *Syracuse, etc., R.R.Co.*, 103 N.Y.58,74). A different question would be here if there were lacking any nexus of relation between the business conducted by the manager and the opportunity brought to him as an incident of management (*Dean* v.

MacDowell, 8 Ch.D.345,354; *Aas* v. *Benham*, 1891, 2 Ch.244, 258; *Latta* v. *Kilbourn*, 150 U.S.524). For this problem, as for most, there are distinctions of degree. If Salmon had received from Gerry a proposition to lease a building at a location far removed, he might have held for himself the privilege thus acquired, or so we shall assume. Here the subject-matter of the new lease was an extension and enlargement of the subject-matter of the old one. A managing coadventurer appropriating the benefit of such a lease without warning to his partner might fairly expect to be reproached with conduct that was underhand, or lacking, to say the least, in reasonable candor, if the partner were to surprise him in the act of signing the new instrument. Conduct subject to that reproach does not receive from equity a healing benediction.

A question remains as to the form and extent of the equitable interest to be allotted to the plaintiff. The trust as declared has been held to attach to the lease which was in the name of the defendant corporation. We think it ought to attach at the option of the defendant Salmon to the shares of stock which were owned by him or were under his control. The difference may be important if the lessee shall wish to execute an assignment of the lease, as it ought to be free to do with the consent of the lessor. On the other hand, an equal division of the shares might lead to other hardships. It might take away from Salmon the power of control and management which under the plan of the joint venture he was to have from first to last. The number of shares to be allotted to the plaintiff should, therefore, be reduced to such an extent as may be necessary to preserve to the defendant Salmon the expected measure of dominion. To that end an extra share should be added to his half.

Subject to this adjustment, we agree with the Appellate Division that the plaintiff's equitable interest is to be measured by the value of half of the entire lease, and not merely by half of some undivided part. A single building covers the whole area. Physical division is impracticable along the lines of the Bristol site, the keystone of the whole. Division of interests and burdens is equally impracticable. Salmon, as tenant under the new lease, or as guarantor of the performance of the tenant's obligations, might well protest if Meinhard, claiming an equitable interest, had offered to assume a liability not equal to Salmon's, but only half as great. He might justly insist that the lease must be accepted by his coadventurer in such form as it had been given, and not constructively divided into imaginary fragments. What must be yielded to the one may be demanded by the other. The lease as it has been executed is single and entire. If confusion has resulted from the union of adjoining parcels, the trustee who consented to the union must bear the inconvenience (*Hart* v. *Ten Eyck*, 2 Johns.Ch.62).

Thus far, the case has been considered on the assumption that the interest in the joint venture acquired by the plaintiff in 1902 has been continuously his. The fact is, however, that in 1917 he assigned to his wife all his "right, title and interest in and to" the agreement with his coadventurer. The coadventurer did not object, but thereafter made his payments directly to the wife. There was a reassignment by the wife before this action was begun.

We do not need to determine what the effect of the assignment would have been in 1917 if either coadventurer had then chosen to treat the venture as dissolved. We do not even need to determine what the effect would have been if the enterprise had been a partnership in the strict sense with active duties of agency laid on each of the two adventurers. The form of the enterprise made Salmon the sole manager. The only active duty laid upon the other was one wholly ministerial, the duty of contributing his share of the expense. This he could still do with equal readiness, and still was bound to do, after the assignment to his wife. Neither by word nor by act did either partner manifest a choice to view the enterprise as ended. There is no inflexible rule in such conditions that dissolution shall ensue against the concurring wish of all that the venture shall continue. The effect of the assignment is then a question of intention (*Durkee* v. *Gunn*, 41 Kan.496,500; *Taft* v. *Buffum*, 14 Pick.322; cf. 69 A.S.R.417, and cases there cited).

Partnership Law (Cons. Laws, ch.39), section 53, subdivision 1, is to the effect that "a conveyance by a partner of his interest in the partnership does not of itself dissolve the partnership, nor, as against the other partners in the absence of agreement, entitle the assignee, during the continuance of the partnership, to interfere in the management or administration of the partnership business or affairs, or to require any information or account of partnership transactions, or to inspect the partnership books; but it merely entitles the assignee to receive in accordance with his contract the profits to which the assigning partner would otherwise be entitled." This statute, which took effect October 1, 1919, did not indeed revive the enterprise if automatically on the execution of the assignment a dissolution had resulted in 1917. It sums up with precision, however, the effect of the assignment as the parties meant to shape it. We are to interpret their relation in the revealing light of conduct. The rule of the statute, even if it has modified the rule as to partnerships in general (as to this see Pollock, Partnership, p.99, §31; Lindley, Partnership [9th ed.], 695; *Marquand* v. *N.Y.M.Co.*, 17 Johns.525), is an accurate statement of the rule at common law when applied to these adventurers. The purpose of the assignment, understood by every one concerned, was to lower the plaintiff's tax by taking income out of his return and adding it to the return to be made by his wife. She was the appointee of the profits, to whom checks were to be remitted. Beyond that, the relation was to be the same as it had been. No one dreamed for a moment that the enterprise was to be wound up, or that Meinhard was relieved of his continuing obligation to contribute to its expenses if contribution became needful. Coadventurers and assignee, and most of all the defendant Salmon, as appears by his own letters, went forward on that basis. For more than five years Salmon dealt with Meinhard on the assumption that the enterprise was a subsisting one with mutual rights and duties, or so at least the triers of the facts, weighing the circumstantial evidence, might not unreasonably infer. By tacit, if not express approval, he continued and preserved it. We think it is too late now, when charged as a trustee, to come forward with the claim that it had been disrupted and dissolved.

The judgment should be modified by providing that at the option of the defendant Salmon there may be substituted for a trust attaching to the lease a trust attaching to the shares of stock, with the result that one-half of such shares together with one additional share will in that event be allotted to the defendant Salmon and the other shares to the plaintiff, and as so modified the judgment should be affirmed with costs.

. . .

POUND, CRANE and LEHMAN, JJ., concur with CARDOZO, Ch.J., for modification of the judgment appealed from and affirmance as modified; ANDREWS, J., dissents in opinion in which KELLOGG and O'BRIEN, JJ., concur.

Judgment modified, etc.

EQUITY

GLOBE WOOLEN COMPANY, Appellant *v.* UTICA GAS AND ELECTRIC COMPANY, Respondent.

CARDOZO, J. The plaintiff, a corporation, sues to compel the specific performance of contracts to supply electric current to its mills. The defendant, also a corporation, answers that the contracts were made under the dominating influence of a common director; that their terms are unfair, and their consequences oppressive; and that hence they may not stand. A referee has sustained the defense; and the Appellate Division, with some modification, has affirmed his judgment.

The plaintiff is the owner of two mills in the city of Utica. One is for the manufacture of worsteds and the other for that of woolens. The defendant generates and sells electricity for light and power. For many years John F.Maynard has been the plaintiff's chief stockholder, its president and a member of its board of directors. He has also been a director of the defendant, and chairman of its executive committee. He received a single share of the defendant's stock to qualify him for office. He returned the share at once, and he has never held another. His property interest in the plaintiff is large. In the defendant he has none.

The history of the transaction may be briefly stated. At the beginning, the mills were run by steam, and the plant was antiquated and inadequate. As early as 1903, one Greenidge, then the superintendent and later the general manager of the defendant's electrical department, suggested to Mr. Maynard the substitution of electric power. Nothing came of the suggestion then. Mr. Maynard was fearful that the cost of equipment would be too great unless the defendant would guarantee a saving in the cost of operation. None the less, a change was felt to be important, and from time to time the subject was taken up anew. In 1904, there was an investigation of the power plant by Greenidge and a written report of its condition. For this service, though he was still in the defendant's employ, he was paid by Mr. Maynard. In 1905, the substitution of electricity was again considered, but dismissed as impracticable because of the plaintiff's continued insistence upon a guarantee of saving. In the fall of 1906, the project was renewed. It was renewed by Maynard and Greenidge, who debated it between themselves. There were other officers of the defendant who knew that the project was afoot, but they took no part in formulating it. Maynard still insisted on a guarantee of saving. The plaintiff's books were thrown open to Greenidge, who calculated for himself the cost of operation with steam and the probable cost with electricity. When the investigation was over, a contract was closed. It took the form of letters exchanged between Greenidge and Maynard. In the letter signed by Greenidge, the defendant proposed to supply the plaintiff's worsted mill with electricity at a maximum rate of $.0104 per kilowatt hour, and to guarantee that the cost for heat and light and power would show a saving each month of $300 as compared with the cost for the corresponding month in the year previous to the change. There was to be a trial period ending July 1, 1907. Then, at the plaintiff's option, the contract was to run for five years, with a privilege of renewal for a like term. In a letter signed by Maynard on October 22, 1906, the plaintiff accepted the proposal. At once, the defendant made preparations to install the new equipment. Six weeks later, on December 1, 1906, Mr. Maynard laid the contract before the defendant's executive committee. He went to the meeting with Mr. Greenidge. The contract was read. Mr. Lewis, the vice-president, asked Mr.

Greenidge what the rate would be, and was told about $.0104 per kilowatt hour. Mr. Beardsley, another director, asked whether the contract was a profitable one for the company, and was told by Mr. Greenidge that it was. Mr. Maynard kept silent. A resolution was moved and carried that the contract be ratified. Mr. Maynard presided at the meeting, and put the resolution, but was excused from voting.

This settled the problem of power for the worsted mill. Attention was next directed to the woolen mill. Again, Mr. Maynard and Mr. Greenidge put the project through, unaided. In February, 1907, letters, similar in most things to the earlier ones, were exchanged. The guarantee of saving for this mill as for the other was to be $300 a month. There were, however, new provisions to the effect that the contract should apply to "current used for any purposes in any extensions or additions to the mills," and that in case of shortage of electricity the plaintiff should be preferred in service over all other customers except the city of Utica. At a meeting of the executive committee, held February 11, 1907, this contract was ratified. The statement was made by Mr. Greenidge, in the presence of Mr. Maynard, that it was practically a duplicate of the first contract, except that it related to another mill. Nothing was said about the new provisions. Mr. Maynard presided and put the resolution, but did not vote.

At a cost to the plaintiff of more than $21,000, the requisite changes in the mills were made, and the new power was supplied. It quickly appeared that the defendant had made a losing contract; but only gradually did the extent of the loss, its permanence and its causes unfold themselves. Greenidge had miscalculated the amount of steam that would be required to heat the dye houses. The expenditure for coal mounted by leaps and bounds. The plaintiff dyed more yarn and less slubbing than before. But the dyeing of yarn takes twice as much heat as that of slubbing, and thus doubles the cost of fuel. These and like changes in the output of the mills had not been foreseen by Greenidge, and Maynard had not warned of them. In 1909, the defendant became alarmed at the mounting loss. Various tests and palliatives were suggested and adopted, but there was no change in the result. Finally, in February, 1911, the defendant gave notice of rescission. At that time, it had supplied the plaintiff with electricity worth $69,500.75 if paid for at the maximum rate fixed by the contract, and $60,000 if paid for at the lowest rate charged to any customer in Utica. Yet not only had it received nothing, but it owed the plaintiff under its guarantee $11,721.41. The finding is that a like loss prolonged to the end of the term would amount to $300,000.

These are the contracts which the courts below have annulled. The referee annulled them absolutely. The Appellate Division imposed the condition that the defendant reimburse the plaintiff for the cost of installation. The defendant makes no complaint of the condition. The plaintiff, appealing, stands upon its bargain.

We think the evidence supports the conclusion that the contracts are voidable at the election of the defendant. The plaintiff does not deny that this would be true if the dual director had voted for their adoption (*Munson* v. *Syracuse, G. & C.R.R.Co.*, 103 N.Y.58). But the argument is that by refusing to vote, he shifted the responsibility to his associates, and may reap a profit from their errors. One does not divest oneself so readily of one's duties as trustee. The refusal to vote has, indeed, this importance: it gives to the transaction the form and presumption of propriety, and requires one who would invalidate it to probe beneath the surface (*Davids* v.

Davids, 135 App.Div.206,209). But "the great rule of law" (ANDREWS, J., in *Munson* v. *Syracuse, G. & C.R.R.Co.*, *supra*, p.73) which holds a trustee to the duty of constant and unqualified fidelity, is not a thing of forms and phrases. A dominating influence may be exerted in other ways than by a vote (*Adams* v. *Burke*, 201 Ill.395; *Davids* v. *Davids*, *supra*). A beneficiary, about to plunge into a ruinous course of dealing, may be betrayed by silence as well as by the spoken word. The trustee is free to stand aloof, while others act, if all is equitable and fair. He cannot rid himself of the duty to warn and to denounce, if there is improvidence or oppression, either apparent on the surface, or lurking beneath the surface, but visible to his practised eye (*Davids* v. *Davids*, *supra*; *Crocker* v. *Cumberland Mining & Milling Co.*, 31 S.Dak.137, 146; *Fort Payne Rolling Mill* v. *Hill*, 174 Mass.224; *Wyman* v. *Bowman*, 127 Fed.Rep.257,274).

There was an influence here, dominating perhaps, and surely potent and persuasive, which was exerted by Mr. Maynard from the beginning to the end. In all the stages of preliminary treaty, he dealt with a subordinate, who looked up to him as to a superior, and was alert to serve his pleasure. There was no clean-cut cleavage in those stages between his conflicting offices and agencies (*Hoyle* v. *Plattsburgh & M.R. R.Co.*, 54 N.Y.314,328,329). No label identified the request of Mr. Maynard, the plaintiff's president, as something separate from the advice of Mr. Maynard, the defendant's chairman. Superior and subordinate together framed a contract, and together closed it. It came before the executive committee as an accomplished fact. The letters had been signed and delivered. Work had been begun. All that remained was a ratification, which may have been needless, and which even if needful, took the aspect of a mere formal-ity. There was some attempt to show that Mr. Lewis, the vice-president, had seen the letters before. The testimony of Mr. Greenidge indicates the contrary. In support of the judgment, we accept his testimony as true. That the letters had been seen by others, there is not even a pretense. The members of the committee, hearing the contract for the first time, knew that it had been framed by the chairman of the meeting. They were assured in his presence that it was just and equitable. Faith in his loyalty disarmed suspicion.

There was, then, a relation of trust reposed, of influence exerted, of superior knowledge on the one side and legitimate dependence on the other (*Sage* v. *Culver*, 147 N.Y.241,247; *Davids* v. *Davids*, *supra*). At least, a finding that there was this relation has evidence to sustain it. A trustee may not cling to contracts thus won, unless their terms are fair and just (*Crocker* v. *Cumberland Mining & Milling Co.*, *supra*, and cases there cited; *Dougan* v. *MacPherson*, 1902, A.C.197, 200; Thompson on Corp.1228,1231). His dealings with his beneficiary are "viewed with jealousy by the courts, and may be set aside on slight grounds" (*Twin Lick Oil Co.* v. *Marbury*, 91 U.S.587,588). He takes the risk of an enforced surrender of his bargain if it turns out to be improvident. There must be candor and equity in the transaction, and some reasonable proportion between benefits and burdens.

The contracts before us do not survive these tests. The unfairness is startling, and the consequences have been disastrous. The mischief consists in this: that the guarantee has not been limited by a statement of the conditions under which the mills are to be run. No matter how large the business, no matter how great the increase in the price of labor or of fuel, no matter what the changes in the nature or the proportion of the products, no matter even though there be extensions of the plant, the defendant has pledged its word that for ten years there will be a saving of $600 a month, $300 for each mill, $7,200 a year. As a result of that pledge it has supplied the plaintiff with electric current for nothing, and owes, if the contract stands, about $11,000 for the privilege. These elements of unfairness, Mr. Maynard must have known, if indeed his knowledge be material. He may not have known how great the loss would be. He may have trusted to the superior technical skill of Mr. Greenidge to compute with approximate accuracy the comparative cost of steam and electricity. But he cannot have failed to know that he held a one-sided contract, which left the defendant at his mercy. He was not blind to the likelihood that in a term of ten years there would be changes in the business. The swiftness with which some of the changes followed, permits the inference that they were premeditated. There was a prompt increase in the proportion of yarns as compared with slubbing when the guarantee of saving charged the defendant with the greater cost of fuel. But whether these and other changes were premeditated or not, at least they were recognized as possible. With that recognition, no word of warning was uttered to Greenidge or to any of the defendant's officers. There slumbered within these contracts a potency of profit which the plaintiff neither ignored in their making nor forgot in their enforcement.

It is no answer to say that this potency, if obvious to Maynard, ought also to have been obvious to other members of the committee. They did not know, as he did, the likelihood or the significance of changes in the business. There was need too of reflection and analysis before the dangers stood revealed. For the man who framed the contracts, there was opportunity to consider and to judge. His fellow members, hearing them for the first time, and trustful of his loyalty, would have no thought of latent peril. That they had none is sufficiently attested by the fact that the contracts were approved. There was inequality, therefore, both in knowledge and in the opportunity for knowledge. It is not important in such circumstances whether the trustee foresaw the precise evils that developed. The inference that he did, might not be unsupported by the evidence. But the indefinite *possibilities* of hardship, the opportunity in changing circumstances to wrest unlooked for profits and impose unlooked for losses, these must have been foreseen. Foreseen or not, they were there, and their presence permeates the contracts with oppression and inequity.

We hold, therefore, that the refusal to vote does not nullify as of course an influence and predominance exerted without a vote. We hold that the constant duty rests on a trustee to seek no harsh advantage to the detriment of his trust, but rather to protest and renounce if through the blindness of those who treat with him he gains what is unfair. And because there is evidence that in the making of these contracts, that duty was ignored, the power of equity was fittingly exercised to bring them to an end.

The judgment should be affirmed with costs.

HISCOCK, Ch.J., CHASE, COLLIN, CUDDEBACK and POUND, JJ., concur; ANDREWS, J., absent.

Judgment affirmed.

LEGAL ETHICS

In the Matter of JACOB ROUSS, an Attorney, Appellant.
THE ASSOCIATION OF THE BAR OF THE CITY OF NEW YORK, Respondent.

CARDOZO, J. In 1912 the appellant, Jacob Rouss, was the attorney for one Eugene Fox. Fox, a member of the police force in the city of New York, had been brought before a magistrate on the charge of collecting bribes from the keeper of a disorderly house. The keeper of the house, one George A.Sipp, had been served with a subpœna, or at least there had been to his knowledge an attempt to serve him. Rouss and Sipp's attorney entered into an arrangement that Sipp for a money consideration would keep without the state. The money was paid; Sipp fulfilled his bargain; and Fox was discharged. Indictments were later found against five inspectors of police for conspiracy to obstruct justice through the suppression of Sipp's testimony. On the trial of those indictments, Rouss was a witness for the People. His testimony as there given is in substance a confession of guilt. Charges of professional misconduct were afterward preferred against him. To these charges, he makes answer that he is immune from discipline by force of section 584 of the Penal Law, which says that "no person shall be excused from attending and testifying, or producing any books, papers or other documents before any court, magistrate or referee, upon any investigation, proceeding or trial, for a violation of any of the provisions of this article, [Art. 54 defining and punishing conspiracy], upon the ground or for the reason that the testimony or evidence, documentary or otherwise, required of him may tend to convict him of a crime or to subject him to a penalty or forfeiture; but no person shall be prosecuted or subjected to any penalty or forfeiture for or on account of any transaction, matter or thing concerning which he may so testify or produce evidence, documentary or otherwise, and no testimony so given or produced shall be received against him, upon any criminal investigation, proceeding or trial." The question is whether disbarment is a penalty or forfeiture within the meaning of that statute.

Membership in the bar is a privilege burdened with conditions. A fair private and professional character is one of them. Compliance with that condition is essential at the moment of admission; but it is equally essential afterwards (*Selling* v. *Radford*, 243 U.S.46; *Matter of Durant*, 80 Conn.140 147). Whenever the condition is broken, the privilege is lost. To refuse admission to an unworthy applicant is not to punish him for past offenses. The examination into character, like the examination into learning, is merely a test of fitness. To strike the unworthy lawyer from the roll is not to add to the pains and penalties of crime. The examination into character is renewed; and the test of fitness is no longer satisfied. For these reasons courts have repeatedly said that disbarment is not punishment (*Ex parte Wall*, 107 U.S.265; *Matter of Randall*, 11 Allen, 473,480; *Matter of Randel*, 158 N.Y.216; *Boston Bar Assn.* v. *Casey*, 211 Mass.187,192; *Matter of Durant*, *supra*). "The question is," said Lord MANSFIELD, "whether, after the conduct of this man, it is proper that he should continue a member of a profession which should stand free from all suspicion" (*Ex parte Brounsall*, Cowp. 829). "It is not," he continued, "by way of punishment; but the court, on such cases, exercise their discretion whether a man whom they have formerly admitted, is a proper person to be continued on the roll or not." This ruling was announced after consultation with all the judges, "as it is for the dignity of the profession that a solemn opinion should be given." On that high plane the jurisdiction was thus early placed, and in that high spirit it has been exercised. Even pardon will not elude it. Pardon blots out the offense, and all its penalties, forfeitures and sentences; but the power to disbar remains (*Matter of an Attorney*, 86 N.Y.563). We do not need to inquire now whether the power is so essential and inherent that the legislature may not take it away (*State ex rel. Wood* v. *Raynolds*, 158 Pac.Rep.413, and cases there cited). At least we will not hold it to have been taken away by words of doubtful meaning. We will not declare, unless driven to it by sheer necessity, that a confessed criminal has been intrenched by the very confession of his guilt beyond the power of removal.

The problem before us, let it be recalled, is one solely of statutory construction. There is no question of constitutional right. The Constitution says that no person "shall be compelled in any criminal case to be a witness against himself" (Const.art.1, sec.6). A proceeding looking to disbarment is not a criminal case (*Matter of Randel, supra*). We do not suggest that the witness is protected by the Constitution only when testifying in the criminal courts. The law is settled to the contrary. But to bring him within the protection of the Constitution, the disclosure asked of him must expose him to punishment for crime. There may be a broader privilege by statute or at common law. If that is so, the Constitution does not assure its preservation (*Perrine* v. *Striker*, 7 Paige, 598,602; *People ex rel. Hackley* v. *Kelly*, 24 N.Y.74,82,83; *Counselman* v. *Hitchcock*, 142 U.S.547,562). Where speech will expose to penalties unrelated to crime, the legislature may withdraw the privilege of silence. It has done so in the past (*Perrine* v. *Striker, supra; Robinson* v. *Smith*, 3 Paige, 222, 231). It may do so again.

We think that section 584 of the Penal Law was designed to give an immunity as broad as the constitutional privilege, and no broader (*State* v. *Jack*, 69 Kan.387). Its origin is not doubtful. The rule has always been that disclosure of crimes may be compelled if there is adequate immunity. The difficulty has been to know when the immunity is adequate. *People ex rel. Hackley* v. *Kelly* (24 N.Y.74, decided in 1861) held it to be a compliance with the Constitution that the testimony of the witness could not be used, though he was still subject to prosecution through the testimony of others. *People ex rel. Lewisohn* v. *O'Brien* (176 N.Y.253,268, decided in 1903) overruled *People ex rel. Hackley* v. *Kelly,* followed *Counselman* v. *Hitchcock* (142 U.S.547), and closed with the suggestion that "if the interests of the People are deemed to require it, it is, of course, quite competent, and proper, for the legislative body to provide for an exemption of the witness from liability to prosecution, as broad in its effect as is the constitutional privilege." Following that suggestion, section 584 of the Penal Law and like statutes (see, *e.g.*, Penal Law, secs. 380 and 381) were enacted. Their purpose was to make the Constitution and the statute coextensive and consistent. Penalties and forfeitures, as the words are used in this exemption, are penalties and forfeitures imposed upon an offender as part of the punishment of his crime (*U.S.* v. *Reisinger,* 128 U.S.398; *Boyd* v. *U.S.,* 116 U.S.616; *Lees* v. *U.S.,* 150 U.S. 476; *U.S.* v. *Regan,* 232 U.S.37; *La Bourgoyne,* 104 Fed.Rep. 823). The statute is a grant of amnesty. The witness is to have the same protection as if he had received a pardon (*Brown* v. *Walker,* 161 U.S.591,599; *Burdick* v. *U.S.,* 236 U.S.79). It is inconceivable that the intention was to give him even more. But a pardon, as we have seen, though it blots out penalties and forfeitures, does not render the courts impotent to protect their honor by disbarment (*Matter of an Attorney,* *supra*). The legislature cannot have believed that in the interpretation of a grant of amnesty exemption from penalties and forfeitures would receive a broader meaning. Disbarment, therefore, is not within the range of the exemption. That was the ruling in *Matter of Biggers* (24 Okla.842; *S.C.,* 25 L.R.A. [N.S.] 622) in circumstances not to be distinguished from those before us. It is a ruling well sustained by precedent and reason.

There are two other lines of argument which by different methods of approach lead to the same goal. One argument is purely verbal. It points to the concluding words of the statute: "no testimony so given or produced shall be received against him, upon any *criminal* investigation, proceeding or trial" (Penal L. §584). The use of the word "criminal" helps to explain and characterize the kinds of penalties and forfeitures within the range of the exemption. But there is another argument more significant than any verbal one. The argument is that unless the immunity is limited to criminal penalties and criminal forfeitures, the state has promised more than it can perform, and the whole statute becomes illusory. There was an ancient rule in chancery that discovery would never be granted in aid of an action for a forfeiture (*Earl of Mexborough* v. *Whitwood Urban District Council* [L.R.1897] 2 Q.B. 111,118; *Jones* v. *Jones* [L.R.] 22 Q.B.D.425; *Martin* v. *Treacher* [L.R.] 16 Q.B.D.507; *Lansing* v. *Pine*, 4 Paige, 639; *Perrine* v. *Striker*, 7 Paige, 598,601; *Abernethy* v. *Society of the Church of the Puritans*, 3 Daly, 1,8,9). It was merely a branch of the broader principle that forfeitures are abhorred in equity. Cases which illustrate its application are cited by counsel for the appellant: *Honeywood* v. *Selwin* (3 Atk.276), where the defendant, being a member of Parliament, was held privileged from discovery because by statute the acceptance of other office vacated a seat in Parliament (Wigmore, section 2256 [note 9]); *Firebrass's Case* (2 Salk.550), where the chief ranger of Enfield Chase was held privileged from discovery which might lead to the forfeiture of his place; and other cases where discovery would have shown a violation of the statute against simony. The precedents are collated by Wigmore (section 2256). We are asked to hold that forfeitures within the meaning of the rule in equity and forfeitures within the meaning of this act of amnesty are the same thing. But the consequences of such a holding would be impossible. The argument proves too much. A forfeiture as viewed by courts of chancery had a range and breadth which no exemption granted by the state could rival. One illustration among many will suffice. The loss of an estate for breach of a condition subsequent was a forfeiture within the rule in equity (*Earl of Mexborough* v. *Whitwood, etc.*; *Jones* v. *Jones*; *Martin* v. *Treacher*; *Abernethy* v. *Church, supra*). Nice distinctions were drawn in early cases between the determination of the estate by act of the party himself and its determination by some event not subject to his control. Nice distinctions were also drawn between conditions and conditional limitations. A decision by Chancellor KENT in *Livingston* v. *Tompkins* (4 Johns.Ch.415,420) swept these distinctions aside; the estate, however lost, was forfeited; and the forfeiture would find no aid in equity. That was not a rule of evidence. It was one of the principles regulating the exercise of chancery jurisdiction (*Livingston* v. *Tompkins, supra*).

Side by side with this principle of chancery jurisdiction there grew up a rule of evidence—a privilege of witnesses— which was enforced in courts of law. Its origin is obscure. At one time the law of evidence may have known no privilege at all (Wigmore, section 2250). When the privilege first came, its scope was uncertain. There was doubt, indeed, whether a witness could be compelled to answer if by so doing he would subject himself to a civil action, or charge himself with a debt (2 Taylor on Ev.sec.1463; Wigmore on Ev. sections 2223, 2254). Discussion of the subject in *Lord Melville's* case led to the statute 46 Geo.3, ch.37. That statute is the precursor of section 837 of our own Code (Code Civ.Pro. §837). It established the rule that the witness must testify unless the answer will tend to accuse him of a crime or expose him to a penalty or forfeiture. The penalties and forfeitures, however, were not defined. Whether they are as broad as penalties and forfeitures within the meaning of the rule in equity is still an open question, and one not now before us. Chief Justice COCKBURN expressed his doubts upon that subject in *Pye* v. *Butterfield* (5 B. & S.829,836). (See also Wigmore, section 2256.) But the thing which concerns us now is not the meaning of the statutory privileges of silence where that privilege survives. We are concerned with the extent of the *exemption* where the privilege has been taken away. The forfeitures and penalties which the state undertakes to remit cannot be the forfeitures and penalties which equity refused to aid; and this for the simple reason that the state would be powerless to remit them effectively. Again, a single illustration serves our purpose. The witness on a trial for conspiracy who shows that he has violated a condition of his lease, has thereby exposed himself to forfeiture of his estate at the election of his landlord. The forfeiture, however, is one which no act of amnesty can waive. We cannot suppose that the legislature attempted to waive it. We cannot impute to the lawmakers a futile and frivolous intent. The alternative is to hold that the forfeitures remitted are forfeitures imposed by the sovereign power as part of the punishment of crime. If some other construction is possible, there is none so reasonable and obvious. Punishment of crime may for this purpose include the recovery from the offender of penalties and forfeitures through the form of civil actions (*U.S.* v. *Regan, supra,* at p.50; *Hepner* v. *U.S.,* 213 U.S.103,111). But punishment there must be.

Our decision in *Matter of Kaffenburgh* (188 N.Y.49) is

pressed upon us as controlling. But we think it is inapplicable. Kaffenburgh had refused to answer when called as a witness upon the trial of an indictment for conspiracy. He put his refusal on the ground that the answer would tend to criminate him. That was before the enactment of section 584 of the Penal Law. Disbarment proceedings were afterwards begun, and the charge was made that the refusal to answer was professional misconduct. That charge was not sustained either in the Appellate Division or in this court. Disbarment was ordered, but on other grounds. Much that was said was in reality unnecessary to the decision. There was no occasion to determine whether Kaffenburgh's refusal to testify was proper because it tended to expose him to a forfeiture of office. He had placed his refusal on the ground of a tendency to criminate him, and that of itself was sufficient to sustain him. We may assume, however, the binding force of the opinion in all its parts. If we give it that force, it does not reach this case. It defines at the utmost the scope of section 587 of the Code of Civil Procedure. It measures the statutory privilege when no part of the privilege has been withdrawn. In the case at hand, the privilege has been withdrawn. It has been withdrawn by section 584 of the Penal Law. In return for the loss of the privilege there has been the grant of a new exemption. It is that exemption and not the vanished privilege, which is now to be defined. *Matter of Kaffenburgh* did not decide that disbarment for professional misconduct is a penalty or forfeiture within the meaning of an act of amnesty (*Matter of an Attorney*, 86 N.Y.563). If it did, we could not follow it.

Consequences cannot alter statutes, but may help to fix their meaning. Statutes must be so construed, if possible, that absurdity and mischief may be avoided. The claim of immunity from disbarment cannot survive the application of that test. If the exemption protects lawyers, it must equally protect physicians, whose licenses have long been subject to revocation for misconduct (Public Health Law, §170; Consol. Laws, ch.45; 1 R.S.452, §3; *Matter of Smith*, 10 Wend. 449; *Allinson* v. *Gen. Council of Medical Education* [L.R. 1894] 1 Q.B.750). Two great and honorable professions have in that view been denied the right to purify their membership and vindicate their honor. The charlatan and rogue may assume to heal the sick. The knave and criminal may pose as a minister of justice. Such things cannot have been intended, and will not be allowed.

The order of disbarment should be affirmed.

HISCOCK, Ch.J., CHASE, McLAUGHLIN, CRANE and ANDREWS, JJ., concur; HOGAN, J., not voting.

Order affirmed.

CORPORATIONS

MINNIE B.BERKEY, Respondent, *v.* THIRD AVENUE RAILWAY COMPANY, Appellant.

CHARLES P.BERKEY, Respondent, *v.* THIRD AVENUE RAILWAY COMPANY, Appellant.

CARDOZO, J. The plaintiff boarded a street car at Fort Lee Ferry and One Hundred and Twenty-fifth street on October 4, 1916, in order to go east on One Hundred and Twenty-fifth street to Broadway, and thence south on Broadway to Columbia University at One Hundred and Seventeenth street. She was hurt in getting out of the car through the negligence of the motorman in charge of it. The franchise to operate a street railroad along the route traveled by the plaintiff belongs to the Forty-second Street, Manhattanville and Saint Nicholas Avenue Railway Company (described for convenience as the Forty-second Street Company) and no one else. Substantially all the stock of that company is owned by the Third Avenue Railway Company, the defendant, which has its own franchise along other streets and avenues. Stock ownership alone would be insufficient to charge the dominant company with liability for the torts of the subsidiary (*Elenkrieg* v. *Siebrecht*, 238 N.Y.254; *Stone* v. *C.,C.,C. & St. Louis Ry.Co.*, 202 N.Y.352). The theory of the action is that under the screen of this subsidiary and others, the defendant does in truth operate for itself the entire system of connected roads, and is thus liable for the torts of the consolidated enterprise (*Chicago, etc., Ry.Co.* v. *Minn. Civic Assn.*, 247 U.S.490; *Davis* v. *Alexander*, 269 U.S.114).

We are unable to satisfy ourselves that such dominion was exerted. The Forty-second Street Company deposits in its own bank account the fares collected on its route. It pays out of that account and no other the wages of the motormen and conductors engaged in the operation of its cars. It was not organized by the defendant as a decoy or a blind. It was not organized, so far as the record shows, by the defendant at all. There is no evidence that at the time of its formation the defendant had any interest in it as shareholder or otherwise. Its franchise goes back to the year 1884, and through all the intervening years it has preserved its corporate organization with property adequate to the maintenance of life. Its balance sheet for the year ending July, 1917, shows assets of $12,456,-847.86. The values there stated are much in excess of the debts and liabilities, including in the reckoning of liabilities the outstanding capital stock. In no possible view, even if they are to be scaled down to some extent, are they unsubstantial or nominal. True, the subsidiary lost money that year, but so also did its parent. The fact remains that it was functioning as a corporation continuously and actively. It was so functioning at the trial in 1924. There is no evidence or suggestion that it has ceased to function since.

The question is whether other circumstances yet to be noted neutralize these indicia of separate life and operation. The defendant, as we have seen, was the owner in 1916 of substantially all the stock of the subsidiary corporation. Its president in reporting to the stockholders the financial situation at the end of the fiscal year informed them that to make the picture accurate, the statement must exhibit the consolidated income, and this was obviously true. Other ties must be shown in addition to the one resulting from ownership of shares. The members of the two boards of directors were nearly, though not quite the same. Each road had the same executive officers, *i.e.*, the same president, treasurer, general manager, paymaster and counsel. The parent has made loans to the subsidiary from time to time, sometimes for construction, sometimes for operating expenses. The loan for construction expenses ($6,415,152.92) is represented by a demand note. There is nothing to show whether the money was borrowed for the original construction in 1884 or for later changes of construction when the road was electrified. The parent is also the holder of the second mortgage bonds, $1,487,000, the first mortgage bonds, however ($1,200,000), being issued to the public. The operating loans are temporary advances for electric power, for materials or supplies and for the salaries of executive officers. As a matter of convenience these are made in the first instance out of the treasury of the parent company. They are then charged to the account of the subsidiary, and repaid generally the following month, and not later than the following year. Repayment is inconsistent with an understanding that the parent in making the advances was operating on its own account the cars of a connecting line. The charges are more than book entries, mere devices of an accountant. Drafts are drawn upon the subsidiary and paid with its own money. The unpaid advances for operation in July, 1917, were only $253,029.37, and this at the end of a poor year. We are not to confuse the salaries of the executive officers with the wages of motormen and conductors. The latter, as already pointed out, were paid in the first instance as well as ultimately by the subsidiary itself. So were many other expenses for maintenance and repair. So were the many judgments for personal injuries recovered in the past.

One other circumstance or group of circumstances is the subject of much emphasis in the arguments of counsel. The defendant was the dominant stockholder, not only in this subsidiary, but also in many others. The routes when connected cover an area from the lower part of Manhattan at the south to Yonkers and other points in Westchester at the north. All the cars, wherever used, are marked "Third Avenue System." On the other hand, the transfer slips bear the name in each instance of the company that issues them. The cars, when new ones become necessary, are bought by the defendant, and then leased to the subsidiaries, including, of course, the Forty-second Street Company, for a daily rental which is paid. The cars leased to one road do not continue along the routes of others. The motormen and conductors do not travel beyond their respective lines. With the approval of the Public Service Commission, transfer slips are issued between one route and another, but transfers could have been required by the Commission if not voluntarily allowed (Public Service Comm. Law, §49, subds.3 and 6; Cons. Laws, ch.48).

Upon these facts we are to say whether the parent corporation, the owner of a franchise to operate a street railroad on Third Avenue and the Bowery and a few connected streets, has in truth operated another railroad on Broadway and Forty-second Street, and this in violation of the statutes of the State. The plaintiff's theory of the action requires us to assume the existence of a contract between the defendant on the one side and the Forty-second Street Company on the other. The several circumstances relied upon—community of interest and in a sense community of management—are important only in so far as they are evidence from which the existence of a contract may fairly be inferred. The contract in the plaintiff's view was one between the two corporations by which the defendant was to use and operate the other's franchise as its own. If such a contract was made, it was not only *ultra vires*, but illegal, because prohibited by statute. By Public Service Commission's Law (§54), "no franchise nor any right to or under any franchise, to own or operate a railroad or street railroad shall be assigned, transferred or leased, nor shall any contract or agreement with reference to or affecting any such franchise or right be valid or of any force or effect whatsoever, unless the assignment, transfer, lease, contract or agreement shall have been approved by the proper commission." By section 56 any violation of the provisions of the statute exposes the offending corporation to continuing fines of large amounts, and its officers and agents to prosecution and punishment as guilty of a misdemeanor. If a written contract had been made for the operation by the defendant of the subsidiary's line, no one would doubt that such contract would fall within the condemnation of section 54 of the act. The contract is not the less illegal because made by word of mouth.

We cannot bring ourselves to believe that an agreement, criminal in conception and effect, may be inferred from conduct or circumstances so indefinite and equivocal. Community of interest there must obviously be between a subsidiary corporation and a parent corporation, the owner of its stock. This community of interest would prompt the parent, not unnaturally, to make advances for operating expenses to the subsidiary when convenience would be thus promoted. The advances so made have for the most part been repaid, and in so far as they remain unpaid have been carried as a debt. During all this time the cars have been manned by the subsidiary's servants, who are paid for their work out of the subsidiary's fares. We do not stop to inquire whether the inference of unified operation would be legitimate in a case where a contract for such an extension of the area of activity would be permitted by the law. We feel assured that no such inference is to be drawn from acts so uncertain in their suggestions where the inference is also one of the commission of a crime. The law prohibits a contract for operation by the parent of a franchise other than its own without the consent of the appropriate commission. It does not prohibit stock ownership, or at least did not, so far as the record shows, when the defendant bought the shares. We are now asked to draw from conduct appropriate to the ownership of stock, and fairly explicable thereby, the inference of a contract prohibited by law. We do not obviate the difficulty when we say that the stockholders by acquiescence have ratified any departure from the restrictions of the charter. They could do this so as to wipe out the transgression of their officers if the act constituting the transgression were *ultra vires* only. They could not do so where the act was one prohibited by law (*Kent* v. *Quicksilver Mining Co.*, 78 N.Y.159). The statute is aimed at more than the protection of the stockholders. It protects the creditors also, and beyond the creditors the public. Creditors are to be guarded against an increase of liabilities and an impairment of assets by an extension of corporate activities not approved by the Public Service Commission, the representative of the State. The public is to be guarded against like consequences, for the public which rides upon the cars has an interest, not to be ignored, in cheap, continuous and efficient operation. These benefits cannot be enjoyed if a road has been plunged into insolvency by improvident extensions. "The business of a railroad [*i.e.*, a street railroad] is to run its own lines. The law does not permit it at its pleasure to run the lines of others" (*Doran* v. *N.Y.City Int.Ry.Co.*, 239 N.Y. 448).

We do not mean that a corporation which has sent its cars with its own men over the route of another corporation may take advantage of the fact that its conduct in so doing is illegal to escape liability for the misconduct of its servant (*Nims* v. *Mt. Hermon Boys School*, 160 Mass.177; *Bissell* v. *Mich. R.R.Co.*, 22 N.Y.258). There is no room for varying constructions when operation results from acts so direct and unequivocal. A defendant in such circumstances is liable for the tort, however illegitimate the business, just as much as it would be if its board of directors were to order a motorman to run a traveler down. We do mean, however, that an intention to operate a route in violation of a penal statute is not to be inferred from acts which reasonably interpreted are as compatible with innocence as with guilt (*Shotwell* v. *Dixon*, 163 N.Y.43,52). Such, it seems to us, whether viewed distributively or together, are the acts relied on here to establish an agreement between two corporations that the business of one shall be the business of the other. Many arrangements for

economy of expense and for convenience of administration
may be made between carriers without subjecting them to liability as partners or as coadventurers "either *inter sese* or as
to third persons" (*Ins.Co.* v. *Railroad Co.*, 104 U.S.146,
158). For like reasons such arrangements may be made without establishing a relation of principal and agent. Where the
coadventure or the agency, if created, carries consequences
along with it that are offensive to public policy, the law will
not readily imply the relation it condemns. The basis for the
implication must be either intention or estoppel. We perceive no evidence sufficient to support a finding of estoppel.
Intention is presumed, unless the inference of innocence is
belied with reasonable certainty, to be conformable to law.

There is no need to enter into a minute analysis of cases
such as *Davis* v. *Alexander* (269 U.S.114); *Lehigh Valley
R.R.Co.* v. *Dupont* (128 Fed.Rep.840); *Lehigh Valley R.R.
Co.* v. *Delachesa* (145 Fed.Rep.617); *A.,T. & S.F.R.R.Co.* v.
Davis (34 Kan.199); *Wichita Falls etc., Ry.Co.* v. *Puckett* (53
Okla. 463); and many others that might be added. In none
of them was an illegal agreement imputed to the dominant
railroad by force of conduct fairly compatible with an innocent construction. On the contrary, the defendant in every
case would have acted wholly within its rights if it had assumed liability as principal by an unequivocal engagement.
Thus, in *Davis* v. *Alexander* (*supra*) a contract for the carriage
of goods was made in Texas, the transportation to begin on
the route of the parent corporation and to continue over the
line in the ownership of the subsidiary. There is no doubt
that at common law a corporation doing business as a carrier
of passengers or goods may charge itself with liability for loss
on a connecting line, and to that end may enter, within reasonable limitations not yet accurately defined, into a joint

adventure with another (*Swift* v. *Pac. Mail S.S.Co.*, 106 N.Y.206,216,217). The situation was the same in *Lehigh Valley R.R.Co.* v. *Dupont* and *Lehigh Valley R.R.Co.* v. *Delachesa* (*supra*). Indeed, in the *Dupont* case the court was at pains to point out that the contract of carriage, if extended to the connecting route, was not even *ultra vires* (128 Fed.Rep. at p.845). Other differences are exposed when we press the process of dissection farther. Thus, in *Davis* v. *Alexander* (*supra*) the case was submitted to the jury upon the theory that the proceeds of operation over the two routes were commingled in a single fund. Not only that, but engines and cars were used indiscriminately, and so also were the crews. The jury were told that all these facts must be found to coexist before the wrong of the subsidiary could be charged against the parent. The Supreme Court in its opinion does not catalogue the circumstances supporting the inference of unity of control. The opinion is confined to the statement that "the shippers introduced substantial evidence in support of their allegations." The facts are disclosed when we examine the record on appeal. So in *Wichita Falls Ry.Co.* v. *Puckett* (*supra*) the same employees worked on the entire route, and a common treasury received the proceeds of the system. Between such cases and the one before us there exists a distinction plain upon the surface. This being so, there is no need to choose between the Federal doctrine and our own, if indeed when they are understood, there is any difference between them. Liability of the parent has never been adjudged when the subsidiary has maintained so consistently and in so many ways as here the separate organization that is the mark of a separate existence, and when the implication of a contract for unity of operation would be the implication of a contract for the commission of a crime.

The whole problem of the relation between parent and subsidiary corporations is one that is still enveloped in the mists of metaphor. Metaphors in law are to be narrowly watched, for starting as devices to liberate thought, they end often by enslaving it. We say at times that the corporate entity will be ignored when the parent corporation operates a business through a subsidiary which is characterized as an "alias" or a "dummy." All this is well enough if the picturesqueness of the epithets does not lead us to forget that the essential term to be defined is the act of operation. Dominion may be so complete, interference so obtrusive, that by the general rules of agency the parent will be a principal and the subsidiary an agent. Where control is less than this, we are remitted to the tests of honesty and justice (Ballantine, Parent & Subsidiary Corporations, 14 Calif. Law Review, 12,18,19,20). The logical consistency of a juridical conception will indeed be sacrificed at times when the sacrifice is essential to the end that some accepted public policy may be defended or upheld. This is so, for illustration, though agency in any proper sense is lacking, where the attempted separation between parent and subsidiary will work a fraud upon the law (*Chicago, etc., Ry.Co.* v. *Minn. Civic Assn.*, 247 U.S.490; *United States* v. *Reading Company*, 253 U.S.26,61,63). At such times unity is ascribed to parts which, at least for many purposes, retain an independent life, for the reason that only thus can we overcome a perversion of the privilege to do business in a corporate form. We find in the case at hand neither agency on the one hand, nor on the other abuse to be corrected by the implication of a merger. On the contrary, merger might beget more abuses than it stifled. Statutes carefully framed for the protection, not merely of creditors, but of all who travel upon railroads, forbid the confusion of liabilities by extending operation over one route to operation on another. In such circumstances, we thwart the public policy of the State instead of defending or upholding it, when we ignore the separation between subsidiary and parent, and treat the two as one.

The order of the Appellate Division should be reversed, and the judgment of the Trial Term affirmed with costs in the Appellate Division and in this court.

. . .

HISCOCK, Ch.J., McLAUGHLIN, ANDREWS and LEHMAN, JJ., concur; CRANE, J., dissents in opinion in which POUND, J., concurs.

Ordered accordingly.

DAMAGES

JACOB & YOUNGS, INCORPORATED, Respondent, *v.* GEORGE E.KENT, Appellant.

CARDOZO, J.   The plaintiff built a country residence for the defendant at a cost of upwards of $77,000, and now sues to recover a balance of $3,483.46, remaining unpaid. The work of construction ceased in June, 1914, and the defendant then began to occupy the dwelling. There was no complaint of defective performance until March, 1915. One of the specifications for the plumbing work provides that "all wrought iron pipe must be well galvanized, lap welded pipe of the grade known as 'standard pipe' of Reading manufacture." The defendant learned in March, 1915, that some of the pipe, instead of being made in Reading, was the product of other factories. The plaintiff was accordingly directed by the architect to do the work anew. The plumbing was then encased within the walls except in a few places where it had to be exposed. Obedience to the order meant more than the substitu-

tion of other pipe. It meant the demolition at great expense
of substantial parts of the completed structure. The plaintiff
left the work untouched, and asked for a certificate that the
final payment was due. Refusal of the certificate was followed
by this suit.

The evidence sustains a finding that the omission of the
prescribed brand of pipe was neither fraudulent nor willful.
It was the result of the oversight and inattention of the plaintiff's subcontractor. Reading pipe is distinguished from
Cohoes pipe and other brands only by the name of the manu-
facturer stamped upon it at intervals of between six and seven
feet. Even the defendant's architect, though he inspected the
pipe upon arrival, failed to notice the discrepancy. The plaintiff tried to show that the brands installed, though made by
other manufacturers, were the same in quality, in appearance,
in market value and in cost as the brand stated in the contract—that they were, indeed, the same thing, though manu-
factured in another place. The evidence was excluded, and a
verdict directed for the defendant. The Appellate Division
reversed, and granted a new trial.

We think the evidence, if admitted, would have supplied
some basis for the inference that the defect was insignificant
in its relation to the project. The courts never say that one
who makes a contract fills the measure of his duty by less than
full performance. They do say, however, that an omission,
both trivial and innocent, will sometimes be atoned for by
allowance of the resulting damage, and will not always be the
breach of a condition to be followed by a forfeiture (*Spence* v.
Ham, 163 N.Y.220; *Woodward* v. *Fuller*, 80 N.Y.312; *Glacius*
v. *Black*, 67 N.Y.563,566; *Bowen* v. *Kimbell*, 203 Mass.364,
370). The distinction is akin to that between dependent and
independent promises, or between promises and conditions

(Anson on Contracts [Corbin's ed.], sec.367; 2 Williston on Contracts, sec.842). Some promises are so plainly independent that they can never by fair construction be conditions of one another. (*Rosenthal Paper Co.* v. *Nat. Folding Box & Paper Co.*, 226 N.Y.313; *Bogardus* v. *N.Y. Life Ins.Co.*, 101 N.Y.328.) Others are so plainly dependent that they must always be conditions. Others, though dependent and thus conditions when there is departure in point of substance, will be viewed as independent and collateral when the departure is insignificant (2 Williston on Contracts, secs.841,842; *Eastern Forge Co.* v. *Corbin*, 182 Mass.590,592; *Robinson* v. *Mollett*, L.R., 7 Eng. & Ir.App.802,814; *Miller* v. *Benjamin*, 142 N.Y.613). Considerations partly of justice and partly of presumable intention are to tell us whether this or that promise shall be placed in one class or in another. The simple and the uniform will call for different remedies from the multifarious and the intricate. The margin of departure within the range of normal expectation upon a sale of common chattels will vary from the margin to be expected upon a contract for the construction of a mansion or a "skyscraper." There will be harshness sometimes and oppression in the implication of a condition when the thing upon which labor has been expended is incapable of surrender because united to the land, and equity and reason in the implication of a like condition when the subject-matter, if defective, is in shape to be returned. From the conclusion that promises may not be treated as dependent to the extent of their uttermost minutiæ without a sacrifice of justice, the progress is a short one to the conclusion that they may not be so treated without a perversion of intention. Intention not otherwise revealed may be presumed to hold in contemplation the reasonable and probable. If something else is in view, it must not be left to implication. There will be no assumption of a purpose to visit venial faults with oppressive retribution.

Those who think more of symmetry and logic in the development of legal rules than of practical adaptation to the attainment of a just result will be troubled by a classification where the lines of division are so wavering and blurred. Something, doubtless, may be said on the score of consistency and certainty in favor of a stricter standard. The courts have balanced such considerations against those of equity and fairness, and found the latter to be the weightier. The decisions in this state commit us to the liberal view, which is making its way, nowadays, in jurisdictions slow to welcome it (*Dakin & Co.* v. *Lee*, 1916, 1 K.B.566,579). Where the line is to be drawn between the important and the trivial cannot be settled by a formula. "In the nature of the case precise boundaries are impossible" (2 Williston on Contracts, sec.841). The same omission may take on one aspect or another according to its setting. Substitution of equivalents may not have the same significance in fields of art on the one side and in those of mere utility on the other. Nowhere will change be tolerated, however, if it is so dominant or pervasive as in any real or substantial measure to frustrate the purpose of the contract (*Crouch* v. *Gutmann*, 134 N.Y.45,51). There is no general license to install whatever, in the builder's judgment, may be regarded as "just as good" (*Easthampton L. & C.Co., Ltd.,* v. *Worthington*, 186 N.Y.407,412). The question is one of degree, to be answered, if there is doubt, by the triers of the facts (*Crouch* v. *Gutmann; Woodward* v. *Fuller, supra*), and, if the inferences are certain, by the judges of the law (*Easthampton L. & C.Co., Ltd.,* v. *Worthington, supra*). We must weigh the purpose to be served, the desire to be gratified, the excuse for deviation from the letter, the cruelty of enforced adherence. Then only can we tell whether literal fulfilment is to be implied by law as a condition. This is not to say that the parties are not free by apt and certain words to effectuate a purpose that performance of every term shall be a condition of recovery. That question is not here. This is merely to say that the law will be slow to impute the purpose, in the silence of the parties, where the significance of the default is grievously out of proportion to the oppression of the forfeiture. The willful transgressor must accept the penalty of his transgression (*Schultze* v. *Goodstein*, 180 N.Y.248,251; *Desmond-Dunne Co.* v. *Friedman-Doscher Co.*, 162 N.Y.486, 490). For him there is no occasion to mitigate the rigor of implied conditions. The transgressor whose default is unintentional and trivial may hope for mercy if he will offer atonement for his wrong (*Spence* v. *Ham, supra*).

In the circumstances of this case, we think the measure of the allowance is not the cost of replacement, which would be great, but the difference in value, which would be either nominal or nothing. Some of the exposed sections might perhaps have been replaced at moderate expense. The defendant did not limit his demand to them, but treated the plumbing as a unit to be corrected from cellar to roof. In point of fact, the plaintiff never reached the stage at which evidence of the extent of the allowance became necessary. The trial court had excluded evidence that the defect was unsubstantial, and in view of that ruling there was no occasion for the plaintiff to go farther with an offer of proof. We think, however, that the offer, if it had been made, would not of necessity have been defective because directed to difference in value. It is true that in most cases the cost of replacement is the measure (*Spence* v. *Ham, supra*). The owner is entitled to the money which will permit him to complete, unless the cost of completion is grossly and unfairly out of proportion to the good to be attained. When that is true, the measure is the difference in value. Specifications call, let us say, for a foundation built of granite quarried in Vermont. On the completion of the building, the owner learns that through the blunder of a sub-contractor part of the foundation has been built of granite of the same quality quarried in New Hampshire. The measure of allowance is not the cost of reconstruction. "There may be omissions of that which could not afterwards be supplied exactly as called for by the contract without taking down the building to its foundations, and at the same time the omission may not affect the value of the building for use or otherwise, except so slightly as to be hardly appreciable" (*Handy* v. *Bliss*, 204 Mass.513,519. *Cf. Foeller* v. *Heintz*, 137 Wis.169, 178; *Oberlies* v. *Bullinger*, 132 N.Y.598,601; 2 Williston on Contracts, sec.805, p.1541). The rule that gives a remedy in cases of substantial performance with compensation for defects of trivial or inappreciable importance, has been developed by the courts as an instrument of justice. The measure of the allowance must be shaped to the same end.

The order should be affirmed, and judgment absolute directed in favor of the plaintiff upon the stipulation, with costs in all courts.

. . .

Hiscock, Ch.J., Hogan and Crane, JJ., concur with Cardozo, J.; Pound and Andrews, JJ., concur with McLaughlin, J.

Order affirmed, etc.

SURETY

CHARLES FOSMIRE, Respondent, *v.* NATIONAL SURETY COMPANY, Appellant.

CARDOZO, J. In June, 1916, Wagner & Braun entered into a contract with the state of New York for the construction of part of the state highway in the village of Saugerties. The Highway Law (Consol. Laws, chap.25, sec.130, subd.7) requires every such contractor to execute a bond in the form prescribed by the commission with sufficient sureties, conditioned for the performance of the work in accordance with the contract, for the commencement and completion thereof within the prescribed time, and for the payment of any direct or indirect damages that shall be suffered or claimed on account of such construction during the time thereof and until the highway is accepted. In obedience to that statute, Wagner & Braun, as principals, and the defendant, National Surety Company, as surety, made their bond in favor of the People of the State of New York, in the sum of $25,245, with a condition which reads as follows: "Now, therefore, the condition of this obligation is such that if the said principal shall well, truly and faithfully perform the work in accordance with the terms of the contract and with the plans and specifications, and will commence and complete the work within the time prescribed in the contract on his part to be kept and performed according to the terms and tenor of said contract and shall protect the said State of New York against and pay any excess of cost as provided in said contract and all amounts, damages, costs, and judgments which may be recovered against said State or its officers or agents or which the said State of New York may be called upon to pay to any person or corporation by reason of any damages, direct or indirect, arising or growing out of the doing of said work, or suffered or claimed on account of said construction or improvement during the time thereof and until the final completion and acceptance of the work, or the manner of doing the same, or the neglect of the said principal, or his agents, or servants, or the improper performance of the said work by the said principal, or his agents, or servants, or from any other cause, and if the above bounden principal, his heirs, executors, administrators, or assigns, shall and do well and truly pay or cause to be paid in full the wages stipulated and agreed to be paid to each and every laborer employed by the said principal or by his agents, then this obligation shall be null and void, otherwise to remain in full force and virtue."

The plaintiff, a laborer employed upon the work, brings this action against the surety to recover unpaid wages due from the contractors to himself and a fellow laborer whose assignment he holds. The question is whether the bond gives a cause of action in his favor.

We think the cause of action is in favor of the People solely (*Eastern Steel Co.* v. *Globe Indemnity Co.*, 227 N.Y.586; *Buffalo Cement Co.* v. *McNaughton*, 90 Hun, 74; affd., on opinion below, 156 N.Y.702). In so holding, we put our decision upon the single ground that the bond, read in its entirety, is inconsistent with an intention that the plaintiff and others in like position should have the right to sue upon it. If that intention is absent, the right to sue will be denied (*Simson* v. *Brown*, 68 N.Y.355). A different question would be here if the bond had been conditioned for the payment of wages and nothing else. The interest of the state in the welfare of those who labor on its public works might then point to an intention to create a cause of action in their favor (*Matter of Int.Ry.Co.* v. *Rann*, 224 N.Y.83; Williston on

Contracts, secs.372,402. Cf. 28 U.S.Stat.278; 33 id.811; *Texas P.Cement Co*. v. *McCord*, 233 U.S.157). For the purpose of this opinion, we assume, without attempting to decide, that when such an intention is revealed, there is no legal obstacle in the way of its enforcement (*Seaver* v. *Ransom*, 224 N.Y.233; *Lawrence* v. *Fox*, 20 N.Y.268; Williston, *supra*). But the difficulty which the plaintiff meets at the threshold of his case is in making out the intention that such a right should be conferred (*Simson* v. *Brown, supra*; *Garnsey* v. *Rogers*, 47 N.Y.233; *Knickerbocker L.Ins.Co*. v. *Nelson*, 78 N.Y.137, 153; *Pardee* v. *Treat*, 82 N.Y.385; *White* v. *Race*, 97 N.Y.296; *Standard Gas Power Corp*. v. *New England Casualty Co*., 90 N.J.L.570). The dominant purpose of this bond was protection to the state. That is plain alike from its terms and from those of the statute which required that security be given (Highway Law, *supra*). This dominant purpose will be defeated if laborers may ignore the People, and sue in their own right. They may then sue for wages as often as there is default, and exhausting the penalty of the bond, leave nothing for the state. That danger was pointed out in *Buffalo Cement Co*. v. *McNaughton* (*supra*) where a like bond was given to a city by the contractors for a sewer. "Such actions might have been brought before the completion of the sewer, and the penalty named in the bond exhausted, and the city thereby deprived of the protection which the bond was intended to give to it." (*Buffalo Cement Co*. v. *McNaughton, supra*, at p.79. *Lancaster* v. *Frescoln*, 203 Penn.St.640,644). The state did not intend to make the employees of its contractors the beneficiaries of a cause of action to be enforced in hostility to its own. There is nothing far-fetched or visionary in the danger that would follow the recognition of such competing claims of right. In this very case, we have the admission of counsel that the state completed the work on the default of the contractors, and did so at increased cost and heavy loss, for which the bond was the security. The outcome illustrates the possibilities of a divided right of action.

The plaintiff fails, therefore, to establish that he and his fellow laborers were the donees of a right to sue (Anson on Contracts [Huffcut's ed.], p.282; [Corbin's ed.], p.338). The concession of such a right would do more than frustrate the purpose of the bond. It would frustrate the purpose of the statute which directed that a bond be given. The statute does not permit, and the Commission in exacting the bond did not intend, that the security should be exhausted at the instance and for the benefit of persons other than the state itself. What the defendant's liability would be if the action were prosecuted by the People, we need not now determine. That question is not here. This case is decided when we hold, as we now do, that the action will not lie at the suit of the plaintiff now before us.

The order of the Appellate Division should be reversed, and that of the Special Term affirmed, with costs in the Appellate Division and in this court, and the question certified answered in the negative.

HISCOCK, Ch.J., CHASE, HOGAN, McLAUGHLIN, CRANE and ELKUS, JJ., concur.

Ordered accordingly.

INSURANCE

IDA SILVERSTEIN, Respondent, v. METROPOLITAN LIFE INSURANCE COMPANY, Appellant.

CARDOZO, Ch.J. Defendant issued its policy of insurance whereby it insured plaintiff's husband against the results of bodily injuries "caused directly and independently of all other causes by accidental means," the insurance in the event of his death to be payable to his wife. The policy was not to "cover accident, injury, disability, death or other loss caused wholly or partly by disease or bodily or mental infirmity or medical or surgical treatment therefor."

The insured, while lifting a milk can into an ice box, slipped and fell, the can striking him on the abdomen and causing such pain that he was unable to get up. A surgeon, opening the abdomen, found a perforation at the junction of the stomach and the duodenum, through which the contents of the stomach escaped into the peritoneum, causing peritonitis and, later, death. At the point of perforation there had been a duodenal ulcer, about the size of a pea. The existence of this ulcer was unknown to the insured, and, were it not for the blow, would have had no effect upon his health, for it was dormant, and not progressive, or so the triers of the facts might find. Even so, there had been a weakening of the wall in some degree, with the result that the impact of the blow was followed by perforation at the point of least resistance. The question is whether death was the result of an accident to the exclusion of other causes.

We think the evidence sustains a finding that the ulcer was not a disease or an infirmity within the meaning of the policy. Left to itself, it would have been as harmless as a pimple or a tiny scratch. Only in the event that it was progressive would it become a source of pain or trouble. If dormant, as it was found to be, it was not only harmless in itself, but incapable of becoming harmful except through catastrophic causes, not commonly to be expected. In a strict or literal sense, any departure from an ideal or perfect norm of health is a disease or an infirmity. Something more, however, must be shown to exclude the effects of accident from the coverage of a policy. The disease or the infirmity must be so considerable or significant that it would be characterized as disease or infirmity in the common speech of men (*Eastern Dist. Piece Dye Works v. Travelers Ins.Co.*, 234 N.Y.441,453). "Our guide is the reasonable expectation and purpose of the ordinary business man when making an ordinary business contract" (*Bird v. St. Paul F. & M.Ins.Co.*, 224 N.Y.47,51; *Goldstein v. Standard Acc.Ins.Co.*, 236 N.Y.187,183; *Van Vechten v. American Eagle Fire Ins.Co.*, 239 N.Y.303). A policy of insurance is not accepted with the thought that its coverage is to be restricted to an Apollo or a Hercules.

A distinction, then, is to be drawn between a morbid or abnormal condition of such quality or degree that in its natural and probable development it may be expected to be a source of mischief, in which event it may fairly be described as a disease or an infirmity, and a condition abnormal or unsound when tested by a standard of perfection, yet so remote in its potential mischief that common speech would call it not disease or infirmity, but at most a predisposing tendency (*Leland v. Order of U.C. Travelers*, 233 Mass.558,564; *Collins v. Casualty Co.*, 224 Mass.327; *Mutual Life Ins.Co. v. Dodge*, 11 Fed.Rep. [2d] 486; cert. denied, 271 U.S.677; *Taylor v. N.Y. Life Ins.Co.*, 176 Minn.171,174). There will be no recovery under a policy so written where an everyday act, involving ordinary exertion, brings death to an insured because he is a sufferer from heart disease (*Allendorf v. Fid. & Cas.Co.*, 250 N.Y.529; *Leland v. Order of U.C. Travelers, supra*). On the other hand, a recovery will not be denied to the sufferer from hernia who has had a predisposition to rupture because the inguinal canal was not closed as it ought to have been (*Collins v. Cas.Co., supra*), or to one whose hip has been fractured because his bones have become brittle with the advent of old age (cf. *Taylor* v. *N.Y. Life Ins.Co.*, *supra*). "If a man with an abnormally thin skull be struck a blow which would not seriously injure a normal man, but which causes his death, it is perfectly plain that the cause of death is not the thinness of the skull, but the receipt of the blow" (*Mutual Life Ins.Co.* v. *Dodge*, *supra*, p.489). An appendix already gangrenous is one thing (*Stanton* v. *Travelers Ins.Co.*, 83 Conn.708), and quite another is an appendix, not presently malignant, though a potential source of infection in the future if left within the body. The governing principle has been stated by RUGG, C.J., with clearness and precision: "If there is no active disease, but merely a frail general condition, so that powers of resistance are easily overcome, or merely a tendency to disease which is started up and made operative, whereby death results, then there may be recovery even though the accident would not have caused that effect upon a healthy person in a normal state" (*Leland* v. *U.C. Travelers*, *supra*, at p.564). An ulcer as trivial and benign as an uninfected pimple, is at most a tendency to an infirmity, and not an infirmity itself.

Any different construction would reduce the policy and its coverage to contradiction and absurdity. The infinite interplay of causes makes it impossible to segregate any single cause as operative at any time and place to the exclusion of all others, if cause is to be viewed as a concept of science or philosophy (*Schwarz* v. *Commercial Travelers Mut.Acc. Assn.*, 254 N.Y.523, affg. 227 App.Div.711; 132 Misc.Rep. 200; *Lewis* v. *Ocean Acc. & G.Corp.*, 224 N.Y.18,20). The courts have set their faces against a view so doctrinaire, an estimate of intention so headed toward futility. "We are to follow the chain of causation so far, and so far only, as the parties meant that we should follow it. 'The causes within their contemplation are the only causes that concern us'" (*Goldstein* v. *Standard Acc.Ins.Co.*, *supra*).

The judgment should be affirmed with costs.

POUND, CRANE, KELLOGG, O'BRIEN and HUBBS, JJ., concur; LEHMAN, J., not sitting.

Judgment affirmed.

WILLS

In the Matter of the Will of CHARLES F.FOWLES, Deceased.

DOROTHY E.SMITH et al., Appellants; GERTRUDE F. BROWNE et al., Respondents.

CARDOZO, J. The will of Charles Frederick Fowles, made on April 29, 1915, is before us for construction. By the second article of the will he gave to his wife, Frances May Fowles, $5,000. By the fourth article he gave her the contents of his estate "Fairmile Court." By the eighth article he gave his residuary estate to trustees to divide into three parts, the first part to consist of forty-five per cent thereof, and each of the other parts to consist of twenty-seven and one-half per cent thereof. The income of the first part was to be paid to his wife during her life, and upon her death the trust was to cease and the corpus to be divided. Half of the corpus (22½ per cent of the entire residue) was to be paid by the trustees "pursuant to the provisions of such last will and testament as my said wife may leave (hereby conferring upon my said wife the power to dispose of the said one-half by last will and testament duly executed by her)." If she failed to execute the power, the corpus was to be held in trust for his daughters by a former wife, with remainder to their children. To them also were given upon like trusts, and with like remainders, the other shares of the residue.

These provisions are not obscure, and their validity is not doubtful. The controversy grows out of the ninth article which reads as follows: "In the event that my said wife and myself should die simultaneously or under such circumstances as to render it impossible or difficult to determine who predeceased the other, I hereby declare it to be my Will that it shall be deemed that I shall have predeceased my said wife, and that this my Will and any and all its provisions shall be construed on the assumption and basis that I shall have predeceased my said wife."

Husband and wife were lost at sea on May 7, 1915, with the steamship *Lusitania*. There is nothing to show which was the survivor. The wife left a will made at the same time as the husband's. She recites the power of appointment, and undertakes to execute it. She gives her residuary estate (including the property affected by the power) to trustees for the use of a sister during life with remainder over. Whether this gift in its application to the husband's estate is made valid and effective by the ninth article of his will is the chief question to be determined.

Of his intention, there can be no doubt. In that, we all agree. He was about to set sail with his wife upon a perilous journey. He knew that disaster was possible. He knew that if death came, there would be no presumption to whom it had come first (*Newell* v. *Nichols*, 75 N.Y.78; *St. John* v. *Andrews Institute*, 117 App.Div.698; 191 N.Y.254). He told the courts what he wished them to do if all other tests of truth should fail. They were to distribute his estate as they would if his wife were the survivor. We cannot know whether she was in truth the survivor or not: there is no break in the silence and obscurity of those last hours. The very situation which was foreseen has thus arisen. If intention is the key to the problem, the solution is not doubtful. We are now asked to hold that under the law of the state of New York, a testator may not lawfully declare that a power executed by one who dies under such conditions shall be valid to the same extent as if there were evidence of survivorship.

Two rules of law are supposed to stand in the way. One is the rule that a power created by will lapses if the donee dies before the will takes effect. The other is the rule that wills must be executed in compliance with statutory formalities, and are not to be enlarged or diminished by reference to extrinsic documents which may not be authentic. A testator is not permitted at his pleasure to violate these rules. He does violate them, it is said, by indirection, if he may dispense with evidence of survivorship and still sustain the gift which purports to execute the power. If the wife had survived a single second, the gift would certainly be valid. That would be so though she had signed her will while her husband was yet alive and before the power took effect (*Stone* v. *Forbes*, 189 Mass.163,168; *Airey* v. *Bower*, 12 A.C.263; *Hirsch* v. *Bucki*, 162 App.Div.659,665). It is possible that she did survive, but it is also possible that she did not. The latter possibility, it is said, renders the gift void. We do not think it does.

It is true that a power created by will lapses if the donee of the power dies before the maker of the will (*Curley* v. *Lynch*, 206 Mass.289; Sugden on Powers [8th ed.], 460; Farwell on Powers [2d ed.], p.226). That is because a will has no effect till the death of the testator. Whatever power it creates, comes into being at that time. But to say this, does not answer the question before us. The question is not whether this power of appointment lapsed. The question is whether the testator has avoided the consequences of a lapse. More concretely, it is whether the law permits him to provide that if the donee's survivorship is incapable of proof, he will give his estate none the less to whomever she has named. That is what this testator said, not in words, but in effect. His will in this respect has a parallel in the one construed in *Matter of Greenwood* (1912, 1 Ch.Div.392). There gifts were made to relatives, with the provision that if the legatees died leaving issue, the benefits of the gifts should not lapse, "but should take effect as if his or her death had happened immediately after mine." These words were held equivalent to a gift to the personal representatives of the legatees named. So here, there is by implication a gift to the legatees named by the wife, and a ratification of any execution of the power, however premature. The intent to avert the consequences of a lapse is clear. The only question is whether the intent is one to which the law will give effect. One obstacle, and one only, can be thought of. That is the rule against the incorporation of extrinsic documents, testamentary in character but not themselves authenticated in accordance with the statute. It is said that this rule is violated when a testator, to keep a power alive, ratifies its execution, adopts the will which executes it as his own, and thus in effect averts a lapse. We do not share that view.

Everything that this testator did is justified by our decision in *Matter of Piffard* (111 N.Y.410,414,415). The distinction between that case and this is purely verbal. There is none in substance. In that case the testator authorized his daughter to dispose of a share of his estate by will. If she died before him, leaving a will in execution of the power, he directed his executors to transfer the share to her executors or trustees. We upheld the validity of that provision. We said that it might not be "possible to sustain the power of appointment as such." We held, however, that the daughter's will might be referred to "not as transferring the property by an appointment, but to define and make certain the persons to whom and the proportions in which the one-fifth should pass by the father's will in case of the death of the daughter in his lifetime." There was a like decision upon like facts in *Condit v. De Hart* (62 N.J.L.78). The argument is made that the express direction to transfer the share to the daughter's executors or trustees distinguishes the *Piffard* case from the one at bar. But in another form of words, this testator gave the same direction. He directed his executors to turn over his estate to the persons named by his wife. There is no distinction between a direction to pay the *trustees* named in another will, and a direction to pay the *legatees* named in a will. The daughter's trustees in the *Piffard* case were not to take as individuals. They had no beneficial interest. They were to take as trustees. Only by reference to the will which appointed them could the nature of the trust and the names and interests of the beneficiaries be learned. If there was a violation of the rule against incorporation here, there was equally a violation there.

Piffard's case cannot be distinguished. It ought not to be overruled. Only the clearest error would warrant us in baffling the just hopes and purposes of this testator by disregarding a decisive precedent. But there are substantial reasons to support the view that the decision was right. The reasons may appeal with different strength to different minds. For our present purposes, it is enough that they are at least substantial. The rule against incorporation has not been set aside. It has been kept within bounds which were believed to be wise and just. The rule is sometimes spoken of as if its content had been defined by statute, as if the prohibition were direct and express, and not inferential and implied. But the truth is that it is the product of judicial construction. Its form and limits are malleable and uncertain. We must shape them in the light of its origin and purpose. All that the statute says is that a will must be signed, published and attested in a certain way (Decedent Estate Law, §21; Consol. Laws, ch.13). From this the consequence is deduced that the testator's purpose must be gathered from the will, and not from other documents which lack the prescribed marks of authenticity (*Booth* v. *Baptist Church of Christ*, 126 N.Y.215,247). It is a rule designed as a safeguard against fraud and mistake. In the nature of things, there must be exceptions to its apparent generality. Some reference to matters extrinsic is inevitable. Words are symbols, and we must compare them with things and persons and events (4 Wigmore on Ev. §2470). It is a question of degree (*Langdon* v. *Astor's Executors*, 16 N.Y.9,26,31; *Robert* v. *Corning*, 89 N.Y.225,242). Sometimes the distinction is said to be between documents which express the gift and documents which identify it (*Hathaway* v. *Smith*, 79 Conn. 519,521; *Booth* v. *Baptist Church of Christ*, *supra*). But the two classes of cases run into each other by almost imperceptible gradations (*Langdon* v. *Astor's Executors*, *supra*). One may ratify assumptions of power, extinguish debts, wipe out wrongs, confirm rights, by the directions of one's will (*Bizzey* v. *Flight*, L.R.3 Ch.Div.269; 1 Jarman on Wills, 99). In these and other cases, the expressions of the gift and the description of its subject-matter must often coalesce. No general formula can tell us in advance where the line of division is to be drawn.

It is plain, therefore, that we are not to press the rule against incorporation to "a drily logical extreme" (*Noble*

State Bank v. *Haskell*, 219 U.S.104,110). We must look in each case to the substance. We must consider the reason of the rule, and the evils which it aims to remedy. But as soon as we apply that test, the problem solves itself. There is here no opportunity for fraud or mistake. There is no chance of foisting upon this testator a document which fails to declare his purpose. He has not limited his wife to any particular will. Once identify the document as *her* will; it then becomes his own. He authorizes her to act, and confirms her action (*Condit* v. *De Hart, supra,* at p.81). For the purpose of the rule against incorporation, the substance of the situation is thus the same as it always is when a will creates a power. The substance is that a power which would otherwise have lapsed, has been kept alive by the declaration that its execution, however premature, is ratified and approved. But the execution of a power does not violate the rule against incorporation. It can make no difference for that purpose whether the execution is authorized in advance or made valid by relation. There is no greater impairment in the one case than in the other of the principle of the integrity and completeness of testamentary expression. The source of title may be in one case the appointment, and in the other the confirmatory will. But if we go beneath the form and reach realities, the truth is that under the sanction of the will, a power has been executed. That is the principle which underlies the ruling in *Matter of Piffard* and *Condit* v. *De Hart.* We reaffirm it now. To hold that the purpose of this testator has been adequately or inadequately declared according to the accident of time at which death came to him or his wife in the depths of the ocean, is to follow the rule against incorporation with blind and literal adherence, forgetful of its origin, its purpose, and its true and deep significance.

We have spoken thus far of the gift of the residuary estate under the eighth article of the will. Questions also arise under the second and fourth articles. The gifts under these articles did not lapse, but passed to the personal representatives of the legatee. On that subject it is impossible to add anything to what has been written by Judge CRANE.

The order of the Appellate Division should be reversed and the decree of the Surrogate's Court affirmed with costs in the Appellate Division and in this court to be paid out of the estate.

· · ·

HISCOCK, Ch.J., CHASE and ANDREWS, JJ., concur with CARDOZO, J.; CRANE, J., reads dissenting opinion, except as to specific legacies, and CUDDEBACK, J., concurs; McLAUGHLIN, J., reads dissenting opinion.

Ordered accordingly.

DOMESTIC RELATIONS

FANNIE MIRIZIO, Appellant, *v.* COSMO MIRIZIO, Respondent.

CARDOZO, Ch.J. Plaintiff and defendant were joined in wedlock by a civil ceremony in September, 1921. Both were members of the Roman Catholic Church. The understanding was that a religious ceremony would follow. The ceremony did not follow, for the husband refused to join in it. The wife sued him for a decree of separation, alleging non-support. The husband answered that she had refused to live with him as his wife. He did not deny that he could have had her for the asking by adhering to his promise to be married according to the doctrines of the church. He took the ground that she must yield her body to him anyhow, however ruthless his refusal to have it on her terms. A judgment dismissing the complaint was affirmed by the Appellate Division and later by this court (242 N.Y.74).

Our decision was announced on January 26, 1926. The following day, plaintiff wrote a letter to defendant offering to live with him as a wife in every sense. The defendant answered that he would once have greeted the offer with joy, but that the love he once felt had vanished with the years. The plaintiff renewed her offer, but met with no response.

There followed a second action, the one before us now. Plaintiff says in her complaint that she had been advised by her attorney that she had the right "to refuse to live with the defendant" until he consented to a religious ceremony in accordance with the doctrines of her church. She says that, acting on that advice, she insisted upon such a ceremony, "and refused to live and cohabit with the defendant until then." She then avers her change of heart upon learning from this court of her duty as a wife, and prays that the defendant be required to make provision for her support. There was judgment in her favor upon the trial at Special Term. The "refusal to live and cohabit with the defendant" was held to lack the quality of "a permanent abandonment." It was "a temporary one, pending the determination of her legal rights, and did not forfeit her right to separate maintenance and support." The Appellate Division reversed and dismissed the complaint.

The law has been settled by the judgment of this court that the refusal of a religious ceremony did not justify the plaintiff's failure to fulfill her duty as a wife. There was some question upon the first record whether the plaintiff had refused to live with the defendant, or only to have intercourse with him. Upon the record now before us, that question is no longer open. The plaintiff says in her complaint that, acting on the advice of counsel she took the ground that as long as the defendant declined to join in a religious ceremony she would not live with him at all. She makes no pretense that she offered to live with him as a virgin. For people in their social station, dwelling in one or two rooms, such an offer, if made, would have the aspect of a subterfuge. She resorts to no such evasion, at least in her complaint. Later, in her testimony, she hints at something of the kind, but the court paid no heed to it, and held her to her pleading. When the defendant tried to go into the subject, he was checked with the remark that there was no need of testifying to anything back of the date of our decision, and that no matter how the plaintiff might have testified, the complaint with its admissions against interest would be accepted as the truth. The findings follow the admissions.

The question, therefore, is whether the refusal to cohabit with the defendant upon the grounds and in the conditions stated is an abandonment so definitive as to be unaffected by repentance. The plaintiff acted on advice of counsel and under a claim of legal right. She believed that she was not recreant to her duty as a wife when she declined to live with a husband who had shamelessly repudiated a promise to appease her conscience and his own by sanctifying the marriage with the blessing of the church. She had probable cause for that belief, as is sufficiently attested by the close division in this court. It turns out that she was in error. The moment she was so advised, she gave notice to the defendant that she would yield submission to the law. We are told that her error has barred his door to her forever.

Not every separation is an abandonment beyond annulment or recall. One must look to all the circumstances. Of these, time will commonly be the weightiest, yet not always so decisive that it cannot be neutralized by others (*Bowlby* v. *Bowlby*, 25 N.J.Eq.406; *Cornish* v. *Cornish*, 23 N.J.Eq. 208). We have refused to compress within a formula the extenuating possibilities of behavior in all its myriad diversities (*Bohmert* v. *Bohmert*, 241 N.Y.446). "What is reasonable will depend on the circumstances of the case and the conduct of the parties" (*Bohmert* v. *Bohmert*, *supra*, at p.453). Lawless repudiation of duty, an attitude and spirit of mere rebellion or defiance, maintained without repentance after cooling time has passed, may exact a finding of definitive abandonment though the interval is short. Mistake and provocation and hardship and reservations will permit another finding though the interval is long. There are duties too for the deserted spouse as well as the deserter. One who is chargeable with fault contributing to the breach, palliating and explaining it though not excusing it altogether, may not stand back indifferent, refusing the concessions to be expected of gentleness and honor (1 Schouler, Mar., Div. and Sep. §1663; *Hall* v. *Hall*, 60 N.J.Eq.469,470; 65 id.709; *Wood* v. *Wood*, 63 N.J. Eq.688; *Bowlby* v. *Bowlby*, *supra*; *Bradley* v. *Bradley*, 160 Mass.258; cf. as to the wife's duty, *Wilson* v. *Wilson*, 66 N.J.Eq.237). Separation to be abandonment must be obstinate and hardened (cf. 1 Bishop, New Comm. on Mar., Div. and Sep. §1665).

We are to measure the plaintiff's conduct by these and cognate tests of right dealing and humanity. She was the victim of mistake. She acted, as we have seen, in accordance with the advice of counsel and with probable cause. She was the victim, besides, of provocation and oppression. The defendant had treated her with indifference to her feelings and in wanton disregard of his solemn word of honor. His refusal to fulfill the promise that would have made her his at once, gives color to the belief that he was scheming to be rid of her (cf. *Thorpe v. Thorpe*, 9 R.I.57). He could not have acted differently if he had been seeking from the beginning to provoke her to a course of conduct that would free him from the performance of his duty as her husband. With all these affronts, she maintained her wifely station. In declining to live with him, she did so with reservations and conditions: she would live apart till he kept faith with her, and then she would be his. We have said that she was wrong (242 N.Y.75). The adjudication then made binds us, however emphatic the dissent. We have no thought to depart from it. Plainly, however, she was not wrong in such a sense or in such a degree as to betoken defiance of duty, a "rebellious and unrepentant" spirit (*Bohmert v. Bohmert, supra,* p.452), a will to live apart whether the law approved or frowned. She invoked the law to aid her. The moment it condemned her, she bowed to its command.

We think a term of separation may not be said to constitute as a matter of law a definitive abandonment when it is bounded by a law suit, maintained upon reasonable grounds and with sincerity of conviction for the very purpose of determining whether the separation shall continue. No doubt the interval has been a long one, nearly five and a half years, between marriage and submission. At first the husband was the plaintiff in an unfounded action for annulment. The wife postponed, it seems, her suit for separation until his had been dismissed. But if the time has been long, the defendant could have made it short. There has never been a day in all these years when he might not have had the plaintiff as his own if he had done what a man of honor and a gentleman should have been prompt and glad to do. One is not aggrieved by a separation thus fostered and prolonged.

A plea of former judgment has been urged. It has no basis

in the record. There was no holding in the former suit that the plaintiff's conduct toward her husband had the force of an abandonment. There was not even a holding that she had refused to make her home with him. The holding was merely this, that in refusing him the privilege of sexual intercourse she was guilty of such misconduct as to bar her claim for support while the misconduct continued (242 N.Y.74). The defendant did not counterclaim for a separation either on the ground of abandonment or on any other. If a decree for separation had been given him, another question would be here (*Silberstein* v. *Silberstein*, 218 N.Y.525).

Whatever her errors may have been, the plaintiff is the defendant's wife. He has never offered her a home, nor paid a dollar to maintain her. Not yet has the law released him from the duty of support.

The judgment of the Appellate Division should be reversed, and that of the Special Term affirmed, with costs in the Appellate Division and in this court.

POUND, CRANE, ANDREWS, and LEHMAN, JJ., concur; KELLOGG and O'BRIEN, JJ., dissent.

Judgment accordingly.

NEGOTIABLE PAPER

BESSIE M. STRANG, Appellant, *v.* WESTCHESTER COUNTY NATIONAL BANK, Respondent.

CARDOZO, J. Plaintiff had a deposit account with the defendant bank. She informed the cashier that she wished to make a draft for $1,100, payable to one Homer E.Remsen, to whom she was to loan the money on bond and mortgage. The cashier told her to make the draft to her own order, and to indorse it to the order of Remsen. She brought the draft thus indorsed to one Bushnell, a lawyer. Bushnell gave her in return a bond, signed, as it seemed, by Homer E. Remsen and Alice, his wife; exhibited a mortgage signed in the same way; and made out a certificate that the mortgagors were the owners of the mortgaged property, free from all incumbrances. In truth, there were no such persons. The owner was Bushnell, and his supposed clients were fictitious. He told the plaintiff that he had once been the owner of the property, but that he had sold it two years before to Remsen, and owned it no longer. The draft was paid by the bank upon the indorsement of the attorney in the name of the fictitious client. His suicide a few days afterwards laid bare his crime. The plaintiff notified the bank that the draft had been paid without right, and sued to recover the money charged to her account. The Trial Term gave judgment in her favor. The Appellate Division reversed and granted a new trial. An appeal to this court followed.

We think the appeal must be sustained. The defendant was without authority to disburse the plaintiff's money except in accordance with her orders. It acted at its peril if it paid upon a forged indorsement (*Shipman* v. *Bank of State of N.Y.*, 126 N.Y.318). It did pay upon such an indorsement, and must answer for the consequences. A different case would be here if the plaintiff had dealt with Bushnell in the belief that he was Remsen, intending to make payment to the person then before her, though lured into that intention by his assumption of a fictitious name. In such circumstances, nice distinctions would have to be drawn to determine whether the crime was forgery or something else (*Phelps* v. *McQuade*, 220 N.Y.232; *Mercantile Nat. Bank of the City of N.Y.* v. *Silverman*, 148 App.Div.1; affd. on opinion below, 210 N.Y.567; *First Nat. Bank* v. *Am.Ex.Nat. Bank*, 170

N.Y.88; 3 Williston on Contracts, §1517). That is not what happened. The plaintiff did not intend to deal with Bushnell, either under that name or any other. She did not know Remsen, who was represented to be the owner, but she knew that he was not Bushnell, for Bushnell so informed her. He told her, as we have seen, that the property had once been his, but that he had parted with his ownership. In these circumstances, the crime of forgery was committed when he signed the names of Homer and Alice Remsen to the bond which charged them with the debt (*United Cigar Stores Co. v. American Raw Silk Co., Inc.*, 184 App.Div.217; affd., 229 N.Y.532; *Nat. Surety Co. v. Nat. City Bank*, 184 App.Div. 771; *Mercantile Nat. Bank v. Silverman, supra; Phelps v. McQuade, supra*). The crime was committed again when he signed their names to the mortgage, adding a certificate of acknowledgment in the name of a fictitious notary. It was committed once again upon his indorsement of the check. What he did was not the less a forgery because it has turned out in the end that the borrower was a myth (*Shipman v. Bank of State of N.Y., supra; Seaboard Nat. Bank v. Bank of America*, 193 N.Y.26; *United Cigar Stores Co. v. American Raw Silk Co., Inc., supra; People v. Browne*, 118 App.Div. 793,799; Penal Law, §883; Cons. Laws, ch.40). The myth did not exist with the consent or knowledge of the lender (Neg. Inst. Law [Cons. Laws, ch.38], §28).

The argument is made that the bank acted within its rights when it paid the check to Bushnell, because Bushnell was in truth the owner of the mortgaged land. The record does not tell us whether his title was unincumbered, but ownership, though absolute, would not change the nature of his crime. The plaintiff did not loan her money to Bushnell, content to accept him as a borrower. He of all men was excluded. She loaned it upon the bond of Homer and Alice Remsen, with a mortgage as collateral. Undoubtedly, she believed, when she drew her check upon the bank, that Remsen was an owner of the property, and that the mortgage was a valid lien. This belief did not mean that some one else who had been expressly excluded as a borrower, had the right, because he was the owner, to step into the borrower's shoes. Remsen, if a real person, might have indorsed the draft without liability as a forger, however fraudulent the statement that he was the owner of the land (*Phelps* v. *McQuade, supra*). Bushnell, having asserted that the borrower was some one other than himself, was not at liberty to indorse, whether he was the owner of the land or not. No doubt there are border cases where the line is hard to draw between the impostor who appropriates what is intended for another, and the impostor who deceives by misrepresenting his responsibility or character. We have an illustration in *Hartford* v. *Greenwich Bank of City of N. Y.* (157 App.Div.448; 215 N.Y.726), a case which later opinions have said is not to be extended (*United Cigar Stores Co.* v. *American Raw Silk Co., Inc., supra; Nat. Surety Co.* v. *Nat. City Bank of Brooklyn*, 184 App.Div.771). In the case at hand the line of division is reasonably clear. The plaintiff had no thought that she was accepting Bushnell's bond. The maker of the bond was to be the holder of the check.

The order of the Appellate Division should be reversed, and the judgment of the Trial Term affirmed, with costs in this court and in the Appellate Division.

· · ·

HISCOCK, Ch.J., HOGAN, POUND, and ANDREWS, JJ., concur with CARDOZO, J.; MCLAUGHLIN, J., reads dissenting opinion in which CRANE, J., concurs.

Order reversed, etc.

PUBLIC UTILITIES

THE PEOPLE OF THE STATE OF NEW YORK ex rel.
LEHIGH VALLEY RAILWAY COMPANY et al., Appellants,
v. STATE TAX COMMISSION, Respondent.

CARDOZO, Ch.J. The question in this case is the one left open and undecided in *People ex rel. Western N.Y. & Penn. Ry.Co.* v. *State Tax Commission* (244 N.Y.596). We are to determine "whether the right to erect a railroad bridge resting on abutments on private property across a stream, the bed of which is in private ownership, even though to some extent the river can be used for navigation, constitutes a special franchise unless the bridge so erected does actually interfere and obstruct the use to which the public could subject the stream."

The Lehigh Valley Railway Company is the owner of two bridges within the limits of the city of Ithaca, one across Cascadilla creek and the other across Six Mile creek. Both creeks are navigable streams, though only for small craft. Motor boats, rowboats, rafts and skiffs navigate the two streams above and below the crossings. The railroad company is the owner of the bed of the creeks and also of the banks on which the abutments rest. The bridges do not interfere either with existing navigation, or with any navigation that is possible without deepening the beds.

We think the maintenance of a bridge by a public service corporation across navigable waters involves the enjoyment of a special franchise subject to taxation, though the bed is in private ownership and the bridge is at such a height that navigation is unobstructed.

The power of the State to regulate or prohibit bridges or other structures above a navigable stream is not at all de-

pendent upon the ownership of the soil below. It is an incident to the public duty to maintain for the public benefit
waterways that supply the natural avenues of commerce.
Title to the bed of most of the rivers of the State is in the
owners of the uplands (*Fulton L., H. & P.Co.* v. *State,*
200 N.Y.400). The Hudson and the Mohawk may be exceptions, but the exceptions have their roots in the antiquities of
history (*Danes* v. *State,* 219 N.Y.67; *Waterford El.L., H. &
P.Co.* v. *State,* 208 App.Div.273; 239 N.Y.629). So large and
important a stream as the Oswego river was held in a leading
case to be subject to the general rule (*Fulton L., H. & P.Co.*
v. *State, supra*). The difference between the navigable quality
of such a river and that of the creeks spanned by these bridges
is one solely of degree. We cannot doubt that a railroad corporation, the owner of land along the banks of the Oswego,
would be in the enjoyment of a special franchise within the
meaning of the statute (Tax Law, §2, subd 6; Cons.Laws,
ch.60), if it were to throw a bridge across the river, no matter
at how high a point above the level of the water. The franchise
would be unrelated to the title to the bed below (*Trustees* of
Town of Southampton v. *Jessup,* 162 N.Y.122).

The truth indeed is that a bridge, however placed across a
navigable stream, is a potential interference with navigation
in such a sense and to such a degree as to preclude its construction by force of common right or without the license or
approval of the appropriate agencies of government. Cascadilla creek and Six Mile creek are navigable waters within
the accepted definition (*Morgan* v. *King,* 35 N.Y.454; *U.S.*
v. *Holt Bank,* 270 U.S.49,56). Until Congress interferes, the
State may develop as it will their navigable quality (*International Bridge Co.* v. *N.Y.,* 254 U.S.126,132; *U.S.* v. *Chand-
ler-Dunbar Co.,* 229 U.S.53). It may say that bridges shall

not be built at all if it finds the risk too great. It may say that they may be built, but only upon conditions (*Gilman* v. *Philadelphia*, 3 Wall. [U.S.] 713). One who builds or maintains them enjoys a special privilege, not due of common right or as incident to ownership. This uncommon privilege, which, even if now irrevocable, might once have been withheld, is chargeable with a special tax, if the State elects to tax it.

We have said that a bridge over a navigable stream is subject in its construction to the veto of the State since it involves a menace, at least potential, to the unobstructed flow of commerce. Interference with navigation can come from piers or other obstacles narrowing the channel. It can come from the elevation of the structure, as where the bridges are so low that boats cannot go under them. These are the main impediments, but not the only ones. There may be dangers from above. Navigation is impeded if objects falling from a bridge cause damage to the craft below, or expose the traveler to peril. The State has the right to say to what extent such perils, even though slight, shall be permitted. It may determine what may be built above its waterways as above its highways on the land (*Tilly* v. *Mitchell & Lewis Co.*, 121 Wis.1,13; 2 Elliott on Roads & Streets, §830; cf. *People ex rel. N.Y.C. R.R.Co.* v. *Tax Comm.*, 239 N.Y.183).

Support is found for this conclusion in decisions that define the regulatory power of Congress in respect of navigable streams. The United States is not the owner of the beds of such streams within the limits of the States. Whatever power belongs to Congress to control the course of navigation is a branch of its power to regulate interstate and foreign commerce, and is limited thereby. The law is settled, none the less, that its power to prohibit or control the erection of bridges over navigable waters is as broad as any that would belong to it if it had title to the bed. Riparian owners may not escape the effect of its veto by proof that in the circumstances of a given case the obstruction would be negligible. They must submit to the enactments which ordain that in some instances Congress itself must authorize the bridge and that in all instances there must be the license and approval of administrative officers (*Cummings* v. *Chicago,* 188 U.S.410, 429; *Stone* v. *Southern Ill. Bridge Co.,* 206 U.S.267,274; *Int. Bridge Co.* v. *N.Y.,* *supra*; *Miller* v. *Mayor of N.Y.,* 109 U.S. 385; *Gilman* v. *Philadelphia, supra*; *People* v. *Hudson River Connecting R.R.Corp.,* 228 N.Y.203,217,218; River & Harbor Act of March 3, 1899; 30 Stat. §1151, §9; Mason's U.S. Code, vol.2, p.2414, title 33, § 401; Blair, Federal Bridge Legislation, 36 Yale L.J.808, and cases there cited). Much in point is the ruling in a recent case (*Economy Light Co.* v. *U.S.,* 256 U.S.113). There the question was whether the Desplaines river, a stream navigable by small craft, was subject to the Federal statute. "We concur in the opinion of the Circuit Court of Appeals that a river having actual navigable capacity in its natural state and capable of carrying commerce among the States, is within the power of Congress to preserve for purposes of future transportation, even though it be not at present used for such commerce, and be incapable of such use according to present methods, either by reason of changed conditions or because of artificial obstructions. And we agree that the provisions of section 9 of the Act of 1899 (30 Stat.1151) apply to such a stream." (*Economy Light Co.* v. *U.S., supra*.) If Congress may exact a license, so also may the State, whose power of regulation is plenary till Congress intervenes (*Gilman* v. *Philadelphia, supra*; *Int. Bridge Co.* v. *N.Y., supra*).

The Lehigh Valley Railway Company, the owner of these

bridges, is organized as a corporation under the laws of this State, and must look to those laws for the definition of its powers. The railroad corporation acts for the better part of a century have treated the right to span a stream as a privilege or franchise. We see this in the act of 1850 (L. 1850, ch.140, §28, subd.5). Provision is there made that a railroad corporation may construct its road across any stream of water or watercourse, provided the stream or watercourse be restored to substantially its former state. "Nothing in this act contained," however, "shall be construed to authorize the erection of any bridge, or any other obstructions across, in or over any stream or lake navigated by steam or sail boats, at the place where any bridge or other obstructions may be proposed to be placed." We see the same thought in the later Railroad Act of 1890 (L. 1890, ch.565, §11) which in this respect continues the act of 1850 with changes merely verbal. We see the same thought, emphasized and developed, in the Railroad Act in force at the time of the assessment (L. 1910, ch.481, as amended by L. 1913, ch.743, and L. 1916, ch.109; Consol.Laws, ch.49). In that act there is a re-enactment of the provisions of the earlier statutes with the addition that the consent of the Public Service Commission shall be obtained whenever a bridge is built across a navigable creek. A railroad corporation submits in the acceptance of its charter to the restrictive reservations accompanying the grant.

The right to bridge a stream is not an inseparable incident to riparian ownership (*Enfield Toll Bridge* v. *Hartford R.R. Co.*, 17 Conn.40,63), like the right, *e.g.*, to build a dock or a pier (*Town of Brookhaven* v. *Smith*, 188 N.Y.74). This is so though the bridge has been constructed without objection. In the absence of a grant, the State may revoke such license, if any, as may be inferred from acquiescence, and resume dominion to itself. Dams across rivers and even across creeks have been held to be unlawful if built without license, express or implied, at points where the stream would otherwise be navigable (*Willson* v. *Black Bird Creek Marsh Co.*, 2 Pet. [U.S.] 245; *Pound* v. *Turck*, 95 U.S.459; *U.S.* v. *Bellingham Bay Boom Co.*, 176 U.S.211; *Waterford El.L., H. & P.Co.* v. *State*, 208 App.Div.273, at pp.286,287,288, explaining *Commissioners of Canal Fund* v. *Kempshall*, 26 Wend.404). If there have been loose statements to the contrary, they have been made for the most part in jurisdictions where the building of a dam had the sanction, either express or implied, ot the provisions of a statute (see, *e.g.*, *Newbold* v. *Mead*, 57 Penn.St.487; *Pearson* v. *Rolfe*, 76 Me.380,386; *Foster* v. *Spool & Block Co.*, 79 Me.508,511; *Kretzschmar* v. *Meehan*, 74 Minn.211,214). The erection of a bridge involves a kindred exercise of power (*Gilman* v. *Philadelphia, supra*; Gould on Waters, §132). "There are three cases in which authority from the Legislature is necessary to erect a bridge over a stream. One is when the stream is navigable; 2d, when the State owns the bed of the stream; and 3d, when the right to take toll is desired." (*Fort Plain Bridge Co.* v. *Smith*, 30 N.Y. 44,63.)

Distinctions have at times been attempted between streams navigable for boats and those floatable for logs (Gould on Waters, §110; 1 Farnham on Waters, §29, p.138; cf., however, *Morgan* v. *King*, 35 N.Y.454,459). There are statements that in the one class of waters the public right extends to the full width at the stream (*Sullivan* v. *Jernigan*, 21 Fla.264, 279), and that in the other it is more restricted. We do not need to go into these distinctions now. The line between navigable and non-navigable waters is not always an easy one to draw (*Egan* v. *Hart*, 165 U.S.188). Much will often depend upon the acquiescence of the State. Even an unlawful obstruction may not be abated as a nuisance at the suit of private persons if the State does not complain, and there is no showing of special damage by the champions of the public right (*Fort Plain Bridge Co.* v. *Smith, supra,* at p.62). Here the State itself is asserting its own dominion, never surrendered, but on the contrary, in the very creation of its corporations, explicitly reserved. The relator has no immunity against a challenge so august.

The order should be affirmed with costs.

POUND, CRANE, ANDREWS, LEHMAN, KELLOGG, and O'BRIEN, JJ., concur.

Order affirmed, etc.

CONFLICT OF LAWS

AMELIA F. DEAN, Respondent, *v.* ROBERT J. DEAN, Appellant.

CARDOZO, J. Plaintiff and defendant were married in Ontario, Canada, and lived there together till February, 1919. The husband then left the matrimonial domicile, and abandoned his wife and children. He lived for a time in Buffalo, and later in Erie, Pennsylvania. While domiciled in Pennsylvania, he brought suit against his wife for divorce in the courts of that State, charging her with desertion. Upon the false statement that he did not know her whereabouts, he obtained an order for the service of process by publication. He was granted a judgment of divorce on November 5, 1923. Soon afterwards he came back to Buffalo after having married again. The present plaintiff, his first wife, did not appear in the Pennsylvania divorce suit, and did not know that it was pending. She remained in Ontario until March, 1924, when she took up her home in Buffalo. She found her husband living with another woman, and sued him for divorce.

We have said that the husband abandoned his wife and children when he left the matrimonial domicile. There is evidence for the conclusion, and against it. The husband on his side maintained that the wife refused to follow him. The trial judge, weighing the probabilities, gave credence to the wife. It is true that in his decision he did not find the fact of abandonment in so many words. He stated it, however, in his opinion as his inference from the evidence. He found, moreover, in his decision that on November 5, 1923, the date of the Pennsylvania judgment, the wife was domiciled in Ontario. If the husband had not abandoned her, her domicile would have followed his. Reading the opinion and the decision together, we cannot doubt that in the view of the trier of the facts the husband was at fault. A finding of abandonment will, therefore, be implied (*Ogden* v. *Alexander*, 140 N.Y.356,362).

The situation then is this: The husband after deserting his wife in the matrimonial domicile in Ontario, obtained upon constructive service of process a divorce in Pennsylvania. The full faith and credit clause of the Constitution of the United States (Art.4, §1) does not command us to accord recognition to a judgment so procured (*Haddock* v. *Haddock*, 201 U.S.562). The only question is whether comity or public policy, or, to put it differently, our own interpretation of the conflict of laws, should prompt us to concede a recognition that we are at liberty to refuse. We do not need to inquire what our conclusion would be if the issue of abandonment had been resolved in favor of the husband. In that event, the wife, though she remained in Ontario, would have been under a duty to live with her husband wherever he offered her a home. In the view of the law, his domicile would have been hers. A different problem would be before us for solution if it thus appeared that the Pennsylvania court, in decreeing a divorce, was adjudicating the status of parties whose domicile was there (cf. *Cheely* v. *Clayton*, 110 U.S.701,705; *Franklin* v. *Franklin*, 190 Mass.349; *Loker* v. *Gerald*, 157 Mass.42,45; and *O'Dea* v. *O'Dea*, 101 N.Y.23, explained in *Ball* v. *Cross*, 231 N.Y.329). We do not even have to forecast the decision that would be made if they had been living separate by consent (cf. *Winston* v. *Winston*, 165 N.Y.553,555). We confine ourselves to the facts as found. The wife having been deserted by her husband, might maintain a domicile of her own (*Williamson* v. *Osenton*, 232 U.S.619; *Perkins* v. *Perkins*, 225 Mass. 82), and she chose to maintain one in Ontario, till later she changed it to New York. She has never consented that her husband acquire a home apart from her, nor barred herself by misconduct from objecting to his doing so. In these circumstances, the incapacity of the divorce decree of Pennsylvania to affect the status of the abandoned wife, does not depend upon some local policy established by New York for the protection of citizens or residents. It does not have its origin in the need of preserving the domestic law against evasion by one spouse to the prejudice of the other. It results from the general principles that govern the extraterritorial recognition of jurisdiction in actions of divorce (*Perkins* v. *Perkins, supra*; *Haddock* v. *Haddock, supra,* at p.570; *Ball* v. *Cross, supra*).

We do not mean that these principles have validity as law, *ex proprio vigore*, irrespective of conflicting conceptions of expediency or justice. The policy behind them is always local in the sense that each State, aside from constitutional restrictions, may formulate its own conception for itself. The like may be said of the conflict of laws generally. The conception of justice prevalent at home will override an opposing conception prevalent abroad, but the conception prevalent at home may exact justice to the stranger as well as justice to the resident. So we think it does. The wife domiciled in Canada and there abandoned by her husband, became by her marriage a party to a relation which the courts of Pennsylvania have attempted to destroy. They have done this, though there has been no submission to the jurisdiction by her, upon the basis of a domicile which the erring husband has wrongfully set up apart from her. We think the judgments of this court leave no escape from the conclusion that according to the standards of justice prevalent among us, injustice would be done if that attempt were to prevail. This being so, the divorce decree of Pennsylvania ought not to be recognized as valid in New York unless it would have been recognized as valid in the country in which the wife was domiciled at the time when the decree was made (*Ball* v. *Cross, supra; Perkins* v. *Perkins, supra*). If the courts of her domicile were satisfied, we might follow where they led (*Armitage* v. *Attorney-General*, 1906 P.135; *Ball* v. *Cross, supra*). But Canada does not recognize the binding force of the decree. The law of Ontario to that effect was proved upon the trial (*King* v. *Brinkley*, 14 Ontario L.R.434). We find nothing in our public policy to justify a holding that the wife, who remained a wife while she kept her domicile in Ontario, should be deemed to have ceased to be one when she changed her domicile to New York.

If there is need of other support for this conclusion, it is given by the husband's fraud. He obtained an order for the publication of the summons in local newspapers of Erie county, Pennsylvania, upon the false suggestion that the wife's whereabouts were unknown. The purpose as well as the effect of this misstatement was to keep her in ignorance of the suit. We do not need to say that for such a fraud alone the judgment would be disregarded if jurisdiction, as recognized internationally, were otherwise complete. At least the fraud will help us to determine whether a recognition dependent upon conceptions of public policy and justice, shall be granted or withheld. An abandoned and defrauded wife asks us to maintain her status as it was fixed by the law of her domicile at the date of the fraudulent decree. We cannot say that conceptions of public policy and justice require us to change it.

The judgment should be affirmed, with costs.

. . .

HISCOCK, Ch.J., POUND, McLAUGHLIN and ANDREWS, JJ., concur with CRANE and CARDOZO, JJ.; LEHMAN, J., dissents in opinion.

Judgment affirmed.

TRUSTS

In the Matter of the Will of ROBERT J.HORNER, Deceased. LILLIAN HORNER, Appellant; GRACE B.SIMMS et al., Respondents.[1]

CARDOZO, J. The proceeding is one for the construction of a will.

Robert J.Horner directed that his residuary estate be con-

---

1. This highly technical opinion has been included for the sake of a more complete picture. For a recent attack on the rule here involved (which occasions so much technical difficulty) and a suggestion for its simplification, see New York State Legislative Document No. 65 (H), 1936, *Communication and Study Relating to Rule against Perpetuities and Related Matters* by Richard R.Powell and Henry E.Whiteside. This study was undertaken for the Law Revision Commission which is New York's "ministry of justice."

verted into money and then disposed of it as follows: One-fourth he gave to his daughter Grace B.Simms; the remaining three-fourths he gave to trustees to divide into three equal funds, of which the first was to be called "A trust for the benefit of children of Grace B.Simms;" the second, "A trust for the benefit of children of Robert J.Horner, Jr.," and the third, "A trust for the benefit of Robert J.Horner, Jr." The validity of these trusts is the question now before us. The next of kin of the testator acquiesce in the decree. The wife alone appeals.

Convenience will be promoted if the second of the three trusts be considered at the outset. Its provisions are as follows:

"*Tenth.* I direct my Trustees to pay out of the interest accruing upon the trust created for the benefit of children of Robert J.Horner, Jr., such sums as they shall deem advisable for the maintenance and education of Elsie Horner, Muriel Horner, Robert J.Horner, Jr., and Constance Horner. Upon any of said children reaching the age of twenty-one (21) years, I direct my Trustees to pay to said child his or her interest in said trust fund as shall be determined by the number of the said children then surviving and after all of the said children herein mentioned have reached the age of twenty-one (21) years and the payments herein provided have been made, the trust created for their benefit shall thereupon terminate. Should any of said children die before reaching the age of twenty-one years, leaving issue him or her surviving, the said issue shall receive the portion of said fund the parent would have received if living."

If the dominant purpose is the creation of a single trust subsisting during four minorities, absolute ownership is illegally suspended (Pers.Prop. Law [Cons. Laws, ch.41] §11), and the trust in its entirety is void, even though in some contingencies it may end within the statutory term (*Central Trust Co. of N.Y.* v. *Egleston,* 185 N.Y.23; *Leach* v. *Godwin,* 198 N.Y.35). On the other hand, if the dominant purpose in the creation of the trust is that of division into separate shares terminable by separate minorities or lives, the trust to that extent may be upheld, even though in some other contingency it is to be illegally prolonged (*Matter of Colegrove,* 221 N.Y. 455). We must say whether unity or pluralism is the preponderating note. The choice at best is between two obscurities, and yet the stress, it would seem, is upon shares into which an aggregate is conceived of as at least constructively divided, and not upon an aggregate in which shares have been submerged. We see this when we trace the disposition of the fund in the several contingencies suggested by the will. If there is no death before majority, then, as each minority ends, an equal share is to be set free. If death occurs before majority, but issue are left, a share, still conceived of as appropriated to the parent during life, will be passed on to the issue, who will stand as the parent's representatives, and again will be set free. "The said issue shall receive the portion of said fund the parent would have received if living." Even while minority continues and the trust is in force, the trustees are authorized by another subdivision of the will, the thirteenth, to pay to each child in any year out of the principal of the fund a sum not exceeding $500, which, is to be charged "as an advancement." Trouble arises for the first time in the contingency of death during minority without issue. In that contingency, the share that would have gone to the child so dying if he had survived until majority is not to be severed from the bulk, but is to be held within the trust for the use of the survivors. This must be the meaning, for only thus can effect be given to the direction that a child arriving at majority is to receive a share that shall be determined, not by a division into fourths, but by the number of children surviving when division is to be made. A possible result will be that the primary share will be kept within the trust for three lives or minorities beyond the life of the child who would have taken it if he had lived to be of age. Either there must be excision at some point before the expiration of two lives, or the gift must perish altogether. We had before us in *Matter of Colegrove* (*supra*) a will almost the same as this one in the effect of its provisions, though differing in form. A way was found, while removing what was unsound, to preserve what was essential. So here the vital parts of the plan are untouched by the excrescence. The provision that in given circumstances a share shall fall back into the general body of the trust and remain unsevered from the bulk is so subordinate in importance and so separable in function that we are at liberty to cut it off and preserve what goes before.

We have said that the offending provision has not only a function that is separate but an importance that is subordinate. The ends that were uppermost in the thought of the testator assume division rather than unity for their effectual attainment. Shares will be severed and distributed at the successive periods of majority if hope and expectation, reasonably entertained in view of the ages of the children, are not thwarted by events. Consolidation or absorption will at best be the fulfillment of a secondary purpose, to take effect only as a substitute when the primary one has failed. We said in *People ex rel. Alpha Portland Cement Co.* v. *Knapp* (230 N.Y. 48,60), considering the question whether a statute was to be enforced with the invalid part cut out or was to be rejected altogether, that "the answer must be reached pragmatically, by the exercise of good sense and sound judgment, by considering how the statutory rule will function if the knife is laid to the branch instead of at the roots." The same thing may be said of the surgery of wills (*Carrier* v. *Carrier*, 226 N.Y.114,124). Here also the principle of division is not solely a principle of form. In part, though not wholly, it is a principle of function (*People ex rel. Alpha Portland Cement Co.* v. *Knapp, supra*). The tests of presumable intention and probable desire will be commonly of greater potency than those that have their origin in the separation of the good from the bad by paragraph or sentence (*Oxley* v. *Lane*, 35 N.Y.340, 349; *Harrison* v. *Harrison*, 35 N.Y.543,547). Viewing the problem in this spirit, we shall hesitate to lay emphasis upon differences of form where there is no difference in effect, as we should be doing if we were to establish a distinction between the Colegrove will and this one. No doubt, there will be times when differences merely formal will be, none the less, controlling (Gray on the Rule against Perpetuities, §349), yet we will not press them farther than we must. The persuasive thought will rather be whether the differences are of such a nature as to suggest varying conceptions of what is vital in the scheme. We may be fairly sure that this testator was not troubling himself with distinctions between shares which lose their identity in certain contingencies through fusion or absorption into the whole, and a whole which loses its identity through dissolution into shares. What he had in mind was a primary desire that each child at majority should have an equal share of the principal, a fourth of the entire fund, with a secondary desire that if this became impossible, the fourth should go to issue, and, in default of issue, should be retained as an accretion to the whole. It could hardly have occurred to him to hesitate when driven to a choice between the destruction of the whole and the loss of the accretion. We carry out his purpose when we treat the four shares of principal as having a several existence in his thought from the beginning, and as subject from the beginning to the vicissitudes of several limitations (*Vanderpoel* v. *Loew*, 112 N.Y. 167,177,180; *Everitt* v. *Everitt*, 29 N.Y.39,85; *Wells* v. *Wells*, 88 N.Y.323,333).

We do not overlook the argument that the only direction for division to be found in the will is one proportioning the shares to the number of children surviving when majority is reached. The assumptions of the argument do not accord altogether with the facts, for there may be an earlier division in the event of death during minority with issue (cf. *Everitt* v. *Everitt*, *supra*). Except in that contingency, however, division is postponed until one of the four children is of age, if by division we mean a physical severance of shares which till then have been physically undivided, and a payment upon severance to the ultimate donees. We might have said the same thing in *Matter of Colegrove* (*supra*). It is precisely for this reason that the trust before us here, like the one before us there, involves in some contingencies an illegal limitation. That feature lacking, we should have nothing to lop off and nothing to discuss. But to say that there is no direction for division in the sense of payment is not to say that there is none for a constructive division into shares, atoms within the mass, each with its several life (*Vanderpoel* v. *Loew*, *supra*). Such a severance is not always the outcome of express command. There are times when it is rather the product of a state of mind. The shares exist as shares if the testator thought of them as shares. Whether he so thought of them will be determined by many things; by the way that he has dealt with them in alternative contingencies; by all the subtle suggestions of an assumption or an intention imperfectly expressed. We find, indeed, when analysis is pressed, that the determining considerations are much the same as those that distinguish a joint tenancy from a tenancy in common (cf. FINCH, J., in *Hillyer* v. *Vandewater*, 24 N.E.Rep.999; memo. of decision, 121 N.Y.681). Unity of ownership is the characteristic of the one estate (4 Kent's Comm.358), and unity of possession the characteristic of the other. Each tenant in common "is considered to be solely or severally seized of his share" (4 Kent's Comm.358; cf. *Allen* v. *Almy*, 87 Conn.517,526). If we were asked to define the estate in remainder, dependent upon the termination of the trust, that is given to each child, we should find it impossible to do so in terms of joint tenancy. We should have to say that each child has a remainder, contingent upon his attaining his majority, in a portion of the fund which, if that contingency is satisfied, cannot be less than a fourth, but which may be increased, by force of a provision for cross remainders among survivors, in the additional contingency that another child shall die a minor without issue (4 Kent's Comm.201; *Houghton* v. *Brantingham*, 86 Conn.630). The gift to survivors is not secured to them by virtue of a *jus accrescendi* attaching as an inseparable incident to a joint ownership of the whole. The gift is a cross remainder involving succession to a part. The will in this respect is not unlike the one considered by the Supreme Court of Connecticut in *Houghton* v. *Brantingham* (*supra*), where the court said: "This was not the creation of a joint tenancy with right of survivorship, but the creation of a freehold estate in one-half of the property of the testatrix in each of the sons during their joint lives with a contingent remainder in fee of the entire estate in the surviving son." Survivorship as the result of an alternative limitation is very different in its implications from survivorship attaching as an incident of tenure. These general considerations are fortified by others when we attempt by closer scrutiny to extract the thought of the testator. Two tokens of understanding stand out especially significant. One is the direction that each child may receive an annual advancement upon his portion of the principal, to be charged to him as such in the accounts of the trustees (cf. *Schermerhorn* v. *Cotting*, 121 N.Y.48,62). No bookkeeper would find it easy, or, it may be, possible, to comply with that direction without entries that would import a division into shares. The point of view of the testator, who was, it seems, a business man, and not a lawyer, is fairly reflected in the point of view of an accountant, keeping the books of account to which business is accustomed. Even more significant are the marks of the testator's understanding that upon death during minority, what has been appropriated to the child so dying is something that may be identified and segregated and appropriated anew, passing to issue or to survivors according to the event. If the express direction that in such a contingency the share should go to issue, had been supplemented by an express direction that, in default of issue, it should be added to the trusts for the survivors, the latter direction, almost beyond question, would be separable, though illegal (*Matter of Colegrove, supra*). We think it is not less separable because it is implied.

The line of cleavage thus drawn between what is to be kept and what destroyed, does not divide a mere continuum and split into parts a gift essentially unbroken (cf. Gray on the Rule against Perpetuities, §§355,349; *Smith* v. *Bence*, 1891, 3 Ch.242,249; *Hancock* v. *Watson*, 1902, A.C.14,22; *Gray* v. *Whittemore*, 192 Mass.367,372,373). It is not arbitrarily interjected by the court at a point where the testator had no thought of a resting place, a pause, a stage upon the journey.

It follows seams and contracts suggested by the will itself. In the thought of the testator, the death of a child during minority is the signal for a halt and a new reckoning (*Carrier v. Carrier*, 226 N.Y.114,124). The trustees must inquire whether his next of kin are descendants or collaterals, and shape the trust accordingly. In one contingency, death with issue, the new apportionment will be valid. In another, death without issue, the new apportionment will be void upon the expiration of the second life, if not upon the expiration of the first one. Whatever the advance, the significance of the halt remains. The will in all its provisions is instinct with the thought that each of the four children has a share or interest of his own, which upon majority or death must be distributed anew. If the grafted shoots are to be sacrificed the parent stock may be preserved (*Oxley* v. *Lane, supra; Schey* v. *Schey,* 194 N.Y.368,375). We go along with the testator as far forward as we may.

The next subject to be considered is the trust for the benefit of the children of Mrs. Simms. Its provisions are as follows:

"*Ninth.* I direct my trustees to pay the interest upon the trust for the benefit of children of Grace B.Simms from time to time, for the maintenance and education of said children. Upon any child of Grace B.Simms reaching the age of twenty-one (21) years, I direct my trustees to pay to said child his or her interest in said trust fund as shall be determined according to the number of children of Grace B.Simms then living, and after all the children of said Grace B.Simms then living have reached the age of twenty-one (21) years and the payments herein provided have been made, the trust created for their benefit shall thereupon terminate. Should any of the children of said Grace B.Simms die before reaching the age of twenty-one (21) years, leaving issue him or her surviving, the said issue shall receive the portion of said fund the parent would have received, if living. In case there shall be no children of the said Grace B.Simms living at the time this trust goes into effect, I direct my trustees to pay the interest upon said trust fund to my daughter, Grace B.Simms, during the term of her natural life unless thereafter there should be children of her blood. In case of the death of my said daughter, Grace B.Simms, without leaving child or children her surviving, I direct my trustees to pay over the principal sum of said trust fund with accumulations of interest, to the trust fund created for the benefit of children of Robert J.Horner, Jr."

At the date of the decree, as at the death of the testator, Mrs. Simms had only one child, a daughter Gladys, an infant of tender years. The trust, however, was established for the benefit not only of the child then in being, but also of any other children that might thereafter be born to the mother. In so far as its duration is measured by the lives or minorities of persons not in being, its provisions are in plain conflict with the prohibition of the statute. The only question is whether the share for the benefit of Gladys is capable of being severed from the shares for afterborn issue. We are confronted here by difficulties not present in the second trust, the one for the children of Mr. Horner. There the beneficiaries were determinate persons, four in number, named in the will. Here they are a fluctuating class to be determined in the future by the accidents of birth and death (*Bentinck* v. *Duke of Portland*, 7 Ch.D.693,698; *Webster* v. *Boddington*, 26 Beav. 136,138; 1 Jarman on Wills [6th ed.], 239). We think the provisions for the benefit of afterborn children are so entangled with those for the benefit of Gladys as to make severance impossible. Let us suppose, for example, that two other children are born before the majority of Gladys and before the death of Mrs. Simms. What is then to be done with two-thirds of the income while Gladys is a minor? We may not pay the whole to her, for the will gives her but a part. We may not pay a third to each of the other children during the minority of Gladys, and then stop, for this would be to measure by *her* minority the portions that under the will are to be measured by theirs, a mutilation of the trust in the very essence of its plan. We may not continue the payments to the others after Gladys becomes of age or dies, for in so doing we shall be measuring the duration of the trust by lives not in being at the death of the testator. We may not drop from the trust a proportionate share of the principal as soon as another child is born, thus limiting the trust for Gladys upon each birth to a constantly diminishing share and adjudging intestacy as to the shares released, for the will gives no hint that such a severance was expected, but on the contrary tells us in effect that if afterborn children die without issue during minority, Gladys is again to have the income of the whole until she reaches her majority, and thereupon the principal, *i.e.*, the whole and not a part. The trust for the children of Mr. Horner is so framed that it was possible to start at the death of the testator with four enumerated shares which, for their primary terms at least, were held upon lawful limitations, and ran against the statute only when later subdivided. The trust for the benefit of the children of Mrs. Simms gives us, not determinate shares, but shares in a state of flux, the provisions for the living child hopelessly commingled, indistinguishably fused, with those for the use of children to be born in the future (*Central Trust Co. of N.Y.* v. *Egleston,* 185 N.Y.23,31; *Leach* v. *Godwin,* 198 N.Y.35; *Bailey* v. *Buffalo L.T. & S.D.*

Co., 213 N.Y.525,538; cf. 22 Halsbury Laws of England, Perpetuities, 696, and cases cited). We find no line of cleavage here which permits us to separate what is good from what is bad without destroying the testator's will, and making a new one of our own. It is of no moment that Gladys is even now the only child. The settled rule is that "in determining the validity of a trust and whether testamentary dispositions contravene the statute forbidding the suspension of the absolute ownership of personal property for more than two lives in being, we must consider not what has actually happened since the death of the testator, but what might have happened" (*Matter of Mount,* 185 N.Y.162,169; *Schettler* v. *Smith,* 41 N.Y.328; *Haynes* v. *Sherman,* 117 N.Y.433,438; *Central Trust Co. of N.Y.* v. *Egleston, supra; Matter of Hitchcock,* 222 N.Y.57,71). A single organic plan had been conceived by the testator, a plan for the benefit of a fluctuating class (*Central Trust Co. of N.Y.* v. *Egleston, supra*). We extract the heart of this plan when we condemn its fluctuating element (cf. *Benedict* v. *Webb,* 98 N.Y.460,466; *Bentinck* v. *Duke of Portland; Webster* v. *Boddington, supra*). There is significance in the disposition to be made of the fund if no children are in being when the will shall take effect. In that event, the income is to go to Mrs. Simms during life, but not without conditions; it is to go to her "unless thereafter there should be children of her blood." This is the dominant motive, never relaxed and unmistakably expressed. We feel its pulse in every line.

Our ruling in *Matter of Mount* (185 N.Y.162,169) is pressed upon us as decisive. That case went to the verge of permissable excision. It did not go so far as we shall have to go now if this trust is to be upheld. There the testator created a trust for life for the benefit of his sister, and directed that at the end of that estate the fund should be divided *per stirpes* into as many shares as there were children of his nephew then living and issue of deceased children, with separate trusts for each of them. We sustained this limitation for the benefit of the children alive at the testator's death, though we pronounced it void as to the others. The judgment went upon the ground that there was present in that will the precise element that is lacking in the trust for the children of Mrs. Simms, a direction for the severance of the shares, so that the good was not inextricably commingled with the bad (185 N.Y. at pp.169,170; cf. *Mount* v. *Mount*, 234 N.Y.568; *Boughton* v. *James*, 1 Coll.26; Gray, the Rule against Perpetuities, §389). Here, as we have seen, the poison interpenetrates the system.

The question remains, since the daughter and the son, the only next of kin, acquiesce in the surrogate's decision, whether the decree is to be disturbed as to any one except the wife, the sole appellant in this court. The decree under review upholds the trust for Gladys during the term of her minority and no longer. Such a trust, thus limited, is not subject to the objection that it does violence to the public policy of the state. If that were its effect, the court might feel constrained to interfere, though the parties in interest were silent (*Carrier* v. *Carrier*, 226 N.Y.114,122,123). The objection to the trust as declared by the decree is that it has been made over by the court, and the good separated from the bad, to such an extent that it is no longer the trust declared by the testator. This, however, is an objection that the next of kin, who with the wife would take the fund if the trust were avoided altogether, are competent to waive so far as their own interests are concerned. They might declare such a trust themselves, and by the same token and to the same extent they may confirm and approve its declaration by the court (*Carrier* v. *Carrier*, *supra*). Wife and next of kin take under the Statute of Distributions as tenants in common, and not jointly. In such circumstances, a reversal of the judgment as to the wife who appeals does not affect the shares of others who have preferred to acquiesce (*St. John* v. *Andrews Institute*, 192 N.Y.382; *Matter of Union Trust Co. of N.Y.*, 219 N.Y.537).

We do not need to enter upon a discussion of the validity of the third trust, the one for Robert J.Horner, Jr. It shares the fate of the trust for the benefit of his children.

The order of the Appellate Division and the decree of the Surrogate's Court should be modified by adjudging the invalidity as to the appellant of the trust for the benefit of the children of Grace B.Simms, and as so modified the order and the decree should be affirmed, with costs to all parties separately appearing and filing briefs in this court, payable out of the estate.

HISCOCK, Ch.J., POUND, McLAUGHLIN, CRANE, ANDREWS and LEHMAN, JJ., concur.

Ordered accordingly.

SALES

HENRY GLASS & CO., Appellant, *v.* ABRAHAM MISROCH, Respondent.

CARDOZO, J. In October, 1918, plaintiffs agreed to sell and defendant to buy 6,000 yards of material, described as Palm Beach suitings, to be delivered at defendant's place of business on January 15, 1919, and to be paid for seventy days thereafter. Tender of delivery was made at the prescribed time, and rejected by the buyer's agent. The sellers thereupon gave notice to the buyer that the goods would be resold for his account and that he would be charged with the deficiency. Thus warned, the buyer telegraphed the sellers: "Had instructed receiving clerk to accept invoice of January fifteenth." At the same time his attorneys wrote that their client had need of the goods, and had not intended to reject them. "You will please send them in and if they are in accordance with the contract they will be paid for." Obeying these directions, the plaintiffs, on January twentieth, sent the goods again by their truck to the defendant's place of business and tendered them to the defendant, who received them without reservation or condition. The following day, January twenty-first, he wrote that the goods were defective, and that payment would be refused. He reiterated this position later. This action followed for the recovery of the price.

The jury found the goods to be of merchantable quality and in accordance with the contract. Upon their verdict to that effect there was a judgment for the plaintiffs. The Appellate Division reversed and dismissed the complaint upon the ground that the contract was executory and that the remedy was by action for the damages resulting from the breach.

"Where, under a contract to sell or a sale, the property in the goods has passed to the buyer, and the buyer wrongfully neglects or refuses to pay for the goods according to the terms of the contract or the sale, the seller may maintain an action against him for the price of the goods" (Pers.Prop. Law [Cons. Laws, ch.41], §144, subd.1).

There has been wrongful refusal by this defendant to pay for the goods in accordance with the contract. The question is whether the property had passed to him at the time of the refusal. Up to the time of the Sales Act, the answer to that question would have been unimportant in New York. Till then, the seller, upon tender of goods in conformity with the contract, might have maintained an action for the price, if the tender was wrongfully rejected, though there had been no transfer of the title (*Dustan* v. *McAndrew*, 44 N.Y.72,78; *Hayden* v. *DeMets*, 53 N.Y.426; *Mason* v. *Decker*, 72 N.Y. 595; *Van Brocklen* v. *Smeallie*, 140 N.Y.70). All this has now been changed. With exceptions not now important (Pers. Prop. Law, §144, subds.2 and 3), the right of action is dependent upon a transfer of the property. To determine whether the property has passed, we look to the intention of the parties; and for the ascertainment of their intention, the statute has its rules (Pers.Prop. Law, §100). Rules 4 and 5 are the ones applicable here. Subdivision 1 of rule 4 is to the effect that "where there is a contract to sell unascertained or future goods by description and goods of that description and in a deliverable state are unconditionally appropriated to the contract, either by the seller with the assent of the buyer, or by the buyer with the assent of the seller, the property in the goods thereupon passes to the buyer. Such assent may be expressed or implied, and may be given either before or after the appropriation is made." Subdivision 2 of the same rule is to the effect that "where, in pursuance of a contract to sell, the seller delivers the goods to the buyer, or to a carrier or other bailee (whether named by the buyer or not) for the purpose of transmission to or holding for the buyer, he is presumed to have unconditionally appropriated the goods to the contract, except in the cases provided for in the next rule and in section 101." Rule 5 provides that "if the contract to sell requires the seller to deliver the goods to the buyer, or at a particular place, or to pay the freight or cost of transportation to the buyer, or to a particular place, the property does not pass until the goods have been delivered to the buyer or reached the place agreed upon." The goods in controversy were delivered by the sellers to the buyer and in a deliverable state (§156, subds.1 and 4). The sellers by that act are presumed to have unconditionally appropriated to the contract the goods so delivered. If the buyer by his conduct assented to the appropriation, the property has passed.

The defendant insists that the goods are not appropriated to a contract with the assent of the buyer until the buyer has so manifested his approval of their quality as to preclude him thereafter from giving notice of rescission (Pers.Prop. Law, §128, subd.1; §129). In that view, the passage of title may be indefinitely postponed, for the reasonable time within which a buyer is privileged to return goods found to be defective will vary with many circumstances, as, for instance, the nature of the defects, whether patent or concealed (*Schnitzer* v. *Lang*, 239 N.Y.1; *Bierman* v. *City Mills Co.*, 151 N.Y.482). We think assent to appropriation is something more immediate and certain. It does not signify an acceptance so definitive and deliberate as to bar rescission for defects (Williston, Sales, §482). It signifies the buyer's willingness to take as his own the goods appropriated by the seller, subject to rescission and return if defects are afterwards discovered. The cases are many in which goods are shipped by carriers who receive them for the buyers. An order for such shipment is an assent that the goods be appropriated by the seller, and title passes when they are delivered to the carrier "in a deliverable state" (*Standard Casing Co., Inc.,* v. *California Casing Co., Inc.,* 233 N.Y.413; *Rosenberg Bros. & Co.* v. *Buffum Co., Inc.,* 234 N.Y.338,343; *Kinney* v. *Horwitz*, 93 Conn.211,219; *Levy* v. *Radkay*, 233 Mass.29). This does not mean that a buyer is helpless if the goods when they reach their destination are found to be defective. His assent to the appropriation of goods in a deliverable state is not assent to the appropriation of any goods, though of a kind or quality at variance with the contract. On the other hand, his assent will stand, and may not be retracted, if the variance is pretended. There is no distinction in this respect between delivery to the buyer through a carrier or other intermediary and delivery to the buyer personally. The question in each case is whether delivery is made in such circumstances as to indicate assent to the appropriation by the seller. *Delaware, Lackawanna & Western R.R.Co.* v. *U.S.* (231 U.S.363) was a case where hay was delivered to a railroad company not as carrier but as buyer, under a contract that delivery should be made at Buffalo, with privilege to the buyer to transport to other places on its route and there inspect (p.371). The ruling was that title passed upon delivery, subject to the right of rescission if defects were afterwards discovered (p.372). Acceptance, as it is there shown (p.372), means different things in different contexts, and the shifting shades of meaning are a fruitful source of error (cf. *Rodgers* v. *Phillips*, 40 N.Y.519; *Stone* v. *Browning*, 68 N.Y.598,600; Williston, Sales, §482). The courts of Massachusetts, long before the adoption of the Uniform Sales Act, upheld the rule, which prevailed in England also, that an action for the price would not lie until there had been a transfer of the property. They held, however, that where delivery had been made at the place of business of the buyer in accordance with the contract, the action would not fail because the buyer gave notice of rejection for defects that were unreal (*Nichols* v. *Morse*, 100 Mass.523; *Roach* v. *Lane*, 226 Mass.598,604; cf. *Katz* v. *Delohery Hat Co.*, 97 Conn.665,673; *Pacific Iron Works* v. *L.I.R.R.Co.*, 62 N.Y.272,274; *Burrowes* v. *Whitaker*, 71 N.Y.291; *Rosenberg Bros. & Co.* v. *Buffum Co., Inc.*, *supra*, at p.343). Numberless also are the cases where without previous inspection or opportunity for inspection the buyer has received delivery at the place of business of the seller, with ensuing liability to make payment of the price (*Rhode* v. *Thwaites*, 6 *B. & C.* 388; *Leonard* v. *Carleton & Hovey Co.*, 230 Mass.262,264; Williston, Sales, §274; Benjamin on Sales [6th ed.] p.384, *et seq.*). It is not the locality that governs, but the character of the act and the implications that attach to it.

When we speak of delivery, we must be on our guard, none the less, against misleading ambiguities. Delivery to be operative as a transfer of the property must be assented to by the buyer (Williston, Sales, §472; cf. §280, p.592). The seller may not force the goods upon a buyer unwilling to receive them. The buyer, when delivery is tendered, may refuse to assent to it at all (taking, of course, the risk of liability for damages), or may assent subject to the condition that he be allowed to see the goods before delivery or appropriation shall be deemed to be complete. "Unless otherwise agreed, when the seller tenders delivery of goods to the buyer, he is bound, on request, to afford the buyer a reasonable opportunity of examining the goods for the purpose of ascertaining whether they are in conformity with the contract" (Pers. Prop. Law, §128, subd.2). The law was the same before the statute was enacted. "The rule is that a tender of bulky articles in the performance of an agreement must be seasonably made, so that the person may have an opportunity to examine the articles tendered, and see that they are such as they purport to be, and such as he is entitled to demand, before the close of the day on which the delivery is to be made" (*Croninger* v. *Crocker*, 62 N.Y.151,158; cf. *McNeal* v. *Braun*, 53 N.J.L.617; *Lummis* v. *Millville Mfg.Co.*, 72 N.J.L. 25,26; Williston, Sales, §§455,478,479). There is a difference in other words between inspection following delivery, and inspection to determine whether delivery shall be permitted. Until that determination is made, the transaction is *in fieri*. Delivery remains inchoate while the buyer refuses to treat it as perfected. Even taking the goods in, may be so qualified by notice or agreement that possession will not operate as an expression of assent. "The buyer is entitled to examine the goods to decide whether he will become owner, and until the examination is completed or waived, he is under no obligation to accept the goods" (Williston, Sales, §472). The examination *is* waived, however, in so far as it is a condition precedent to the transfer of the property, when there is an assent to delivery without reservation or condition accompanying the receipt and qualifying or postponing or neutralizing its effect. Examination prior to such acceptance is indeed, as we have seen, to be permitted "on request" (Pers.Prop. Law, §128, subd.2), yet even when requested, it is immediate and summary, closing, at least in ordinary conditions, with the close of the day, for which reason tender must be made at a seasonable hour (*Croninger* v. *Crocker, supra*). Undoubtedly, a right survives to examine and reject thereafter, but it survives as a condition subsequent, and its exercise does not bar an action for the price if the goods rejected were in truth in a deliverable state. When we speak of the condition as subsequent, we mean that assent to the appropriation stands unless revoked for a sufficient cause. It is a different question whether in the event of revocation, the seller is relieved of the burden of proving as a condition precedent to recovery that the goods, though appropriated with assent, conform in kind and quality to those called for by the contract (Williston, Sales, §§473, 278; Benjamin, Sales [6th ed.], p.400; Pers.Prop. Law, §100, rule 4, subd.1). Enough for present purpose that the effect of receipt without reservation or disclaimer is to defer the examination indefinitely for the convenience of the buyer (Williston, Sales, §474). True, dissent must be announced within a reasonable time (Pers.Prop. Law, §128, subd.1; §129), but a reasonable time is without determinate limits and varies with the facts. If title does not pass when there is assent to a consummated delivery, the seller will have to bear the risk of the destruction of the goods during a period of indeterminate duration, though he has complied with his contract and the grounds of rejection are capricious or pretended. There can be little doubt that the announcement of such a rule will be a shock to the average merchant who believes that he is through with the transaction upon delivery accepted by the buyer, unless indeed he has made delivery of goods that are defective. If conflicting interpretations of the statute are reasonably possible, our preference should be for the one that keeps it in accord with mercantile practice. There is some suggestion, it is true, of a rule that may be said to occupy a middle ground. Acceptance after inspection survives, we are told, as a condition precedent even though delivery is perfected, yet at some intermediate point, before a reasonable time for rejection has expired, it fades into a condition subsequent. We find no basis in the statute for a distinction that would complicate by the introduction of new refinements an already complicated subject. Assent to delivery, unless otherwise qualified, is assent to appropriation, and thus, subject to rescission, an acceptance of the title.

The defendant argues that his telegram to the plaintiffs and the letter written by his attorneys do qualify the delivery, and in qualifying it rebut the inference of ownership. We do not so construe them. The telegram is in effect a notice to the plaintiffs that the buyer will assent to a delivery, if the tender, rejected by mistake, is made to him again. The letter is merely a reminder by his lawyers that payment will not be due if the goods are not as ordered. To state this is to state the obvious. Nothing in the telegram or in the letter is notice to the plaintiffs that delivery, when accepted, is to be subject to consequences or conditions other than those that by legal implication are inherent in the act.

Two cases, one relied on by the sellers, and the other by the buyer, deserve a word of explanation to avoid misconstruction in the future. *Turner-Looker Co.* v. *Aprile* (234 N.Y. 517) did not hold that an action for the price would lie upon the rejection of a lawful tender though there had been no transfer of the property. The decision went upon the ground that title had passed when the tender was rejected. *Larkin* v. *Geisenheimer* (201 App.Div.741; 235 N.Y.547) did not hold that upon the acceptance of delivery without conditions, the transfer of title is postponed until inspection and approval. There the contract was to deliver upon a vessel, but in the meantime the goods were to be delivered at the buyer's office for the single and stated purpose of examination at his hands. Upon these facts, delivery at the office was held to be, not absolute, but conditional. Title could not pass till the contract had been performed by delivery at the ship.

An error in the admission of evidence necessitates another trial. The plaintiffs' letter of January 28, 1919, contains a scathing arraignment of the defendant's conduct. It was erroneously received as evidence in favor of its authors.

The judgment of the Appellate Division should be modified by granting a new trial, and as so modified affirmed, with costs to abide the event.

HISCOCK, Ch.J., POUND, CRANE, ANDREWS and LEHMAN, JJ., concur; MCLAUGHLIN, J., absent.

Judgment accordingly.

REAL PROPERTY

ALEXANDER ROMAN, Appellant, *v.* JULIANA LOBE, Respondent.

CARDOZO, J. Plaintiff, a broker, having effected a sale of real estate, sues the seller for his commissions. The defendant, admitting the employment and the service, defends upon the ground that the broker was not licensed in accordance with the statute (Real Prop. Law [Cons. Laws, ch.50], art.XII-A). Plaintiff held a license for the year ending September 30, 1923. He did not obtain a renewal license till October 26, 1923. He was thus without a license on October 16, 1923, when the purchaser was procured and the cause of action arose. There was judgment for the defendant, which was unanimously affirmed, first at the Appellate Term and later at the Appellate Division. The sole question in this court is whether the requirement of a license is a constitutional exercise of legislative power.

By article XII-A of the Real Property Law, enacted in 1922, a real estate broker in certain cities and counties may not do business as such until a license has been issued (§440-a). There were amendatory statutes in 1923 (L. 1923, ch.517) and 1924 (L. 1924, ch.579). The applicant must be a citizen of the United States, or have declared his intention to become such a citizen (§440-a, as amd. in 1924). That provision was not in force when the plaintiff's services were rendered. Authority to grant the license resides with the State Tax Commission, and the application shall give such information as the Commission may reasonably require "to enable it to determine the trustworthiness of the applicant." By the amendment of 1924, it may exact such other information as may be necessary to establish the "competency" of the appli-

267

cant "to transact the business of real estate broker * * * in such manner as to safeguard the interests of the public" (§441). This may include "proof that the applicant has a fair knowledge of the English language, a fair understanding of the general purposes and general legal effect of deeds, mortgages, land contracts of sale, and leases, and a general and fair understanding of the obligations between principal and agent, as well as of the provisions of this act" (§441, as amd. by L. 1924, ch.579). The license, if granted, shall be effective up to and including the thirtieth day of September following the date of issue (§441-a). It may, however, be renewed "upon application therefor by the holder thereof, in such form as the commission may prescribe, and payment of the annual fee" (§441). "In case of application for renewal of license, the commission may dispense with the requirement of such statements as it deems unnecessary in view of those contained in the original application for license" (§441). The action of the Commission in granting or refusing a license may be reviewed by the courts on certiorari (§441-e). A license once granted may be revoked by the Commission for fraud or demonstrated misconduct or incompetency (§441-c). In such cases the remedy of certiorari is available again (§441-e). There shall be no refusal of a license and no revocation or suspension without notice to the applicant and opportunity for a hearing (§441-d). From the operation of the act certain classes of persons, e.g., receivers, referees, administrators, executors and attorneys at law, are excluded (§442-g). No action to recover commissions may be maintained without alleging and proving that a license had been issued when the cause of action arose (§442-e).

The Legislature has a wide discretion in determining whether a business or occupation shall be barred to the dishonest or incompetent (*People* v. *Beakes Dairy Co.*, 222 N.Y. 416,427; *Hall* v. *Geiger-Jones Co.*, 242 U.S.539; *State* v. *De Verges*, 153 La.349; C.W.Pound, Constitutional Aspects of Administrative Law in Growth of Administrative Law, 111,112). Callings, it is said, there are so inveterate and basic, so elementary and innocent, that they must be left open to all alike, whether virtuous or vicious. If this be assumed, that of broker is not one of them. The intrinsic nature of the business combines with practice and tradition to attest the need of regulation. The real estate broker is brought by his calling into a relation of trust and confidence. Constant are the opportunities by concealment and collusion to extract illicit gains. We know from our judicial records that the opportunities have not been lost. With temptation so aggressive, the dishonest or untrustworthy may not reasonably complain if they are told to stand aside. Less obtrusive, but not negligible, are the perils of incompetence. The safeguards against incompetence need not long detain us, for they were added to the statute after the services were rendered. We recall them at this time for the light that they cast upon the Legislature's conception of the mischief to be remedied. The broker should know his duty. To that end, he should have "a general and fair understanding of the obligations between principal and agent" (§441, as amd. by L. 1924, ch.579). Disloyalty may have its origin in ignorance as well as fraud. He should know, so the Legislature has said (L. 1924, ch.579), what is meant by a deed or a lease or a mortgage. At any moment he may have to make report as to such matters to expectant buyers or lessees. Often he goes farther, perhaps too far, and prepares a memorandum of the contract. He is accredited by his calling in the minds of the inexperienced or the ignorant with a knowledge greater than their own.

The Legislatures of many States, awaking to these evils, have adopted statutes like to ours. Licenses to be issued after suitable inquiry as to character and competence are required in California (L. 1919, p.1252), Tennessee (L. 1921, ch.98), Kentucky (L. 1924, ch.138), Virginia (L. 1924, ch.461; Virginia Code, §4359, title 38-B), New Jersey (L. 1921, ch.141), Louisiana (Act No. 236 of 1920), Idaho (L. 1921, ch.184), Illinois (L. 1921, ch.153), Michigan (L. 1921, ch.387), Montana (Rev. Code, 1921, §4065), Oregon (L. 1921, ch.223), Wisconsin (Stat. 1923, sec. 136.01), and Wyoming (L. 1921, ch.31). Legislation so general marks a rising tide of opinion which is suggestive and informing (*Klein* v. *Maravelas*, 219 N.Y.383,385). The Supreme Court of California in a careful judgment upheld the act adopted in that State (*Riley* v. *Chambers*, 181 Cal.589). The ruling there made was approved and followed by the Supreme Court of Louisiana (*Zerlin* v. *La. Real Estate Board*, 158 La.111). In accord also is the Supreme Court of Wisconsin (*Payne* v. *Volkman*, 183 Wis. 412). The Court of Appeals of Kentucky at first upheld the Kentucky act (*Hoblitzel* v. *Jenkins*, 204 Ky.122), but afterwards condemned it (*Rawles* v. *Jenkins*, 212 Ky.287). A like statute of Tennessee was before the Supreme Court of the United States in *Bratton* v. *Chandler* (260 U.S.110). By dictum and manifest implication, if not by necessary decision, the statute was sustained. Valid by the judgment of the same court are statutes for the licensing of dealers in securities (*Hall* v. *Geiger-Jones Co.*, 242 U.S.539; *Merrick* v. *Halsey & Co.*, 242 U.S.568), insurance brokers (*La Tourette* v. *McMasters*, 248 U.S.465,468), and brokers dealing in farm produce (*Payne* v. *Kansas*, 248 U.S.112; cf. *State* v. *Payne*, 98 Kan.465; *State* v. *Bowen & Co.*, 86 Wash.23, and *State ex rel. Beek* v. *Wagener*, 77 Minn.483,491; *Lasher* v. *People*,

183 Ill.226,232). One searches vainly for any adequate distinction in respect of legislative control between one broker and another.

Significant, also, is the argument from history. For the better part of a century, real estate brokers in many States, even though not subjected to a test of character and competence, have been prohibited from doing business without a preliminary license. The validity of these requirements has been uniformly upheld. Decisions enforcing them will be found in the Federal courts (*Bradley* v. *City of Richmond*, 227 U.S.477,480), in Illinois (*Braun* v. *City of Chicago*, 110 Ill. 186), in Pennsylvania (*Luce* v. *Cook*, 227 Penn.St.224), in Minnesota (*Buckley* v. *Humason*, 50 Minn.195), and in Arkansas (*City of Little Rock* v. *Barton*, 33 Ark.436). Such forms of regulation are less drastic, indeed, than the system now in question. They have significance, none the less, in marking off the business of the broker as distinct from occupations which by general acquiescence are pursued of common right without regulation or restriction. "We do not readily overturn the settled practice of the years" (*Story* v. *Craig*, 231 N.Y.33,40; cf. *Jackman* v. *Rosenbaum Co.*, 260 U.S.22; *Ownbey* v. *Morgan*, 256 U.S.94; *Biddles, Inc.*, v. *Enright*, 239 N.Y.354,365).

The case circumscribes the judgment. We hold that the Legislature acts within its lawful powers when it establishes a system of licenses for real estate brokers with annual renewals. Farther than that we do not have to go to decide the controversy before us. The plaintiff does not show himself an alien. That being so, the question is not here whether the restriction of the license to citizens and expectant citizens denies to aliens thus excluded the equal protection of the law (*Lehon* v. *City of Atlanta*, 242 U.S.53; *Arkadelphia Co.* v. *St. Louis*

OPINIONS BY CARDOZO

S.W.Ry.Co., 249 U.S.134,149; *Truax* v. *Raich,* 239 U.S. 33; *Yick Wo* v. *Hopkins,* 118 U.S.356). Besides, the discrimination against aliens is the result of subsequent amendment. The plaintiff is not complaining that the test of fitness applied to him has been unreasonable or arbitrary. If he is without the needed license, he has only himself to blame, in that he did not ask for renewal till his license had expired. That being so, the question is not here whether character should be held to qualify, though other competence were lacking. These and other situations that may be imagined must be dealt with as they develop. A workable system would be left though the tests of fitness were diminished (*Weller* v. *N.Y.,* 268 U.S. 319). By section 442-1, "Should the courts of this State declare any provision of this article unconstitutional, or unauthorized, * * * such decision shall affect only the section or provision so declared to be unconstitutional or unauthorized and shall not affect any other section or part of this article" (cf. *Dorchy* v. *Kansas,* 264 U.S.286). The plaintiff is not aggrieved unless the exaction of a license is to be disregarded altogether.

The judgment should be affirmed with costs.

Hiscock, Ch.J., Pound, McLaughlin and Crane, JJ., concur; Andrews and Lehman, JJ., absent.

Judgment affirmed.

PROCEDURE

GEORGE TAUZA, Respondent, *v.* SUSQUEHANNA COAL COMPANY, Appellant.

Cardozo, J. The plaintiff, a resident of this state, has brought suit against the Susquehanna Coal Company, a Pennsylvania corporation. The defendant's principal office is in Philadelphia; but it has a branch office in New York, which is in charge of one Peterson. Peterson's duties are described by the defendant as those of a sales agent. He has eight salesmen under him, who are subject to his orders. A suite of offices is maintained in the Equitable Building in the city of New York, and there the sales agent and his subordinates make their headquarters. The sign on the door is "Susquehanna Coal Company, Walter Peterson, sales agent." The offices contain eleven desks and other suitable equipment. In addition to the salesmen there are other employees, presumably stenographers and clerks. The salesmen meet daily and receive instructions from their superior. All sales in New York are subject, however, to confirmation by the home office in Philadelphia. The duty of Peterson and his subordinates is to procure orders which are not binding until approved. All payments are made by customers to the treasurer in Philadelphia; the salesmen are without authority to receive or indorse checks. A bank account in the name of the company is kept in New York, and is subject to Peterson's control, but the payments made from it are for the salaries of employees, and for petty cash disbursements incidental to the maintenance of the office. The defendant's coal yards are in Pennsylvania, and from there its shipments are made. They are made in response to orders transmitted from customers in New York. They are made, not on isolated occasions, but as part of an established course of business. In brief, the defendant maintains an office in this state under the direction of a sales agent, with eight salesmen, and with clerical assistants, and through these agencies systematically and regularly solicits and obtains orders which result in continuous shipments from Pennsylvania to New York.

To do these things is to do business within this state in such a sense and in such a degree as to subject the corporation doing them to the jurisdiction of our courts. The decision of the Supreme Court in *International Harvester Co.* v. *Kentucky* (234 U.S.579) is precisely applicable. There sales agents in Kentucky solicited orders subject to approval of a general agent in the home state. They did this, not casually and occasionally, but systematically and regularly. Unlike the defendant's salesmen, they did not have an office to give to their activities a fixed and local habitation. The finding was that travelers negotiating sales were not to have any headquarters or place of business in that state, though they were permitted to reside there (234 U.S. at p.584). Yet because their activities were systematic and regular, the corporation was held to have been brought within Kentucky, and, therefore, to be subject to the process of the Kentucky courts. "Here," said the court (p.585), "was a continuous course of business in the solicitation of orders which were sent to another State and in response to which the machines of the Harvester Company were delivered within the State of Kentucky. This was a course of business, not a single transaction." That case goes farther than we need to go to sustain the service here. It distinguishes *Green* v. *Chicago, B. & Q.Ry.Co.* (205 U.S.530) where an agent in Pennsylvania solicited orders for railroad tickets which were sold, delivered and used in Illinois. The orders did not result in a continuous course of shipments from Illinois to Pennsylvania. The activities of the ticket agent in Pennsylvania brought nothing into that state. In the case at bar, as in the *International Harvester* case, there has been a steady course of shipments from one state into the other. The business done in New York may be interstate business, but business it surely is.

The defendant refers to cases in which corporations, whose

situation was not unlike the defendant's, have been held not to be doing business in this state within the meaning of section 15 of the General Corporation Law and kindred statutes (*People ex rel. Tower Co.* v. *Wells*, 98 App.Div.82; 182 N.Y. 553; *Hovey* v. *De Long H. & E.Co.*, 211 N.Y.420; *Cummer Lumber Co.* v. *Assoc.Mfrs.M.F.Ins.Corp.*, 67 App.Div.151; 173 N.Y.633; *Penn Collieries Co.* v. *McKeever*, 183 N.Y.98). But activities insufficient to make out the transaction of business, within the meaning of those statutes, may yet be sufficient to bring the corporation within the state so as to render it amenable to process (*Int. Text Book Co.* v. *Tone*, decided herewith [220 N.Y.313]). In construing statutes which license foreign corporations to do business within our borders we are to avoid unlawful interference by the state with interstate commerce. The question in such cases is not merely whether the corporation is here, but whether its activities are so related to interstate commerce that it may, by a denial of a license, be prevented from being here (*International Text Book Co.* v. *Pigg*, 217 U.S.91). "A statute must be construed, if fairly possible, so as to avoid not only the conclusion that it is unconstitutional but also grave doubts upon that score" (*U.S.* v. *Jin Fuey Moy*, 241 U.S.394,401; *Hovey* v. *De Long H. & E.Co.*, *supra*, at p.429). But the problem which now faces us is a different one. It is not a problem of statutory construction. It is one of jurisdiction, of private international law (Dicey Conflict of Laws, pp.38, 155). We are to say, not whether the business is such that the corporation may be prevented from being here, but whether its business is such that it *is* here. If in fact it is here, if it is here, not occasionally or casually, but with a fair measure of permanence and continuity, then, whether its business is interstate or local, it is within the jurisdiction of our courts

(*International Harvester Co.* v. *Kentucky, supra,* at p.587). To hold that a state cannot burden interstate commerce, or pass laws which regulate it, "is a long way from holding that the ordinary process of the courts may not reach corporations carrying on business within the state which is wholly of an interstate commerce character" (234 U.S. at p.588). The nature and extent of business contemplated by licensing statutes is one thing. The nature and extent of business requisite to satisfy the rules of private international law may be quite another thing. In saying this we concede the binding force of the decision of the Supreme Court in *Riverside & Dan River Cotton Mills* v. *Menefee* (237 U.S.189) and kindred cases (*Bagdon* v. *Philadelphia & Reading C. & I.Co.,* 217 N.Y.432,438; *Pomeroy* v. *Hocking Valley Ry.Co.,* 218 N.Y. 530). Unless a foreign corporation is engaged in business within the state, it is not brought within the state by the presence of its agents. But there is no precise test of the nature or extent of the business that must be done. All that is requisite is that enough be done to enable us to say that the corporation is here (*St. Louis S.W.Ry.Co. of Texas* v. *Alexander,* 227 U.S.218; *Washington-Virginia Ry.Co.* v. *Real Estate Trust Co. of Phila.,* 238 U.S.185; *Int. Harvester Co.* v. *Ky., supra*; *Pomeroy* v. *Hocking Valley Ry.Co., supra*). If it is here it may be served (HALSBURY, L.C., in *La Compagnie Générale Transatlantique* v. *Law,* L.R. [1899 A.C.] 431).

We hold, then, that the defendant corporation is engaged in business within this state. We hold further that the jurisdiction does not fail because the cause of action sued upon has no relation in its origin to the business here transacted. That in principle was our ruling in *Bagdon* v. *Phila. & Reading C. & I.Co.* (217 N.Y.432,438). We applied it there to a case where service had been made on an agent designated by the corporation under section 16 of the General Corporation Law (Consol. Laws, ch.23). It applies, however, with equal force to a case where service has been made upon an officer or managing agent (*Barrow S.S.Co.* v. *Kane*, 170 U.S.100; *Bagdon* v. *Phila. & Reading C. & I.Co. supra*). The essential thing is that the corporation shall have come into the state. When once it is here, it may be served; and the validity of the service is independent of the origin of the cause of action. To the authorities cited in the *Bagdon* case we may add *Logan* v. *Bank of Scotland* (L.R. [1904, 2 K.B.] 495,499), which states the rule in England, and *Rishmiller* v. *Denver & Rio Grande R.Co.* (159 N.W.Rep. [Minn.] 272), which follows the *Bagdon* case and collates the decisions. (See also: *Mooney* v. *Buford & George M.Co.*, 72 Fed.Rep.32; *Denver & R.G. Co.* v. *Roller*, 100 Fed.Rep.738; *Smith* v. *Empire State-Idaho, M. & D.Co.*, 127 Fed.Rep.462.) It is not necessary to show that express authority to accept service was given to the defendant's agent. His appointment to act as agent within the state carried with it implied authority to exercise the powers which under our laws attach to his position (*Lafayette Ins. Co.* v. *French*, 18 How. [U.S.] 404,407,408; *Conn.Mut.L. Ins.Co.* v. *Spratley*, 172 U.S.602,611,613,615; *Commercial Mut.Acc.Co.* v. *Davis*, 213 U.S.245,255). When a foreign corporation comes into this state, the legislature, by virtue of its control over the law of remedies, may define the agents of the corporation on whom process may be served (*Lafayette Ins.Co.* v. *French, supra*). If the persons named are true agents, and if their positions are such as to lead to a just presumption that notice to them will be notice to the principal, the corporation must submit (*Conn.Mut.L.Ins.Co.* v. *Spratley, supra*; *Commercial Mut.Acc.Co.* v. *Davis, supra*). *Old Wayne Mut. Life Assn.* v. *McDonough* (204 U.S.8) and

Simon v. *Southern Ry.Co.* (236 U.S.115) are not to the contrary. They were fully considered in *Bagdon* v. *Phila. & Reading C. & I.Co.* (*supra*). In those cases, the corporations had no agent within the state. The attempt was made to hold them by service on a public officer, whom the statute required them to designate as their agent, but whom they had refused or failed to designate. In the case before us, we have to deal with a very different situation. The corporation is here; it is here in the person of an agent of its own selection; and service upon him is service upon his principal.

The other questions certified to us by the Appellate Division may be quickly disposed of. We think the evidence sustains the conclusion that Peterson was a managing agent within the meaning of section 432, subdivision 3, of the Code of Civil Procedure (*Rochester, H. & L.R.R.Co.* v. *N.Y., L. E. & W.R.R.Co.*, 48 Hun, 190,192; *Palmer* v. *Penn.Co.*, 35 Hun, 369; 99 N.Y.679; *Ives* v. *Met. Life Ins.Co.*, 78 Hun, 32; *Barrett* v. *Am.T. & T.Co.*, 138 N.Y.491; *Tuchband* v. *Chicago & Alton R.R.Co.*, 115 N.Y.437,440). We think, also, that the plaintiff has shown due diligence in the effort to make service on some superior officer.

The order should be affirmed with costs; the first, second and third questions should be answered in the affirmative, and the fifth question in the negative; and it is unnecessary to answer the fourth question.

HISCOCK, Ch.J., CHASE, COLLIN, CUDDEBACK, HOGAN and POUND, JJ., concur.

Order affirmed.

EVIDENCE

In the Matter of WILLIAM F.DOYLE, Appellant. SAMUEL H.HOFSTADER et al., Constituting a Legislative Committee, Respondents.

CARDOZO, Ch.J. By a joint resolution of the Senate and the Assembly of the State of New York, adopted March 23, 1931, it was resolved that a joint legislative committee be constituted to investigate the administration and conduct of the various departments of the city of New York.

The appellant, William F.Doyle, was subpœnaed to attend before the committee, and upon appearing was directed to answer a series of questions relating to his practice before the Board of Standards and Appeals. There had been preliminary testimony from the lips of other witnesses that fees of extraordinary magnitude had been paid for his services during a period of years. The questions put to the appellant were designed to inform the committee whether he had divided these fees with a political leader, or with some one else, in furtherance of a concerted plan of bribery and corruption, and whether he had paid any part of them as a bribe to any public officer.

The appellant has been adjudged in contempt, first by a majority of the joint legislative committee, and then by the Supreme Court, for his refusal to answer the questions propounded. Typical questions are these: "Question: When you practiced before this board, did you split your fees? Answer: Do you mean with the Board of Standards and Appeals? Question: I mean did you split them with anybody? Answer: I never split a nickel with the Board of Standards and Appeals. Question: I asked you whether you split them with anybody, whether they were on the Board of Standards and

279

Appeals or whether they were not? Answer: I refuse to answer on the ground that it might tend to incriminate me." Again, "Question: Dr. Doyle, did you, in reference to cases pending before the Board of Standards and Appeals, bribe any public official? Answer: You are alluding to the Board of Standards and Appeals? No. Question: Now you did not bribe any member of the Board of Standards and Appeals? Answer: No. Question: Did you bribe any other public official? Answer: I refuse to answer on the ground that it might tend to incriminate me. Question: Did you give any of the proceeds of those fees to any political leader in the County of New York? Answer: I refuse to answer that question on the ground that answering might tend to incriminate me."

We are to determine whether the refusal was contumacious or privileged.

The Constitution of the State provides that no person "shall be compelled in any criminal case to be a witness against himself" (Const.art.I, §6).

The privilege may not be violated because in a particular case its restraints are inconvenient or because the supposed malefactor may be a subject of public execration or because the disclosure of his wrongdoing will promote the public weal.

It is a barrier interposed between the individual and the power of the government, a barrier interposed by the sovereign people of the State; and neither legislators nor judges are free to overleap it.

The appellant is, therefore, privileged to refuse to answer questions that may tend to implicate him in a crime, unless by some act of amnesty or indemnity, or some valid resolution equivalent thereto, he has been relieved from the risk of prosecution for any felony or misdemeanor that his testimony may reveal. The immunity is not adequate if it does no more than assure him that the testimony coming from his lips will not be read in evidence against him upon a criminal prosecution. The clues thereby developed may still supply the links whereby a chain of guilt can be forged from the testimony of others. To force disclosure from unwilling lips, the immunity must be so broad that the risk of prosecution is ended altogether (*People ex rel. Lewisohn* v. *O'Brien*, 176 N.Y.253; *Counselman* v. *Hitchcock*, 142 U.S.547; *Heike* v. *United States*, 227 U.S.131,142).

The respondent insists that immunity co-extensive with the requirements of this rule has been assured to the appellant by statute and resolution: by section 381 of the Penal Law as to the completed crime of bribery; by section 584 of the Penal Law as to the crime of conspiracy; and as to any and all crimes by the joint resolution of the two houses of the Legislature.

(1) Penal Law, section 381, provides as follows: "A person offending against any provision of any section of this chapter relating to bribery and corruption, is a competent witness against another person so offending, and may be compelled to attend and testify upon any trial, hearing, proceeding, or investigation, in the same manner as any other person. But the testimony so given shall not be used in any prosecution or proceeding, civil or criminal, against the person so testifying. A person so testifying to the giving of a bribe *which has been accepted*, shall not thereafter be liable to indictment, prosecution, or punishment for that bribery, and may plead or prove the giving of testimony accordingly, in bar of such an indictment or prosecution."

An argument is made for the appellant that the immunity created by this section is in contravention of restrictions established by the Constitution of the State. The Constitution (Art.XIII, §3) authorizes the exemption of the briber who testifies to the giving or offering of a bribe on the "prosecution" of a public officer for accepting it. The statute gives a like exemption to one who testifies to a like effect on "any trial, hearing, proceeding, or investigation." There is no denial by counsel for the committee that the immunity thus recognized is broader than the one that would be conferred by the Constitution if the statute were not here, since it extends to a legislative investigation designed, not to prosecute for crime, but to gather information for legislation in the future. The expansion may be conceded, and the validity of the statute will suffer no impairment. The purpose of the Constitution was to establish one immunity permanently in the fundamental law, but not to foreclose the Legislature from establishing additional ones thereafter. So the path was pointed in 1887 by the judgment in the leading case of *People* v. *Sharp* (107 N.Y.427). What was said and assumed in that case has been confirmed by years of acquiescence too many and too uniform to permit us to disturb it now upon any nicely balanced arguments.

Section 381 of the Penal Law is thus a valid statute, to be accepted at its face value. Whatever immunity it purports to give is the safe and sure possession of any witness who invokes it after being brought within its terms. But the immunity that it purports to give is limited and narrow. The witness is relieved of the risk of prosecution in one situation and one only: he must have testified to the offer or giving of a bribe which has been accepted (*People* v. *Anhut*, 162 App. Div.517; 213 N.Y.643). If there has been a conspiracy to bribe without evidence of acceptance, the supposed exemption fails. If there has been an offer without acceptance, it fails again. The purpose of this section of the statute, following in that respect the purpose of the Constitution (Art.XIII, §3), is to reach the bribe-taker as the chief delinquent, and let the briber go if thereby the taker can be held. There is no token of a purpose that a like immunity shall follow when there has been a mere conspiracy to corrupt, or an offer of a bribe which has been rejected by the officer to whom the tender has been made. Immunity from prosecution for conspiracy or for an attempt not followed by acceptance must find some other basis, if immunity there is. The counsel for the committee, if we understand his argument aright, makes no contention to the contrary. Seeking another basis for immunity, he has found one, he believes, in another section of the same statute (Penal Law, §584), in respect of any prosecution for a criminal conspiracy. He concedes that there is none against a prosecution for an attempt to bribe apart from a conspiracy, but the risk of such a prosecution he believes to be remote and unsubstantial (*Mason* v. *United States*, 244 U.S.362).

(2) We pass then to the question of the immunity offered to the witness against a prosecution for conspiracy.

The risk of such a prosecution is a real one unless a statute has removed it. Let us suppose that there is testimony by the witness that he split his fees with a political leader, or some one other than a public officer. Let us suppose that he did this under an agreement that the sharer of the fees would control by influence or by the payment of money the decisions of the Board of Standards and Appeals. Let us suppose further that there is no evidence establishing the acceptance of the money by any member of the Board or any one connected with it, no tracing of the bribe into the hands of any one invested with the functions of an office. Prosecution of a public officer for the crime of bribery or corruption will be impossible in such conditions. What *will* be possible will be a prosecution of the witness and his confederates for the crime of conspiracy to corrupt, or conceivably for an attempt to bribe. The risk that the prosecution will take the first of these forms is not remote or unsubstantial. We know from recent records of criminal trials that men charged with paying or receiving money as an inducement to official action have not been prosecuted for the completed crime of bribery or corruption, which would have been difficult to prove; they have been tried for conspiracy (cf. *People* v. *Connolly*, 253 N.Y. 330). The prosecutor may wish to make a like election here. If that shall be his choice, will section 584 of the Penal Law stand in the way of putting the choice into effect?

The section reads as follows: "No person shall be excused from attending and testifying, or producing any books, papers or other documents before any court, magistrate, or referee, upon any investigation, proceeding or trial, for a violation of any of the provisions of this article, upon the ground or for the reason that the testimony or evidence, documentary or otherwise, required of him may tend to convict him of a crime or to subject him to a penalty or for forfeiture; but no person shall be prosecuted or subjected to any penalty or forfeiture for or on account of any transaction, matter or thing concerning which he may so testify or produce evidence, documentary or otherwise, and no testimony so given or produced shall be received against him upon any criminal investigation, proceeding or trial."

The statute is not adequate to relieve the witness of his peril. It is limited to an investigation, proceeding or trial before a "court, magistrate or referee," and to such an investigation conducted for a violation of the "provisions of this article," *i.e.*, the article relating to conspiracy. It is very different from the statute considered in the *Sharp* case (Penal Code, §79, now Penal Law, §381; *People* v. *Sharp*, 107 N.Y.427,451,454), which though narrow in the range of the immunity conferred did not attempt to distinguish between an investigation for one purpose and an investigation for another. The immunity was to be the same whether the hearing was before a committee in aid of future legislation or before a judge or a referee for the punishment of crime. Very likely the Legislature would have been willing to broaden the immunity under section 584 by a similar extension if its thought had been directed to a legislative inquiry. We must take the statute as we find it.

If doubt as to its meaning could survive the mere reading of its terms, the history of its enactment would cause the doubt to be dispelled. Section 584 came into the Penal Law in 1910 by the enactment of chapter 395 of the Laws of 1910. The General Business Law (Cons. Laws, ch.20) already contained a provision prohibiting monopolies and authorizing an investigation before a judge or referee in aid of their suppression (Gen.Bus. Law, §§340,344; cf. Laws of 1899, ch.690, §6; Laws of 1897, ch.383, §7). On the same day that section 584 was added to the Penal Law, the Legislature amended the General Business Law by incorporating in it the grant of an immunity in precisely the same form (Gen.Bus. Law, §345, as amd. by Laws of 1910, ch.394). This explains the mention of a referee in each of the two statutes. A witness testifying before a referee appointed under the General Business Law (the so-called Donnelly act) might be indicted (if he was not immune) either for violation of the provisions of that act, or (if the unlawful monopoly was the act of two or more) for the violation of article 54 of the Penal Law, which denounces as a crime a conspiracy to "commit any act injurious * * * to trade or commerce" (Penal Law, §580, subd.6). To make the immunity secure, the two statutes were thus adopted on the same day, one amending section 345 of the General Business Law and the other in the same words amending the Penal Law by adding section 584 thereto. Obviously, the Legislature when it amended the General Business Law by giving immunity to a witness testifying "before any court, magistrate or referee, upon any investigation, proceeding or trial, pursuant to or for a violation of any of the provisions of this article," had in view, not a hearing before a legislative committee to gather information for future legislation, but a hearing before an officer of one of the enumerated classes—a court, magistrate or referee—acting pursuant to the statute for the suppression of monopolies. Obviously too, it had a like thought when it conferred a like immunity upon witnesses testifying before the same officers and disclosing by their testimony, not merely a monopoly, but a criminal conspiracy (cf. the later amendments to the General Business Law by the so-called Martin act; Gen.Bus. Law, §359).

We think the conclusion is inescapable that the witness, if compelled to testify as to any act or agreement not amounting to the completed crime of bribery, will be subject to indictment for conspiracy, and that section 584 of the statute will not render him immune.

The suggestion is not ignored that conspiracy is a misdemeanor, not a felony, and that some of the inquiries have relation to acts or agreements more than two years old, as to which the Statute of Limitations may constitute a bar. A statute of limitations is equivalent to an act of amnesty when the crime erased by lapse of time is one standing by itself, and is not a clue to the commission of other crimes thereafter (*Brown* v. *Walker*, 161 U.S.591,598; 4 Wigmore on Evidence, §2279). Clearly it is no such equivalent when the crime is a continuing conspiracy, unaffected by any limitation till the combination is abandoned (*United States* v. *Kissel*, 218 U.S. 601).

A witness is not required to show, in order to make his privilege available, that the testimony which he declines to give is certain to subject him to prosecution, or that it will prove the whole crime, unaided by testimony from others. It is enough, to wake the privilege into life, that there is a reasonable possibility of prosecution, and that the testimony, though falling short of proving the crime in its entirety, will prove some part or feature of it, will *tend* to a conviction when combined with proof of other circumstances which others may supply.

The privilege is not removed if there are loopholes in the tender of immunity through which a prosecutor can cut a way to indictment and conviction. The immunity must be as broad as the privilege destroyed.

What has been said as to the risks to which the witness is subjected applies to those questions and those only that are directed to a corrupt agreement between the witness and a confederate not occupying a public office, or to an agreement between the witness and an officer not affecting official action, or not consummated thereafter by payment of the bribe. Inquiry as to a consummated bribery stands upon a different footing. The witness may be compelled to state whether payments for corrupt purposes affecting official action were accepted by an officer, for in making proof of the acceptance he brings himself automatically within the indemnity secured by Penal Law, section 381, to one who testifies to a bribe which has been offered and accepted. There was, therefore, contempt of the committee when the witness after stating that he had never bribed any member of the Board of Standards and Appeals, declined to answer this question: "Did you bribe any other public official?" If the bribe is admitted, all the circumstances attending it may thereupon be explored, the name of the officer, the purpose of the payment, and the particulars of time and place.

(3) The effect of the joint resolution of the two houses of the Legislature is still to be considered.

By the terms of the joint resolution creating the legislative committee, the Legislature has said: "Whenever in its judgment the public interest demands, the committee may determine that a person shall not be excused from attending and testifying before said committee * * * on the ground that the testimony * * * required of him may tend to incriminate him or to subject him to a penalty or forfeiture; but no person so attending and testifying * * * who has duly claimed excuse or privilege, which would be sufficient except for this provision of this resolution and which said excuse or privilege has been expressly denied by the committee, shall be subject to prosecution or to any penalty or forfeiture for or on account of the transaction, matter or thing concerning which he may as aforesaid testify * * * in obedience to its subpoena."

This resolution, if valid, is in effect an act of amnesty. It wipes out as to the witness whose claim of privilege has been denied the criminal statutes of the State with all their pains and penalties, and, like a pardon, makes him a new man. A pardon may be granted by the Governor after conviction of the crime (Const.Art.IV, §5). An act of amnesty may be passed, like any other bill, by the Legislature, acting separately in its two houses (Art.III, §15), with the approval of the Governor, or in the event of his veto, by a two-thirds vote thereafter (Art.IV, §9). "Every bill which shall have passed the Senate and Assembly shall, before it becomes a law, be presented to the Governor; if he approve, he shall sign it; but if not, he shall return it with his objections to the house in which it shall have originated" (Const.art.IV, §9). This resolution was never presented to the Governor. It never received his approval or his veto. It is not an act of amnesty; it is not an "act" at all (*People ex rel. Argus Co.* v. *Palmer*, 12 Misc.Rep.392; 146 N.Y.406).

There are precedents in the books for what is sometimes styled a legislative pardon. If they are scrutinized, they will be found in every instance to have been statutes in the usual form. They were acts of amnesty or indemnity adopted by the Legislature with the Governor's approval (*United States* v. *Hughes*, 175 Fed.Rep.238; *United States* v. *Hall*, 53 Fed. Rep.352; *State ex rel. Anheuser-Busch Brewing Assn.* v. *Eby*, 170 Mo.497; *State* v. *Applewhite*, 75 N.C.229; cf. *Brown* v. *Walker*, 161 U.S.591,601; *Matter of Garland*, 4 Wall. [U.S.] 333; 4 Wigmore on Evidence, §2281, and statutes and cases there collated). Never has it been held that a Legislature alone may suspend the criminal law as to a person or a class of persons. In the constitution of that country from whose polity our own institutions derive to a large extent their origin and meaning, the rule is said to be that a resolution of the House of Commons is invalid and of no effect if in conflict with existing law (Anson, Law and Custom of the Constitution, vol.1, pp.182,185,186,192). We cannot bring ourselves to believe that the efficacy of resolutions is any greater in New York.

The argument is made that a legislative body has inherent power to conduct an investigation for the discovery of abuses in the operations of government (*People ex rel. Karlin* v. *Culkin,* 248 N.Y.465,478; *People ex rel. McDonald* v. *Keeler,* 99 N.Y.463; *McGrain* v. *Daugherty,* 273 U.S.135; *Sinclair* v. *United States,* 279 U.S.263; Landis, Constitutional Limitations on the Congressional Power of Investigation, 40 Harvard Law Review, 153), and that the power to give immunity to witnesses and to suspend to that extent the general laws of the State, must be deemed to be a necessary incident of the power to investigate. But it is not such an incident. It may at times be a useful incident, but it is not a necessary one, necessary that is to say, in the sense of being a power so indispensable to the ordinary exercise of the investigating function that it must be taken as implied. Modern scholarship has traced back for centuries the capacity of a legislative body to equip itself for the task of legislation by discovery of the facts (Landis, *supra*). If the power to suspend the laws in furtherance of the inquiry inheres in the inquirer without the aid of any statute, we can only regard it as extraordinary that so many investigations have been able to proceed without an attempt to use it. The parliamentary practice in Great Britain will be referred to later on. For the moment we confine ourselves to the practice in the United States. There is no record in the books of even a single instance, or none in any event has been brought to our attention, in which a witness, claiming privilege, has been compelled to reveal a crime upon the basis of an inherent power in the inquirer to relieve him from its consequences. Many fruitful inquiries have been prosecuted without the hint of such a power in the organic resolution; we may instance the Armstrong investigation of 1905, with the report as to the business of insurance which was the outcome of its labors (See concurrent resolution of July 20, 1905, printed in N.Y. Assembly Journal, 1905, p.1210, and

N.Y. Senate Journal, 1905, p.1126). In the few instances, none of very distant date, in which a power to confer immunity has been recited in the resolution appointing the committee, there is no record of its use. Nor may we stop with Senate and Assembly if implication once begins. The power to suspend the laws, if attributed to these, must belong to others too. Local legislative bodies, such as boards of aldermen, have implied or inherent power to conduct investigations as to matters of local government (*Briggs* v. *Mackellar*, 2 Abb.Pr.30; *People ex rel. Karlin* v. *Culkin*, *supra*). No one would be likely to assert that they have also the inherent power to give their witnesses immunity against the enforcement of the criminal law. The grand jury is an investigating body, but it has no power to pledge immunity to a witness who declines to answer (cf. Penal Law, §2446). So is the Appellate Division when prosecuting an inquiry as to members of the bar or judges of the inferior courts. Even the Governor is at times an inquisitorial officer, as when examining in person or by deputy into the conduct of other officers or the administration of departments (*Matter of Richardson*, 247 N.Y.401). If he is competent when so acting to give immunity to witnesses, the power must have its origin in the provisions of a statute.

The conclusion, we think, is inescapable that a power to suspend the criminal law by the tender of immunity is not an implied or inherent incident of a power to investigate. It may be necessary for fruitful results in a particular instance, but it is not so generally indispensable as to attach itself automatically to the mere power to inquire. Whether the good to be attained by procuring the testimony of criminals is greater or less than the evil to be wrought by exempting them forever from prosecution for their crimes is a question of high policy as to which the law-making department of the government is entitled to be heard. In the State of New York that department is not the Legislature alone, but the Legislature and the Governor, the one as much as the other an essential factor in the process (*People* v. *Bowen,* 21 N.Y.517,519,521; *Matter of City of Long Beach* v. *Pub.Serv.Comm.,* 249 N.Y.480,489, 490). We beg the question when we argue that the Legislature may give immunity because the Legislature is the sole custodian of the legislative power. It is not the sole custodian of that power. The power is divided between the Legislature and the Governor (cf. *Davis* v. *Ohio,* 241 U.S.565; *Hawke* v. *Smith,* 253 U.S.221). Article III, section 1, of the Constitution must be read in conjunction with article IV, section 9 (*People* v. *Bowen, supra; Matter of City of Long Beach* v. *Pub. Serv.Comm., supra*). The Legislature can initiate, but without the action of the Governor it is powerless to complete. Not only do we beg the question when we infer the validity of the immunity from the possession by the Legislature of the full legislative power; we concede by implication that unless the legislative power has been thus committed without division, the immunity must fail. The argument, reduced to that basis, is seen to be self-destructive. The grant of an immunity *is* in very truth the assumption of a legislative power, and that is why the Legislature acting alone is incompetent to declare it. It is the assumption of a power to annul as to individuals or classes the statutory law of crimes, to stem the course of justice, to absolve the grand jurors of the county from the performance of their duties, and the prosecuting officer from his. All these changes may be wrought through the enactment of a statute. They may be wrought in no other way while the legislative structure of our government continues what it is.

The argument is made that the jurisdiction to grant immunity is an incident of the jurisdiction to punish for contempt. It is no more such an incident for a committee of the Legislature (Legislative Law; Cons. Laws, ch.32, §4, subd.5; *Kilbourn* v. *Thompson*, 103 U.S.168; *People ex rel. McDonald* v. *Keeler*, 99 N.Y.463; *Matter of Barnes*, 204 N.Y.108; *Sinclair* v. *United States*, 279 U.S.263; Landis, op.cit., pp.153, 219) than it is for a court or judge. The punishment for contempt may be imposed for disobedience of a lawful mandate. The power thus to punish may not be used as an excuse for the issue of an unlawful mandate and the remission of the pains and penalties of crimes in consideration of obedience.

We are reminded that on three other occasions, once in 1894 and twice in 1921, resolutions in like form were adopted in the grant of authority to other investigating committees. The existence of these resolutions is put before us as evidence of a practical construction. Little significance belongs to them in view of the fact that there is no evidence of an attempt to enforce them against the protest of a witness (*People* v. *Tremaine*, 252 N.Y.27,46,47). Whatever significance they might otherwise have is destroyed by the fact that in 1921 the Attorney-General of the State gave an opinion to the effect that the Legislature was without power to bestow immunity upon a witness through the form of a resolution, and to suspend, in so doing, the operation of the criminal law (Opinions of Attorney-General, 1921, p.424). A practical interpretation of the Constitution sufficient to change the course of the legislative process must find a broader basis.*

The subject is not clarified by reference to the practice of the Congress, whatever it may be. Under the Federal Constitution, "every Order, Resolution or Vote to which the con-

---

* For a cloud of instances in which statutes were enacted, see 4 Wigmore on Evidence, §2281.

currence of the Senate and House of Representatives may be necessary (except on a question of adjournment)" must be submitted to the President for approval or veto in the same manner as a Bill (U.S.Const.art.I, §7, subd.3; cf. Hinds, Precedents of the House of Representatives, vol.4, §§3483, 3484). A resolution so approved has all the authority of a statute.

We have postponed to this stage the consideration of an argument that is drawn from the practice of the British Parliament.

The practice, instead of tending to give support to the validity of a resolution obliterating guilt, tends directly the other way.

The privilege against self-incrimination in so far as it exists in England does not derive its sanction from a written constitution, and is not binding upon the Houses of Parliament in a parliamentary inquiry. The privilege in New York applies to an investigation by a Legislature as fully as to a trial in court (*People* v. *Hackley*, 24 N.Y.74; *People* v. *Sharp supra*; *Sinclair* v. *United States, supra*). The House of Lords does not compel an answer unless complete immunity is given. The House of Commons at times has been satisfied with less.

There is, however, an established practice whereby the members of the House of Commons, its officers, and shorthand writers are prohibited from making public in a court of justice or otherwise any testimony brought out upon a parliamentary inquiry without special leave of the house, which according to usage is not given if the testimony will expose to prosecution for a crime (Cushing, Law & Practice of Legislative Assemblies, §§983,1001,1002,1004; Hansard, Parliamentary Debates, 2d series, p.970; cf. 2 Redlich, The Procedure of the House of Commons, p.193).

None the less, in the event that the testimony is published, whether in violation of the mandate of the house or not, the prosecuting authorities are free to prosecute the offender for the crime thereby revealed (Cushing, *supra*, §1004).

In other words, the prohibition, even in respect of disclosure by members of the house or persons in its service, is limited to the use as a confession of the very testimony given by the witness in the course of the inquiry, and does not relieve him from prosecution for the crime if a case can be proved without the use of the confession, though by following up its clues (Cushing, *supra*, §1005; Hansard, *supra*, vol. 23, pp.1190,1191,1197,1198).

For this there is need of an act of indemnity which requires the concurrence of both houses and the approval of the Crown (Cushing, *supra*, §1005; Hansard, *supra*, vol.23, p.1190 *et seq.*).

Accordingly we hear of a case in the year 1742 where in consequence of the refusal of witnesses to testify before a select committee to inquire into the conduct of the Earl of Oxford, the House of Commons found it necessary to pass a bill to indemnify such witnesses as should testify truly before the committee, but the bill was rejected by the Lords (Cushing, *supra*, §1005, note).

Nearly a century later in the debate on the East Retford Witnesses Bill, the Marquis of Salisbury referred in his speech to the precedents in Shoreham's case (1771 and 1782), and in other cases where an act of indemnity had been passed to make the immunity complete (Hansard, *supra*, vol.23, p.1190 *et seq.*).

The parliamentary precedents are thus of no avail to sustain the resolution in a State where the privilege of silence is created by the Constitution, and is satisfied by nothing less than obliteration of the crime (*Counselman* v. *Hitchcock, supra; People ex rel. Lewisohn* v. *O'Brien, supra*).

Far from sustaining the resolution, they show that in Great Britain the self-same question has arisen, and that the power of a House of Parliament has been limited to a restraint upon the disclosure of the testimony by members of the house or by others in its service, and has never been extended to the grant of an immunity co-extensive with the risk.

We do well to remember in weighing the significance of the English practice that publication of the proceedings of either of the Houses of Parliament, publication even of the debates, is a breach of privilege and a contempt unless the publication is by permission, tacit or express (21 Halsbury, Laws of England, Parliament, §1472; Redlich, Procedure of the House of Commons, vol.2, pp.36–38; Lowell, The Government of England, vol.1, pp.243,244).

Nowhere in the United States does such a privilege exist.

A final argument is made that the risk of prosecution is unreal and unsubstantial, since it is not to be supposed that a District Attorney would prosecute a witness in the face of a solemn declaration of the will of two houses of the Legislature that the witness should go free. This argument ignores the provisions of article XIII, section 6, of the Constitution that "any district attorney who shall fail faithfully to prosecute a person charged with the violation in his county of any provision of this article which may come to his knowledge, shall be removed from office by the Governor, after due notice and an opportunity of being heard in his defense."

The witness is within his privilege in insisting that the basis for his immunity shall be something more substantial than the grace or favor of the prosecutor who may bring him to the bar of justice (Code Crim.Proc. §§671,673; *The Whisky*

Cases, 99 U.S.594; *Temple v. Commonwealth*, 75 Va.892,897; *Matter of Irvine*, 74 Fed.Rep.945,964, per TAFT, J.). To uphold a finding that his conduct amounted to a contempt it must appear that in refusing to answer he was violating a legal, and not merely a moral obligation. The immunity like the obligation must have its source and sanction in the law. An "equitable right to * * * clemency" (*The Whisky Cases*, *supra*, p.606)—a mere "gesture" of benevolence—is not a substitute for protection against indictment and conviction. Clemency may be refused and even if ultimately granted, must be postponed until conviction, the accused being subjected in the meantime to arrest and imprisonment. The King, like the President of the United States (*Brown v. Walker*, 161 U.S. at p.601), is free to pardon before conviction, and may thus intervene promptly for the relief of a witness to whom immunity has been promised by another department of the government, if mercy so inclines him. The Governor may not pardon until the offender has been tried and guilt has been established by the judgment of a court (Const.art.IV, §5).

Nothing to the contrary was intimated in *People v. Whipple* (9 Cow.707). The only question before the judge in that case was whether in the exercise of a sound discretion he would receive the testimony of an accomplice and recommend a pardon. There are statements in the course of the opinion which the Supreme Court in the *Whisky* cases characterized as "unguarded" (*The Whisky Cases*, *supra*, at p.605). If we take them at their face value, they do not rule the case at hand. The recommendation of clemency is stated to be a recommendation and nothing more, and the Executive is free to heed or to reject it. Conceivably he will give not a full pardon, but a limited one, or a pardon coupled with conditions. Neither in the *Whipple* case nor in any other case decided in this State is there a ruling that an accomplice may be compelled against his protest to testify to his crime and to accept as adequate indemnity the hope of pardon in the future (TAFT, J., in *Matter of Irvine, supra*).

We put aside as remote and unsubstantial the supposed peril of exposure to prosecution for the making of false tax returns to State or Federal officers (*Mason* v. *United States*, 244 U.S.362; *Jack* v. *Kansas*, 199 U.S.372).

When upon the face of a question it would seem that to answer could not tend to implicate in crime, a court will exercise a discretion in determining whether to accept the mere conclusion of the witness that the tendency is present (*Mason* v. *U.S., supra*), though in every instance the conclusion is entitled to weight (*People ex rel. Taylor* v. *Forbes*, 143 N.Y.219). On the other hand, when the obvious effect of the question is to call for the confession of criminality, when that indeed is its avowed purpose, immunity is not adequate unless the crime has been obliterated.

The upshot of the whole discussion is, therefore, this: The witness has immunity by force of Penal Law, section 381, sufficient to call for a response as to payments to public officers to affect their public acts. The witness has no immunity by force of section 584 or otherwise sufficient to call for a response as to a mere conspiracy to bribe, not followed or accompanied by payment, or as to any corrupt agreement halting at the stage of mere attempt.

The way to compel disclosure as to conspiracies and attempts is not obscure or devious. A grant of immunity similar to the one contained in the resolution may be embodied in a statute. The Legislature, when it convenes, may pass an act of amnesty with the approval of the Governor, an act of amnesty co-extensive with the privilege destroyed. The appellant as well as other witnesses will then be under a duty to declare the whole truth, irrespective of the number or the nature of the crimes exposed to view. Even if we were able to read a different meaning into the statutes now existing, the time in all likelihood would not be distant when there would be need of supplemental legislation to give immunity for other crimes, for crimes not covered by the sections dealing with conspiracy and bribery. A witness exposed to prosecution for larceny or extortion would be wholly without the pale of the immunity provisions in any statutes now existing, however liberally construed.

We are not unmindful of the public interests, of the insistent hope and need that the ways of bribers and corruptionists shall be exposed to an indignant world. Commanding as those interests are, they do not supply us with a license to palter with the truth or to twist what has been written in the statutes into something else that we should like to see. Historic liberties and privileges are not to bend from day to day "because of some accident of immediate overwhelming interest which appeals to the feelings and distorts the judgment" (HOLMES, J., in *Northern Securities Co.* v. *United States*, 193 U.S.197,400), are not to change their form and content in response to the "hydraulic pressure" (HOLMES, J., *supra*) exerted by great causes. A community whose judges would be willing to give it whatever law might gratify the impulse of the moment would find in the end that it had paid too high a price for relieving itself of the bother of awaiting a session of the Legislature and the enactment of a statute in accordance with established forms.

The order of the Appellate Division and that of the Special Term should be modified by directing that the appellant stand committed until he answers the question whether he has bribed any public officer, such imprisonment not to exceed the period of thirty days, and as so modified affirmed.

. . .

LEHMAN, KELLOGG, O'BRIEN and HUBBS, JJ., concur with CARDOZO, Ch.J.; CRANE, J., concurs in separate opinion; POUND, J., dissents in part and writes for affirmance.

Ordered accordingly.

CONSTITUTIONAL LAW

HELVERING, COMMISSIONER OF INTERNAL REVENUE, ET AL., Petitioners v. DAVIS, Respondent.

MR. JUSTICE CARDOZO delivered the opinion of the Court.

The Social Security Act (Act of August 14, 1935, c.531, 49 Stat.620, 42 U.S.C., c.7 (Supp.)) is challenged once again.

In *Steward Machine Co.* v. *Davis*, decided this day, *ante,* p.548, we have upheld the validity of Title IX of the act, imposing an excise upon employers of eight or more. In this case Titles VIII and II are the subject of attack. Title VIII lays another excise upon employers in addition to the one imposed by Title IX (though with different exemptions). It lays a special income tax upon employees to be deducted from their wages and paid by the employers. Title II provides for the payment of Old Age Benefits, and supplies the motive and occasion, in the view of the assailants of the statute, for the levy of the taxes imposed by Title VIII. The plan of the two titles will now be summarized more fully.

Title VIII as we have said, lays two different types of tax, an "income tax on employees," and "an excise tax on employers." The income tax on employees is measured by wages paid during the calendar year. §801. The excise tax on the employer is to be paid "with respect to having individuals in his employ," and, like the tax on employees, is measured by wages. §804. Neither tax is applicable to certain types of employment, such as agricultural labor, domestic service, service for the national or state governments, and service performed by persons who have attained the age of 65 years. §811 (b). The two taxes are at the same rate. §§801,804. For the years 1937 to 1939, inclusive, the rate for each tax is fixed at one per cent. Thereafter the rate increases ½ of 1 per cent every three years, until after December 31, 1948, the rate for each tax reaches 3 per cent. *Ibid.* In the computation of wages all remuneration is to be included except so much as is in excess of $3,000 during the calendar year affected. §811 (a). The income tax on employees is to be collected by the employer, who is to deduct the amount from the wages "as and when paid." §802 (a). He is indemnified against claims and demands of any person by reason of such payment. *Ibid.* The proceeds of both taxes are to be paid into the Treasury like internal-revenue taxes generally, and are not earmarked in any way. §807 (a). There are penalties for non-payment. §807 (c).

Title II has the caption "Federal Old-Age Benefits." The benefits are of two types, first, monthly pensions, and second, lump sum payments, the payments of the second class being relatively few and unimportant.

The first section of this title creates an account in the United States Treasury to be known as the "Old-Age Reserve Account." §201. No present appropriation, however, is made to that account. All that the statute does is to authorize appropriations annually thereafter, beginning with the fiscal year which ends June 30, 1937. How large they shall be is not known in advance. The "amount sufficient as an annual premium" to provide for the required payments is "to be determined on a reserve basis in accordance with accepted actuarial principles, and based upon such tables of mortality as the Secretary of the Treasury shall from time to time adopt, and upon an interest rate of 3 per centum per annum compounded annually." §201 (a). Not a dollar goes into the Account by force of the challenged act alone, unaided by acts to follow.

Section 202 and later sections prescribe the form of benefits. The principal type is a monthly pension payable to a person after he has attained the age of 65. This benefit is available only to one who has worked for at least one day in each of at least five separate years since December 31, 1936, who has earned at least $2,000 since that date, and who is not then receiving wages "with respect to regular employment." §§202 (a), (d), 210 (c). The benefits are not to begin before January 1, 1942. §202 (a). In no event are they to exceed $85 a month. §202 (b). They are to be measured (subject to that limit) by a percentage of the wages, the percentage decreasing at stated intervals as the wages become higher. §202 (a). In addition to the monthly benefits, provision is made in certain contingencies for "lump sum payments" of secondary importance. A summary by the Government of the four situations calling for such payments is printed in the margin.[1]

This suit is brought by a shareholder of the Edison Electric Illuminating Company of Boston, a Massachusetts corporation, to restrain the corporation from making the payments and deductions called for by the act, which is stated to be void under the Constitution of the United States. The bill tells us that the corporation has decided to obey the statute, that it has reached this decision in the face of the complain-

1. This and subsequent notes of the Court are omitted. *Author.*

ant's protests, and that it will make the payments and deductions unless restrained by a decree. The expected consequences are indicated substantially as follows: The deductions from the wages of the employees will produce unrest among them, and will be followed, it is predicted, by demands that wages be increased. If the exactions shall ultimately be held void, the company will have parted with moneys which as a practical matter it will be impossible to recover. Nothing is said in the bill about the promise of indemnity. The prediction is made also that serious consequences will ensue if there is a submission to the excise. The corporation and its shareholders will suffer irreparable loss, and many thousands of dollars will be subtracted from the value of the shares. The prayer is for an injunction and for a declaration that the act is void.

The corporation appeared and answered without raising any issue of fact. Later the United States Commissioner of Internal Revenue and the United States Collector for the District of Massachusetts, petitioners in this court, were allowed to intervene. They moved to strike so much of the bill as has relation to the tax on employees, taking the ground that the employer, not being subject to tax under those provisions, may not challenge their validity, and that the complainant shareholder, whose rights are no greater than those of his corporation, has even less standing to be heard on such a question. The intervening defendants also filed an answer which restated the point raised in the motion to strike, and maintained the validity of Title VIII in all its parts. The District Court held that the tax upon employees was not properly at issue, and that the tax upon employers was constitutional. It thereupon denied the prayer for an injunction, and dismissed the bill. On appeal to the Circuit Court of

Appeals for the First Circuit, the decree was reversed, one judge dissenting. 89 F. (2d) 393. The court held that Title II was void as an invasion of powers reserved by the Tenth Amendment to the states or to the people, and that Title II in collapsing carried Title VIII along with it. As an additional reason for invalidating the tax upon employers, the court held that it was not an excise as excises were understood when the Constitution was adopted. Cf. *Davis* v. *Boston & Maine R. Co.*, 89 F. (2d) 368, decided the same day.

A petition for certiorari followed. It was filed by the intervening defendants, the Commissioner and the Collector, and brought two questions, and two only, to our notice. We were asked to determine: (1) "whether the tax imposed upon employers by §804 of the Social Security Act is within the power of Congress under the Constitution," and (2) "whether the validity of the tax imposed upon employees by §801 of the Social Security Act is properly in issue in this case, and if it is, whether that tax is within the power of Congress under the Constitution." The defendant corporation gave notice to the Clerk that it joined in the petition, but it has taken no part in any subsequent proceedings. A writ of certiorari issued.

First. Questions as to the remedy invoked by the complainant confront us at the outset.

Was the conduct of the company in resolving to pay the taxes a legitimate exercise of the discretion of the directors? Has petitioner a standing to challenge that resolve in the absence of an adequate showing of irreparable injury? Does the acquiescence of the company in the equitable remedy affect the answer to those questions? Though power may still be ours to take such objections for ourselves, is acquiescence effective to rid us of the duty? Is duty modified still further by the attitude of the Government, its waiver of a defense under §3224 of the Revised Statutes, its waiver of a defense that the legal remedy is adequate, its earnest request that we determine whether the law shall stand or fall? The writer of this opinion believes that the remedy is ill conceived, that in a controversy such as this a court must refuse to give equitable relief when a cause of action in equity is neither pleaded nor proved, and that the suit for an injunction should be dismissed upon that ground. He thinks this course should be followed in adherence to the general rule that constitutional questions are not to be determined in the absence of strict necessity. In that view he is supported by Mr. JUSTICE BRANDEIS, Mr. JUSTICE STONE and Mr. JUSTICE ROBERTS. However, a majority of the court have reached a different conclusion. They find in this case extraordinary features making it fitting in their judgment to determine whether the benefits and the taxes are valid or invalid. They distinguish *Norman* v. *Consolidated Gas Co.*, 89 F. (2d) 619, recently decided by the Court of Appeals for the Second Circuit, on the ground that in that case, the remedy was challenged by the company and the Government at every stage of the proceeding, thus withdrawing from the court any marginal discretion. The ruling of the majority removes from the case the preliminary objection as to the nature of the remedy which we took of our own motion at the beginning of the argument. Under the compulsion of that ruling, the merits are now here.

Second. The scheme of benefits created by the provisions of Title II is not in contravention of the limitations of the Tenth Amendment.

Congress may spend money in aid of the "general welfare." Constitution, Art.I, section 8; *United States* v. *Butler*, 297 U.S.1,65; *Steward Machine Co.* v. *Davis*, *supra*. There have been great statesmen in our history who have stood for other views. We will not resurrect the contest. It is now settled by decision. *United States* v. *Butler, supra.* The conception of the spending power advocated by Hamilton and strongly reinforced by Story has prevailed over that of Madison, which has not been lacking in adherents. Yet difficulties are left when the power is conceded. The line must still be drawn between one welfare and another, between particular and general. Where this shall be placed cannot be known through a formula in advance of the event. There is a middle ground or certainly a penumbra in which discretion is at large. The discretion, however, is not confided to the courts. The discretion belongs to Congress, unless the choice is clearly wrong, a display of arbitrary power, not an exercise of judgment. This is now familiar law. "When such a contention comes here we naturally require a showing that by no reasonable possibility can the challenged legislation fall within the wide range of discretion permitted to the Congress." *United States* v. *Butler, supra,* p.67. Cf. *Cincinnati Soap Co.* v. *United States, ante,* p.308; *United States* v. *Realty Co.,* 163 U.S.427,440; *Head Money Cases,* 112 U.S.580,595. Nor is the concept of the general welfare static. Needs that were narrow or parochial a century ago may be interwoven in our day with the well-being of the Nation. What is critical or urgent changes with the times.

The purge of nation-wide calamity that began in 1929 has taught us many lessons. Not the least is the solidarity of interests that may once have seemed to be divided. Unemployment spreads from State to State, the hinterland now settled that in pioneer days gave an avenue of escape. *Home Building & Loan Assn.* v. *Blaisdell,* 290 U.S.398,442. Spreading from State to State, unemployment is an ill not particular but general, which may be checked, if Congress so determines,

by the resources of the Nation. If this can have been doubtful until now, our ruling today in the case of the *Steward Machine Co., supra,* has set the doubt at rest. But the ill is all one,
or at least not greatly different, whether men are thrown out
of work because there is no longer work to do or because the
disabilities of age make them incapable of doing it. Rescue
becomes necessary irrespective of the cause. The hope behind this statute is to save men and women from the rigors
of the poor house as well as from the haunting fear that such
a lot awaits them when journey's end is near.

Congress did not improvise a judgment when it found that
the award of old age benefits would be conducive to the general welfare. The President's Committee on Economic Security made an investigation and report, aided by a research
staff of Government officers and employees, and by an Advisory Council and seven other advisory groups. Extensive
hearings followed before the House Committee on Ways and
Means, and the Senate Committee on Finance. A great mass
of evidence was brought together supporting the policy which
finds expression in the act. Among the relevant facts are these:
The number of persons in the United States 65 years of age
or over is increasing proportionately as well as absolutely.
What is even more important the number of such persons
unable to take care of themselves is growing at a threatening
pace. More and more our population is becoming urban and
industrial instead of rural and agricultural. The evidence is
impressive that among industrial workers the younger men
and women are preferred over the older. In times of re-
trenchment the older are commonly the first to go, and even
if retained, their wages are likely to be lowered. The plight
of men and women at so low an age as 40 is hard, almost
hopeless, when they are driven to seek for reëmployment.

Statistics are in the brief. A few illustrations will be chosen from many there collected. In 1930, out of 224 American factories investigated, 71, or almost one third, had fixed maximum hiring age limits; in 4 plants the limit was under 40; in 41 it was under 46. In the other 153 plants there were no fixed limits, but in practice few were hired if they were over 50 years of age. With the loss of savings inevitable in periods of idleness, the fate of workers over 65, when thrown out of work, is little less than desperate. A recent study of the Social Security Board informs us that "one-fifth of the aged in the United States were receiving old-age assistance, emergency relief, institutional care, employment under the works program, or some other form of aid from public or private funds; two-fifths to one-half were dependent on friends and relatives; one-eighth had some income from earnings; and possibly one-sixth had some savings or property. Approximately three out of four persons 65 or over were probably dependent wholly or partially on others for support." We summarize in the margin the results of other studies by state and national commissions. They point the same way.

The problem is plainly national in area and dimensions. Moreover, laws of the separate states cannot deal with it effectively. Congress, at least, had a basis for that belief. States and local governments are often lacking in the resources that are necessary to finance an adequate program of security for the aged. This is brought out with a wealth of illustration in recent studies of the problem. Apart from the failure of resources, states and local governments are at times reluctant to increase so heavily the burden of taxation to be borne by their residents for fear of placing themselves in a position of economic disadvantage as compared with neighbors or competitors. We have seen this in our study of the problem of unemployment compensation. *Steward Machine Co. v. Davis, supra.* A system of old age pensions has special dangers of its own, if put in force in one state and rejected in another. The existence of such a system is a bait to the needy and dependent elsewhere, encouraging them to migrate and seek a haven of repose. Only a power that is national can serve the interests of all.

Whether wisdom or unwisdom resides in the scheme of benefits set forth in Title II, it is not for us to say. The answer to such inquiries must come from Congress, not the courts. Our concern here, as often, is with power, not with wisdom. Counsel for respondent has recalled to us the virtues of self-reliance and frugality. There is a possibility, he says, that aid from a paternal government may sap those sturdy virtues and breed a race of weaklings. If Massachusetts so believes and shapes her laws in that conviction, must her breed of sons be changed, he asks, because some other philosophy of government finds favor in the halls of Congress? But the answer is not doubtful. One might ask with equal reason whether the system of protective tariffs is to be set aside at will in one state or another whenever local policy prefers the rule of *laissez faire.* The issue is a closed one. It was fought out long ago. When money is spent to promote the general welfare, the concept of welfare or the opposite is shaped by Congress, not the states. So the concept be not arbitrary, the locality must yield. Constitution, Art.VI, Par.2.

Third. Title II being valid, there is no occasion to inquire whether Title VIII would have to fall if Title II were set at naught.

The argument for the respondent is that the provisions of the two titles dovetail in such a way as to justify the conclusion that Congress would have been unwilling to pass one without the other. The argument for petitioners is that the tax moneys are not earmarked, and that Congress is at liberty to spend them as it will. The usual separability clause is embodied in the act. §1103.

We find it unnecessary to make a choice between the arguments, and so leave the question open.

Fourth. The tax upon employers is a valid excise or duty upon the relation of employment.

As to this we need not add to our opinion in *Steward Machine Co.* v. *Davis, supra,* where we considered a like question in respect of Title IX.

Fifth. The tax is not invalid as a result of its exemptions.

Here again the opinion in *Steward Machine Co.* v. *Davis, supra,* says all that need be said.

Sixth. The decree of the Court of Appeals should be reversed and that of the District Court affirmed.

Reversed.

Mr. JUSTICE McREYNOLDS and Mr. JUSTICE BUTLER are of opinion that the provisions of the act here challenged are repugnant to the Tenth Amendment, and that the decree of the Circuit Court of Appeals should be affirmed.

AFTERWORD TO THE
1969 EDITION

As far back as 1913, a Conference on Law and Social
Philosophy was organized by a group of philosophers
with John Dewey as President and Morris R. Cohen as
Secretary. Looking back years later, Cardozo remarked
that Dewey and Cohen had learned more about law than
lawyers had learned about philosophy. Our Anglo-American legal tradition proceeds out of a basically practical
orientation. It has been the rare lawyer or judge, like
Holmes and Cardozo, who has realized the value of
forging a philosophy of law. Every significant philosopher from Plato to Hegel included a philosophy of law
in his total perspective. Dewey and Cohen revived the
importance of that integral emphasis. With the rise of
the 'legal realist' movement in the Thirties, the torch
passed from philosophers to men of law—to lawyers,
judges, and law professors—who sought to shed light on
the philosophic foundations of judicial methods based
on realistic observation of actual practices. In very recent
years academic philosophers, of the analytic school especially, have re-directed attention to abstract facets of
legal philosophy. There has been some throwback to the
older preoccupation with law as 'rules.'[1] Hopefully, professional philosophers who turn to law and legal scholars
who encompass philosophy will increasingly appreciate
the virtues of cross-fertilization in a broad conception of

1. See Ronald Dworkin, 'Judicial Discretion' (1963) 40 *J. of Philosophy*
624.

both disciplines. 'Jurisprudence, as the jurist's quest for a systematic vision that will order and illumine the dark realities of the law, and legal philosophy, conceived as the philosopher's efforts to understand the legal order and its role in human life, have come close enough together in our land and our generation to warrant a unified approach to these two overlapping fields.'[2] Many difficulties are still to be overcome. We have only to consider the exchange between Lon L. Fuller (the distinguished professor of jurisprudence at Harvard Law School) and Ernest Nagel (the distinguished logician who for many years taught philosophy of law at Columbia College) in which they were unable to come to terms in acceptance of the distinction between 'is' and 'ought,' between 'fact' and 'value.'[3]

Lawyers have had to live down a traditional disdain classically expressed by Plato in his dialogue *Theaetetus*, which presents an invidious contrast between lawyers and philosophers. Plato puts into the mouth of Socrates the caustic comment that when 'you compare men who have knocked about in law courts' with others 'bred in philosophical pursuits,' the one seems to have been trained as a slave while the other seems a free man. 'The free man,' Socrates tells his companion, 'always has time at his disposal to converse in peace at his leisure. He will pass, as we are doing now, from one argument to another. . . . Like us, he will leave the old for a fresh one which takes his fancy more, and he does not care how long or short the discussion may be, if only it attains the truth.' By contrast, the lawyer 'is always talking against time, hurried on by the clock; the adversary stands over

2. M.R.Cohen and F.S.Cohen, *Readings in Jurisprudence and Legal Philosophy* (Prentice-Hall, Englewood Cliffs, 1951) Preface iii-iv.
3. *Natural Law Forum*, vol. 3, No. 1, and vol. 4, No. 1, 1958 and 1959.

him. . . .' The philosopher tries to draw the 'narrow' lawyer 'upward to a height.' The philosopher tries to move the lawyer from preoccupation with some particular injustice to a contemplation of 'justice and injustice in themselves, what each is, and how they differ from one another and from anything else.'

Only in recent years has the study of law come into its own by way of recognition not only as a professional discipline but as a genuine liberal-arts study. In Jacques Barzun's 'house of intellect' the law occupies a royal suite, with Cardozo as an honored guest: 'The law is a model of intellectual work. . . . It is a profession easy to ridicule by its externals and it is criticizable, like other institutions, for its anachronisms. But as an attempt of the *esprit de finesse* to mold conceptions of the true and the just on the restless multiplicity of human life, it is a triumph of articulateness and exactitude. In the United States in recent years . . . the legal intellect is, for whatever reason, at a disadvantage. Some of its troubles come from the dominance of casualness in our mores, which make the law seem to the ordinary citizen a series of expensive quibbles. . . . A deeper cause is the lowered standard of the linguistic power, which accounts also for the fact that only a few judges no longer living— Holmes, Brandeis, Cardozo—furnish us again and again with the verbal concretions of ideas we should be lost without.'[4]

Besides the revolutions in thought reflected in Darwin-

4. Jacques Barzun, *The House of Intellect* (Harper, New York, 1959) 247–8. See Harold J.Berman, 'A Conference on the Teaching of Law in the Liberal Arts Curriculum' (1955) 6 *Harv.L.School Bull.* 12. A pioneering effort to relate law and society as part of a general liberal education has come to fruition in a book co-authored by Harold J. Berman and William R.Greiner, *The Nature and Functions of Law* (Foundation Press, Brooklyn, 1966).

ian biology, Freudian psychology, Einsteinian physics, and Marxist economics, the Twentieth Century has undergone a social and cultural crisis precipitated by the monstrous moral degeneration of Nazism coupled with the threat of nuclear incineration. The Continental philosophy of 'existentialism' reacted to the crisis by confronting the extremities of human existence, its anxieties and dreads and ever-hovering death. England reacted by falling back upon linguistic analysis—a tradition which goes back to Socrates and Aristotle but in its current form has eluded its historic relation to social evaluation. And we in America, after working out our own pragmatic and experimental approach to human problems in their cultural and contemporary context, experienced a failure of social nerve and mirrored the British in their preponderant concentrations.[5]

The ascendency of analytical philosophy in academic circles has had little influence upon what we may call judicial philosophy, concerned not merely with analysis but with facilitating through philosophy the sound adjudication of conflicts. With the gentle irony which often marks his writing, Judge Henry Friendly observed, in praising the value of philosophical study for the lawyer: 'A Harvard graduate student asked me last year, quite seriously and perhaps not without basis, how anyone could become a lawyer, much less a judge, without understanding modern analytical philosophy, particularly Wittgenstein.'[6]

Edmond Cahn is more impatient, protesting that the trouble with contemporary philosophy is that its academic purveyors do not take it seriously enough as a

5. See John Randall, *Career of Philosophy*, vol. II, 1965, 664–5.
6. Henry Friendly, *Benchmarks* (University of Chicago Press, Chicago, 1967) 29.

guide to life. He will have no truck with mere analysis, aloof from social ethics. He reminds us that Cardozo would have maintained that philosophy is not worth disputation unless it has much higher and more responsible pretensions.[7]

If alive, would Cardozo, in the following eulogy of philosophy, have extended his horizons to embrace this technical breed of recent philosophic analysis?

'You think perhaps of philosophy as dwelling in the clouds. I hope you may see that she is able to descend to earth. You think that in stopping to pay court to her, when you should be hastening forward on your journey, you are loitering in by-paths and wasting precious hours. I hope you may share my faith that you are on the highway to the goal. Here you will find the key for the unlocking of bolts and combinations that shall never be pried open by clumsier or grosser tools. You think there is nothing practical in a theory that is concerned with ultimate conceptions. That is true perhaps while you are doing the journey-man's work of your profession. You may find in the end, when you pass to higher problems, that instead of its being true that the study of the ultimate is profitless, there is little that is profitable in the study of anything else.'[8]

Though his own bent did not lie in that direction, I believe Cardozo's hospitable eclecticism would have discerned some link with linguistic analyses. As Sidney Hook has pointed out, long before Wittgenstein appeared on the philosophic scene, we find jurists 'attempting to liberate themselves from linguistic traps and rigidi-

7. Lenore Cahn (ed.), *Confronting Injustice*: *The Edmond Cahn Reader* (Little, Brown, Boston, 1966) *passim*.
8. Cardozo, *The Growth of the Law* (Yale University Press, New Haven, 1924) 13.

ties which their own abstraction created. As a discipline, the law is a pre-eminent illustration of the fact that linguistic analysis affects much more than language and linguistic use, that it reflects and sometimes even redetermines the development of institutions.'[9]

Cardozo's first and, I think, most important and lasting book, *The Nature of the Judicial Process*, was originally a series of lectures given at the Yale Law School in 1921. Forty years later the *Yale Law Journal* took stock of its reverberations in a symposium called 'The Judicial Process Revisited.'[10] Professor Arthur Corbin, who was responsible for the original invitation to Cardozo, has paid him a lovely tribute in the course of revealing the circumstances surrounding the lectures and the birth of the book. Cardozo, he tells us, was 'a man of such beauty of countenance, such personal charm, and such keenness of mind, that to write of him now creates again the poignant joy that he brought to his friends and listeners at Yale more than forty years ago. His smile could melt one's heart to tears, his modesty and quickness of understanding roused instant confidence, and the beauty of his language, written and spoken, made it the perfect expression of his thought.'

One Cardozo on a judicial bench, he adds dithyrambically, was enough to give assurance that the bench would be the dispenser of 'justice that satisfies the imagination and fulfills the hope.'[11] Some judges, he remarks, may still be wedded to 'the conviction that the taught rule is eternal and must not be weakened into variation and uncertainty.' By contrast the mind and spirit of Cardozo

9. Sidney Hook (ed.), *Law and Philosophy* (1946) Preface xii.
10. 71 *YaleL.J.* 195 (1961).
11. *Ibid.*

were 'free' while displaying due respect for inherited
doctrines and the opinions of his colleagues.

When asked to deliver the lectures at Yale, Cardozo
had responded with his usual modesty: 'I have no message
to deliver.' Corbin would not take 'no' for an answer:
'Judge Cardozo, could you not explain to our students
the process by which you arrive at the decision of a case,
with the sources to which you go for assistance?' With a
bird-like movement of the head and a mere moment of
hesitation, he replied: 'I believe I could do that.' This
humble confidence was duly vindicated by the extraordinary ovation he received at the end of the first lecture:
'He bowed and sat down. The entire audience rose to
their feet with a burst of applause that would not cease.
Cardozo rose and bowed, with a smile at once pleased
and deprecatory, and again sat down. Not a man moved
from his tracks; and the applause increased.'[12]

When he was urged to publish the lectures as a book,
he said half-seriously that he 'did not dare' as he was
afraid of being 'impeached.' Far from being impeached,
Cardozo became the darling of the law schools and the
new enlightenment, inevitably linked with Holmes in
what I have called the Great Tradition of American law,
the Holmes-Cardozo philosophic approach. Corbin,
widely regarded as the dean of law professors, was led to
exalt them both in a burst of extravagance: 'No independent mind can accept 100 per cent of the conclusions
and reasonings of another man, even of such worshipful
masters as Cardozo and Holmes. The best one can do
is to smite those who fail to accept them by 95 per cent.'[13]

Lord Evershed has said that anyone in England 'who
wishes to reflect on the broad problems of the law's phi-

12. *Ibid.* 197.
13. *Ibid.* 199.

losophy and the judicial function' will turn to the recent American writings, especially Cardozo's book *The Nature of the Judicial Process,* which 'must always remain a classic.'[14]

Turning to a consideration of changes in the substance of the law since Cardozo's formulations in his opinions, we are indebted to Judge John Van Voorhis (a present member of the New York Court of Appeals) for an inventory of some interesting shifts.[15] (For analyses of Cardozo's original contributions see the joint issues in his honor of the Columbia, Harvard, and Yale law reviews.[16])

In two notable respects Cardozo's cases were prophetic; in two other fields he went against the trend.

In a dissenting opinion in the Twenties, Cardozo wanted to allow recovery for personal injuries suffered by an infant while a fetus in the womb.[17] His views were vindicated thirty years later.[18]

In the *Schmidt* case, Cardozo criticized the old M'-Naghten 'right-wrong' test of insanity as a defense. His analysis may well have brought psychiatry and law closer, precipitated by Judge Bazelon's famous opinion.[19]

In the field of workmen's compensation, the Court, in line with subsequent social thought and developments, has turned out to be more liberal than Cardozo in favoring the claimant.[20]

A sharper rejection of Cardozo's views is surprisingly

14. Lord Evershed, 'The Judicial Process in Twentieth Century England' (1961) *Col.L.Rev.* 761, 771.
15. John Van Voorhis, 'Cardozo and the Judicial Process Today' (1961) 71 *YaleL.J.* 202.
16. 39 *Col.L.Rev.* 1 (1939); 52 *Harv.L.Rev.* 3; 48 *YaleL.J.* 3.
17. Drobner v. Peters, 232 N.Y. 220, 133 N.E. 567, 1921.
18. Wood v. Lancet, 303 N.Y. 349, 102 N.E. 2d 691, 1951.
19. In Durham v. U.S., 214 F 2d 862 (D.C. Cir., 1954).
20. See Mark's Dependents v. Gray, 251 N.Y. 90.

encountered in the highly charged and controversial field of criminal-law enforcement which must remain within the confines of Constitutional safeguards. In *People* v. *Defore* (242 N.Y. 13, 150 N.E. 585, 1926) Cardozo held that evidence obtained through illegal search and seizure could nevertheless be admitted in evidence at the trial. This decision has been condemned as undermining the Constitutional guarantee against illegal searches and seizures. Justice Clark, speaking for the United States Supreme Court in the *Mapp* case,[21] overruled a 'search-and-seizure' decision of the highest court of the State of Ohio and, in doing so, criticized Cardozo's dictum in *Defore* that a criminal is not to go free simply because the police have 'blundered.' If a State engages in an 'ignoble short cut to conviction,' the Supreme Court warned, we 'tend to destroy the entire system of constitutional restraints on which the liberties of the people rest.'[22]

Cardozo was so wrapped up in these processes of judicial change that all he would ask of Saint Peter, he tells us, is that he might one day return to see how his successors have dislodged his opinions.[23]

Of special relevance to our subject is Judge Van Voorhis' report (from the front line of the New York Court of Appeals) on how Cardozo's philosophy of the judicial process has fared. He assures us that no one is likely to quarrel with Cardozo's recipe for the stew of a judicial opinion.[24] In brief, Cardozo had given us four guides to judicial decision: (1) the traditional analogy of precedents *(stare decisis)*, (2) the force of history, (3) the impact of current custom, and (4) social morality (what

21. Mapp v. Ohio, 367 U.S. 643, 1961.
22. 367 U.S. at 660.
23. Cardozo, *Law and Literature* (Harcourt, Brace, New York, 1931) 168.
24. See pp. 46–8.

Cardozo called the 'method of sociology'). As adumbrated in our text, Judge Van Voorhis can now note in retrospect that, as between adherence to precedent *(stare decisis)* and contemporary standards (the 'method of sociology'), the former 'may be somewhat weaker' than when Cardozo 'so conscientiously sought to maintain it in the absence of overriding factors.' And, correspondingly, there has been a development of the method of sociology 'in fields not previously occupied.' Thus Van Voorhis concludes that the 'most important part' of Cardozo's contribution is the 'method of sociology,' inasmuch as 'social reasons are the ones most frequently adduced to justify overruling of precedent' or, indeed, of history or of custom.[25]

Van Voorhis expands upon this point because, as he says, we have become so accustomed to it that we tend to forget the 'static' view which prevailed when Cardozo wrote. Judges at that time were supposed to be deciding cases simply by 'precedents' and they were not supposed to 'read beyond the law books or apply knowledge of life.' To Cardozo it was not only the law which was a seamless web, however, but law and life which constituted a seamless web. Today judges do not hesitate to 'cite sociologists, economists, historians and other writers' bringing knowledge essential to an intelligent decision.[26] Van Voorhis acknowledges Cardozo's prescience in predicting that this method would turn out to be of much potential 'value in the future.' The judicial process was no longer to be a tight and closed system but an 'open-end' production.[27] The job of the judge becomes the judicious assessment of

25. Van Voorhis, 'Cardozo and the Judicial Process Today,' 203, 204, 221.
26. *Ibid.* 204–5.
27. *Ibid.* 216.

all the constituents which he may deem appropriately
to be blended into the brew of his decision.

When it sometimes occurs that the judge is wholly free
to invoke ethical convictions of right and wrong, Van
Voorhis reminds us that Cardozo thought the judge
should not take primary recourse to his own views but
rather to 'the prevailing public belief of the day.'[28] We
shall have occasion to return to further reflection upon
this central philosophic point.

Since in this edition we have retained intact our original text, we include Cardozo's full opinion in the *Schloendorff* case (at p. 159), despite the fact that it has since
been overruled. We are thus presented with both the
need and the opportunity to show how the creative judicial process works over the years. The *Schloendorff*
opinion is not the best example of Cardozo's pioneering
spirit or analytic skill, but it does serve to illustrate our
purpose. The process of overruling is instructive in showing how the judicial process functions in moving from
an outmoded view to one more acceptable to a later day.
In observing the course of the overruling we can also see
the 'method of sociology' exercising its leaven. We encounter in Judge Fuld's comprehensive opinion in the
Bing case, which overruled *Schloendorff*, a notable exhi-
bition of Cardozo's own influence on judicial methods.

Cardozo's opinion[29] set forth for the first time in New
York a studied rationale for exempting charitable hospitals—as distinct from government-run or profit-making
hospitals—from liability for the negligent acts of their
employees. This exemption is unique, inasmuch as all

28. *Ibid.* 214.
29. Schloendorff v. New York Hospital, 211 N.Y. 125, 105 N.E. 92, 1914.

other employers are held liable for their employees' negligence (under a well-settled doctrine known to the law as *respondeat superior*). The plaintiff in the *Schloendorff* case was a patient who had suffered injuries during an operation and sued the hospital to recover for the damages. Cardozo's opinion rested the immunity of the hospital from liability on two pillars: (1) When a patient avails himself of such charitable service there is an 'implied waiver' of any claims which might arise through negligence in the performance of the service. (2) A doctor is an 'independent contractor' even though he is on the payroll; for he is unlike an ordinary employee in that he performs professional services which require special skill and are not supervised by the hospital.

These are alternative grounds for the decision based on the facts of that case but stating as broad principles the legal basis for the decision. The wide scope of the two principles enunciated by Cardozo bred considerable confusion. Homer had nodded.

If there was indeed an 'implied waiver' of any claim because the service was a charitable one, it was unnecessary for Cardozo to go on to distinguish between doctors and other employees. If the hospital was exempt because the doctor, as a professional man, was not like an ordinary employee but like an 'independent contractor,' then it was not necessary to distinguish between charitable hospitals (sustained by philanthropic donations) and other hospitals.

The actual basis for the decision in the social realities emerges at the end of his opinion. Balancing the burden to the injured patient against the burden to be shouldered by the charitable institution, Cardozo argued that it would be socially undesirable to place such a burden upon precariously supported charitable hospitals. That is to say, he made a value judgment based upon the then-existing social situation. We can readily perceive that the decision turned on Cardozo's fourth guide to judicial decision—what he called the method of sociology.[30] If, as I originally ventured to suggest, this method were more freely avowed and given greater prominence, we might have been spared much of the vexatious confusion which ensued because of the technical character of the two pillars upon which Cardozo explicitly and preponderantly rested his opinion.

In the course of time, as we shall see, the lower courts as well as the highest court felt themselves caught by the tension created by the claims of patients and this immunity of the charitable hospital. Judges felt compelled to create further technical distinctions which added to the confusion, until finally the entire immunity concept had to be dropped. How this development took place over the decades can only cursorily be traced here.

In the *Phillips* case[31] in 1924, Judge Pound tried to demolish the 'waiver' pillar and to base the immunity on the 'independent-contractor' pillar. In doing so, he was forced to argue that when a mere orderly had burned a patient by misplacing a hot-water bottle, he was acting as an 'independent contractor,' like a doctor.

In the subsequent *Hamburger* case[32] in 1929, Cardozo himself highlighted the professional status. After Cardozo had left the Court, the waiver pillar was demolished altogether in the *Sheehan* case.[33]

As lower courts were faced with the need to cope with this unusual immunity, they began to stress not so much

30. Set forth at page 60.
31. 239 N.Y. 188, 146 N.E. 199, 1924.
32. 240 N.Y. 328, 148 N.E. 539, 1929.
33. 273 N.Y. 163, 7 N.E. 2d 1937.

the professional status of the doctor as the kind of negligent act involved: *administrative* or *medical*. Many thin distinctions were made. For example, to place upon a patient a hot-water bottle not capped tightly was called an 'administrative' act, from which it followed of course that the hospital could be held liable.

When, in 1953, in the *Bryant* case[34] the Court designated as a 'medical' act the insertion of a needle by a mere student nurse, Judge Froessel decided it was time to blow the whistle. He dissented and took note of the growing criticism of the *Schloendorff* rule.

In the *Berg* case[35] in 1956, a laboratory technician administered a blood test negligently. The Court declined to call this act a medical act and to relieve the hospital of liability. The intimation is given that *Schloendorff* might have 'outlived its usefulness.'

Finally, in 1957, the Court reached the *Bing* case,[36] in which Judge Fuld[37] impressively overruled *Schloendorff*. His notable opinion exemplifies, in its exhaustiveness and social emphases, the methods of approach which Cardozo had formulated after the *Schloendorff* decision. It is an opinion Cardozo would have warmly applauded.

Judge Fuld opens with a frontal attack. The problem, he says plainly at the outset, is the confusion reflected in the cases since *Schloendorff*. The courts had been unhappy with the hospital's freedom from liability and had therefore sought to distinguish between *administrative* acts and *medical* acts, depending upon whether they were disposed to hold the hospital liable or to honor the exemption from liability, playing with the elastic margins

34. 304 N.Y. 538, 110 N.E. 2d 391.
35. 1 N.Y. 2d 499, 136 N.E. 2d 523, 154 N.Y.S. 2d 455, 1956.
36. 2 N.Y. 2d 656, 143 N.E. 2d 3, 163 N.Y.S. 2d 3, 1957.
37. Now occupying the Chief Judgeship as a spiritual as well as titular heir to Cardozo's seat.

of these categories. The time had come, said Fuld, to consider whether hospitals should be exempt at all. In the *Bing* case an injury had occurred during the preparation for an operation. The courts below had divided on the question of whether or not the act was 'medical.' But this very distinction, Fuld noted, had developed because courts were not satisfied with the exemption and sought a way out. Because of the distinction, confusion had ensued, with accompanying uncertainties. The law was no longer giving the guidance of a reasonably clear-cut policy. Here, then, is the forthright statement of the problem in what may be called Point One of the opinion.

Point Two of the opinion is the opening move to jettison *Schloendorff*. We are presented with a canvass of the precedents, going back to the earliest one in this country —based on a still earlier one in England, which is in turn based on a dictum, both of them later repudiated. If we are to go simply by early precedent, there is, therefore, really no basis for the exemption in the originating precedents themselves, when thus carefully reviewed all the way back.

Point Three brings us face to face with the *Schloendorff* case and a critique of Cardozo's technical rationale for the exemption. If we are to rely on the implied waiver for charity hospitals, Judge Fuld asks, how can we justify the subsequent judicial extension of the doctrine to 'non-charity' hospitals? If we are to rely on the independent-contractor doctrine, why should there not also be an exemption, for example, for employers of chemists or airplane pilots?

In Point Four we follow the checkered career of *Schloendorff*. We note that the extended subsequent immunity did not reach out consistently to include also government-owned hospitals; nor was the immunity extended to non-professional employees, as the waiver doctrine would require if followed consistently.

Point Five razes both pillars. The waiver, 'pretty much of a fiction,' is regarded as having been destroyed by *Sheehan* and *Phillips*. The second pillar must also fall since it is an anomaly to regard any salaried employees of hospitals as independent contractors when there is no such exemption for those on the payroll in any other employment area.

Point Six confronts the fear that charitable hospitals will be handicapped by the burden of liability—'the major impetus originally behind the doctrine.' This fear stemmed from the possibility that a large verdict against a charity hospital might ruin it. In fact, research shows that charity hospitals have not been curtailed in those States where liability has been imposed. *Today* insurance coverage for this risk is available. *Today* a hospital is not dependent on a few donations, but receives community-wide support. *Today* hospitals operate large facilities in a business-like way.

Point Seven sketches the recent trend toward liability for hospitals in other States.

Point Eight reminds us that the *Schloendorff* rule had already been seriously criticized.

Point Nine stands on the unchallenged soundness of the doctrine of *respondeat superior* and argues that a hospital, like any other institution serving the public, must accept the obligation to make redress for injuries caused through the carelessness of any of its employees. It is sound morals that even charitable hospitals, as Judge Fuld puts it, must be 'just' before they are 'generous'; and thus it also becomes sound law.[38]

38. It will be noted that a proposition deemed to be sound morals before the *Bing* decision became sound law as a result of the *Bing* decision.

Judge Fuld concludes with an exposition of present-day social realities and a deft justification of the overruling in relation to the doctrine of *stare decisis*:

'The conception that the hospital does not undertake to treat the patient, does not undertake to act through its doctors and nurses, but undertakes instead simply to procure them to act upon their own responsibility, no longer reflects the fact. Present-day hospitals, as their manner of operation plainly demonstrates, do far more than furnish facilities for treatment. They regularly employ on a salary basis a large staff of physicians, nurses and interns, as well as administrative and manual workers, and they charge patients for medical care and treatment, collecting for such services, if necessary, by legal action. Certainly, the person who avails himself of "hospital facilities" expects that the hospital will attempt to cure him, not that its nurses or other employees will act on their own responsibility.

'Hospitals should, in short, shoulder the responsibilities borne by everyone else. There is no reason to continue their exemption from the universal rule of *respondeat superior*. The test should be, for these institutions, whether charitable or profitmaking, as it is for every other employer, was the person who committed the negligent injury-producing act one of its employees and, if he was, was he acting within the scope of his employment.

'The rule of nonliability is out of tune with the life about us, at variance with modern-day needs and with concepts of justice and fair dealing. It should be discarded. To the suggestion that *stare decisis* compels us to perpetuate it until the legislature acts, a ready answer is at hand. It was intended, not to effect a petrifying rigidity, but to assure the justice that flows from certainty and stability. If, instead, adherence to precedent offers not justice but unfairness, not certainty but doubt and confusion, it loses its right to survive, and no principle constrains us to follow it. On the contrary, as this court, speaking through Judge Desmond in *Woods* v. *Lancet,* 303 N.Y. 349, 355, 102 N.E. 2d 691, 694, 27 A.L.R. 2d 1250, declared, we would be abdicating "our own function, in a field peculiarly nonstatutory," were we to insist on legislation and "refuse to reconsider an old and unsatisfactory court-made rule." ' *(Bing* v. *Thunig,* 2 N.Y. 2d 656, 666–7; 143 N.E. 2d 3.)

Thus *Bing* overruled *Schloendorff,* but not precipitately or to the surprise of anyone who had followed the inroads made by the intervening cases. We are left to wonder only why the overruling took so long. We note the substantial attention given to the underlying social reasons. We again raise the question as to whether it is not indeed the wave of the future that such social considerations will be put at the head and front of an opinion, with the technical arguments being even more subordinated.

In this field of conventionally judge-made law, a court naturally and normally faces up to the need to change a rule which it has itself created. One of the prime impediments to such change, however, is that those who may have relied on the old rule—a hospital not properly insured, in our example—would find itself in serious trouble when the new rule is announced. For the new rule is proclaimed as though it had always been the correct rule—as though it had always been the 'law.' That is to say, under our traditional system, a judicial change in the law has retrospective application. The judge is deemed to be merely the announcer of the law which is supposed to be omnipresently brooding, awaiting his rightful articulation. In contrast, a change made by the legislature goes into effect only prospectively, that is, forward from the date of enactment of the statute. Where the situation had become as confused as in this situation, hospitals could hardly know just what they could rely on, and, as Judge Fuld said, by clearing up the confusion the *Bing* case in actuality brought into the picture the relative stability and certainty which *stare decisis* is supposed to provide.

In a clearer or simpler situation where there has been undoubted reliance, however, and the court is reluctant to overrule for that reason, Cardozo was a strong proponent of the judicial innovation of 'prospective overruling.' By this device a court restricts its overruling to the future only, without any retroactive effect, just as a legislature does. Since the spread of prospective overruling has latterly been accelerated as a result of Cardozo's enthusiasm—and this development is one of the most significant sequels of his liberating thought—may I quote from an article of mine on the subject?[39]

'In January, 1932, while still sitting on the New York Court of Appeals, Chief Judge Cardozo made his important address on legal realism to the New York Bar Association. There he espoused prospective overruling. Returning to his concern about the retroactive effect of a needed judicial change in the law, he went over the familiar ground that an outmoded rule is sometimes continued because the court does not want to defeat the reasonable expectations of those who relied upon it. He repeated his strongly held belief that cases of reliance—and genuine disappointment at a change—are not as

39. Matter within double quotes is from the indicated address of Cardozo.

widespread as is usually assumed. But in cases where
actual reliance *is* involved, he thought courts should apply the outworn rule to the case at hand, and, as he said,
"couple their judgment" with the assertion that they
will feel free to apply another rule to transactions consummated in the future. Cardozo's emphasis was rather
on the notice given by the court that the old rule would
not be further applied than on the explicit formulation
by the court of the new rule. Where a defendant would
really suffer an injustice because of his reliance on the
old rule, Cardozo asked if it would not be the sensible
thing to affirm judgment in the defendant's favor but say
in effect to all those who propose to have similar transactions in the future: we give notice here and now that
the earlier statement of the law, now deemed to have been
mistaken, may not be trusted in guiding your course here-
after.

'Cardozo met head-on the objection that the judges on
the court cannot tie the hands of their successors by a
mere dictum which is not part of the judgment itself.
What the court is really doing, he argued, is releasing, not
tying; if anything, it is untying. What the court is saying,
as Cardozo phrased it, is this: "The rule that we are asked
to apply is out of tune with the life about us. It has been
made discordant by the forces that generate a living law.
We apply it to this case because the repeal might work
hardship to those who have trusted to its existence. We
give notice, however, that any one trusting to it here-
after will do so at his peril."

'The effect, he pointed out, would be to leave the law
uncertain as to new transactions until the court could
speak again. Such uncertainty, however, would not be
very grievous, for parties could fairly assume that the
dictum would be followed when the opportunity came to

turn it into decision. Of course no one could be sure
the court would follow along; but when can one ever be
sure what a court will do? "Whatever evil might inhere
in the small margin of uncertainty would be something
hardly to be complained of in a system of case law which
by the very nature of its existence leaves so many other
things unsettled."

'Cardozo thought judges already had the power to
proceed along these lines. But should there be any doubt,
he thought the power should be conferred explicitly
by statute. . . . So strongly did he feel that he added that,
if necessary, the statute should be reinforced by constitutional amendment.

'If this course were pursued, the fruits would be in-
calculably rewarding: "much of the evasion, the pretense,
the shallow and disingenuous distinctions too often manifest in opinions—distinctions made in the laudable endeavor to attain a just result while preserving a semblance
of consistency—would disappear from our law forever. . . !" '⁴⁰

The proliferation of precedents in recent times has
led not only to more recourse to the 'method of sociology'
and to the new device of prospective overruling. The

40. B.H.Levy, 'Realist Jurisprudence and Prospective Overruling' (1960)
109 *U.Pa.L.Rev.* 1, 12–13, reprinted by permission. See citations of
my article in: William v. City of Detroit, N.W. 2d 29; Paul Haskell,
'Justifying the Principle of Distributive Deviation in the Law of
Trusts' (1967) 18 *HastingsL.Rev.* 267; Henry Friendly, 'Reactions of
a Lawyer–Newly Become Judge' (1961) 71 *YaleL.J.* 236 n.105; Freed-
man, 'Prospective Overruling and Retroactive Application in Federal
Courts (1962) 71 *YaleL.J.* 5, 907. See also U.S. Supreme Court cases
dealing with prospective overruling: Linkletter v. Walker 381 U.S. 618
(1965), Tehan v. U.S. ex rel. Shott, 382 U.S. 406 (1966), Johnson v.
New Jersey, 384 U.S. 719 (1966). See also address by Justice Walter V.
Schaefer, 'The Control of "Sunburst": Techniques of Prospective
Overruling,' 22 *Record of the Association of the Bar of the City of
New York* 6 (June 1967) 394.

precedent explosion[41] has also led to more prolific statutory enactment and codifications of various subjects. Our subject here, however, remains the philosophy of the judicial process, particularly its creative aspects, which will always retain a central preoccupation. Our attention is therefore now directed to more recent philosophical analyses which carry along phases of this theme touched upon or precipitated by Cardozo's thought and often directly related to his contributions.

We start with Levi on 'legal reasoning,' followed by Wasserstrom on 'judicial decision.' Friendly comments on Cardozo, Levi, and Wasserstrom and gives us the sobering benefit of his broad experience. Wechsler reminds us of the 'principled' character of legal decisions. Llewellyn's final testament dwells upon the 'situation' involved. Cahn criticizes Cardozo's interest in the development of the law at what seems to be the expense of the individual party. Santayana takes us into deeper waters in the relation of the judge's ideals to social trends. Frank takes Cardozo to task for limiting the judicial process to the appellate process. Jones stresses that the judge must bring traits of character to his task, which must always remain a problem of wise choice.

In Edward H. Levi's analysis of 'legal reasoning' we encounter a subtle amalgam of philosophic erudition, realist emancipation, and traditional moorings. The case-law example of his thesis is provided through a dissection of Cardozo's famous opinion in *MacPherson* v. *Buick*. Judge Friendly informs us that 'Dean Levi's little book will tell you as much as anything I know.'[42]

41. See William O.Douglas, 'Stare Decisis,' 4 *Record of the Association of the Bar of the City of New York* (November 1960) 153.
42. Friendly, *Benchmarks*, 26.

Levi, former Dean of the Law School of the University of Chicago and now President of the University, begins his *Introduction to Legal Reasoning*[43] by reference to what he calls the 'controlling book' of Jerome Frank, *Law and the Modern Mind.* The pivotal reference is that we must no longer be deluded by the long-time 'pretense' that 'law is a system of known rules applied by a judge.'

Levi's thesis is that the basic pattern of 'legal reasoning' is reasoning by analogy or example. The theory of logic upon which he leans is drawn from a passage of Aristotle's *Prior Analytics*: 'Clearly then to argue by example is neither like reasoning from part to whole, nor like reasoning from whole to part, but rather reasoning from part to part. . . .' In the law we have reasoning from case to case. Whatever may be its alleged imperfections in science or in other contexts, this method of reasoning as used in the law is characterized by the following steps: similarity is perceived between cases; from the earlier cases a rule of law is extracted; it is made to govern the new case. The key step is determining the similarity (and differences). Therein lies the crucial function of the judge. We cannot say that a known rule remains unchanged and is applied to later cases, because we know that rules change from case to case. We know that, in a sense, rules are remade with each case, as is inevitable in any dynamic legal system. The meaning of a rule depends on what facts are considered by the judge to be similar, in the perspective of his grasp of our legal system.

Because each judge must make a determination of such

---

43. Edward Levi, *Introduction to Legal Reasoning* (University of Chicago Press, Chicago, 1948); paperback ed., 1961, with new Preface. We are here presenting a summary only of his analysis of case law and not of Constitutional or statutory interpretation.

similarity and is required to reach his own decision, he cannot be said to be 'bound' by the prior judge's enunciation of the rule of law. 'It is not what the prior judge intended that is of any importance; rather it is what the present judge, attempting to see the law as a fairly consistent whole, thinks should be the determining classification.'[44] Thus the present judge may ignore what the prior judge in a past period considered important. The present judge may dwell on factors which cut no ice for the prior judge.

This kind of reasoning is patently one in which a classification changes as it is made: the rules change as they are applied. Levi reminds us that John Dewey points out, in his *Logic: The Theory of Inquiry*, that in a sense all reasoning may be said to be of this type.[45]

Besides the change from one fact-picture to another, people's desires change. As time goes on, people want different things. The legal process must thus be left purposely 'ambiguous' in order to permit the infusion of new wants—to be able to express the emerging ideas of the community. The law continues to be followed as it continues to be changed. As Cohen and Nagel observe in their *Introduction to Logic and Scientific Method*: 'That the law can be obeyed even when it grows is often more than the legal profession itself can grasp.'

No matter to what extent popular folklore about the law may close its eyes to these characteristics of legal reasoning, we have only to look at what is done in court to see the reasoning effectively at work. The court demands that competing examples or analogies be presented. Thereby the views not only of the parties but of the community are reflected and protected.

44. *Ibid.* 3, alluding to George Mead, *The Philosophy of the Act* (University of Chicago Press, Chicago, 1938) *passim*.
45. See also Ovid Lewis, 'Phase Theory and the Judicial Process' (1965) 1 *Cal.W.L.Rev.* 1.

'Reasoning by example in the law is a key to many things. It indicates in part the hold which the law process has over the litigants. They have participated in the lawmaking. They are bound by something they helped to make. Moreover, the examples or analogies urged by the parties bring into the law the common ideas of the society. The ideas have their day in court, and they will have their day again. . . . Moreover, the hearing in a sense compels at least vicarious participation by all the citizens, for the rule which is made, even though ambiguous, will be law as to them.'[46]

Thus, as Cardozo had argued, the 'common ideas of society' play a decisive role in the judicial process, as they continually change and win acceptance. The adoption of any idea by a court 'reflects the power structure in the community,' but 'reasoning by example will operate to change the idea after it has been adopted.'[47]

Students of jurisprudence will have noted the influence of Professor Arthur Goodhardt's theory of *stare decisis* which puts much emphasis on the variation in facts from one case to another, because the English system is still more precedent-oriented than ours. But Levi's fresh re-formulation, which also takes due account of social pressures, is replete with illuminations, especially in his discussion of the ever-hospitable and ambiguous classificatory system. It is this process which leads us to accept the system, rather than any preternatural impartiality ascribable to any ordinary mortal in a robe. So Levi argues with considerable plausibility.

A more recent and more technically philosophical inquiry is proffered by Wasserstrom in *The Judicial Decision—Toward a Theory of Legal Justification* (1961).

46. *Ibid.* 5.
47. *Ibid.* 6.

Wasserstrom proposes to seek an 'ideal' procedure for deciding cases. He does so not by an empirical examination of how judges have in fact proceeded (as Llewellyn has done, in *The Common Law Tradition: Deciding Appeals,* in order to see how the best of them proceed). Nor is he much interested in what judges *qua* judges tell us about how they decide or should decide. His interest in Cardozo's writings, for example, is solely in Cardozo's minor point that the following of precedents has as one of its merits the assurance of efficiency among judges who would otherwise be lost and at loose ends. What he does is to set up a model for a non-existent legal system of his own creation (which only coincidentally resembles the Anglo-American system at various points!). This device immunizes him from certain kinds of attack, but his thought is thereby also robbed of much immediate and practical use to practitioners—judges or lawyers.

Wasserstrom proceeds with a logician's rigor of analysis in his punctilious definitions and classifications. By a radical over-simplification we are presented with an exploration of opposed extremities of theoretical positions. There is an element of confusion and arbitrariness in calling these polarities 'precedent' and 'equity.' By *his* procedure of 'precedent,' a case is decided by appeal to the 'relevant extant legal rules.' By *his* procedure of 'equity,' a case is decided by appeal to that which is just (or equitable) for that particular case. He readily demonstrates that neither of these procedures suffices by itself. He thus sets the stage for his own proposal: a 'two-level procedure' whereby the case is decided with reference to a rule, but the rule is tested by utilitarian criteria—the satisfactions yielded.[48]

48. Richard Wasserstrom, *The Judicial Decision* (Stanford University Press, Stanford, 1961) 6, 7.

In terms of the distinction between 'sufficient' and 'necessary' conditions, Wasserstrom's two-level procedure is different from his 'precedent' paradigm in that the appeal to a rule is a *necessary* condition for a decision, but not a *sufficient* one. His two-level procedure is different from his 'equity' paradigm in that it is not the justice of the particular decision but the justice of the rule which is the *sufficient* condition for the decision. There is a nicety of argument for those who enjoy this type of schematic presentation; and his conclusion is, at the very least, a reminder that we can ignore neither the justice nor the rule.

Of peculiar interest to the student of contemporary moral theory is Wasserstrom's parallel with 'restricted utilitarianism'—an ethical viewpoint upon which he obviously patterns his two-level procedure. By contrast with 'extreme' utilitarianism, which justifies a moral decision on the basis of the consequences of the particular act, 'restricted' utilitarianism justifies the particular act by appeal to some moral rule—which is itself, however, in turn to be justified as having utility in promoting maximal satisfaction.[49]

Wasserstrom's book is an example of the current reversion to the age-old interest in rules. It is the core of his position that a decision must be justified through its derivation from a legal rule (even though the rule itself must be shown to be desirable).[50] Logic and rules—only partial components of what we have seen is involved in

---

49. For a philosophic account of justice as more than such utility, see John Rawls, 'Justice as Fairness' (1957) 54 *J. of Philosophy* 653, and, in concurrence on that point, Robert Wolff, 'A Refutation of Rawls' Theorem on Justice' (1966) 63 *J. of Philosophy* 179, 190. For reservations about any consensus for an overriding function of the legal system as a whole, see Ronald Dworkin's discussion, 'Wasserstrom: The Judicial Decision' (1964) 75 *Ethics* 47, 51.

50. See Wolff, 'A Refutation of Rawls' Theorem on Justice,' 172–3.

the complexities of a judicial decision—are his métier.

While Wasserstrom makes a useful distinction between how judges decide cases (concededly not by formal logic) and how they should justify their decisions, it remains true that the impact of his book is a relapse to the rule-preoccupation of an earlier day. As Professor L. E. Allen observes: 'One cannot help but wonder to what extent such a focus upon logic and rules as the crucial features of the judicial decision process tends to blur the important insight of the legal realists that these are only relatively minor parts of how judicial decisions are in fact (and should be) made.'[51] A master of symbolic logic like Professor Allen is not likely to derogate the role of logic in judicial decision.[52]

If the criteria for choice are our paramount concern, Wasserstrom's theory of judicial decision diverts attention from the totality of the problem while exaggerating the importance of formal deduction which does not aid us in our choice. As Professor Allen says, it is in this respect 'a matter so trivial as to be of almost inconsequential importance in a full contextual analysis of judicial decision making.'[53]

Wasserstrom finds that while he must disagree with many of the contentions of a leading realist like Jerome Frank, he can applaud Frank's observation that there is a sense in which all judging begins 'with a conclusion more or less vaguely formed'; that the judge tries to find proper substantiating arguments for such a tentative conclusion; and, if he cannot, he will reject the proposed conclusion and seek another.[54] He also approves Frank's

51. L.E.Allen, Review of 'The Judicial Decision' (1957) 71 *YaleL.J.* 1579.
52. See Allen's article, 'Symbolic Logic: A Razor-Edged Tool for Drafting and Interpreting Legal Documents' (1957) 66 *YaleL.J.* 833.
53. Allen, Review of 'The Judicial Decision,' 1578.
54. Jerome Frank, *Law and the Modern Mind* (Brentano's, New York, 1930) 100.

observation that the judge will see if his conclusion 'can be linked with the generalized points of view theretofore acceptable. If none such are discoverable, he is forced to consider more acutely whether his tentative conclusion is wise, with respect to the case before him and with respect to possible implications for future cases.'[55] Thus Wasserstrom at his best can join hands with our militant realist at his best. No realist seriously argues that a decision is to be justified simply on the basis of what Shakespeare invidiously called 'a woman's reason—I think him so because I think him so.' The reference to generalized viewpoints and implications for future cases leads directly to the light thrown from still another corner by Professor Wechsler.

Breaking away from more familiar realist grooves, Herbert Wechsler, Professor of Constitutional Law at Columbia Law School and Director of the American Law Institute, brings us an autonomous concern with principles conveyed in his book, *Principles, Politics and Fundamental Law* (1961). Though the principal essay, delivered by him as Holmes Lecturer at Harvard in 1959, 'Toward Neutral Principles of Constitutional Law,' deals with opinions of the United States Supreme Court, his underlying argument compels attention in any conspectus of current analyses of the decisional process. His contribution is upon the rationalistic rather than empirical side. It is 'principle' with which he is indeed engaged, as the title of his book and his lecture both manifest. His submission is a basic reminder: that law, considered in its most fundamental aspect (and as contrasted with politics, say), is under constraint to be principled. To put it in another way, whereas we may be

55. *Ibid.* 131.

pleasantly surprised to encounter a principled account in
support of some political position, we must expect and
require one for a legal decision. That is to say, it is the
unique character of the judicial process that a court
should not be an organ of naked power, operating by
what Professor Lon Fuller has called 'fiat,' but should
rest upon and support its decisions by a principled justification. A court must show how its decision in a particular case is related to and applies a principle—a principle of law. While it is true that the court is deciding
that case—and only that case—the principle involved
must nevertheless have 'adequate neutrality and generality.' The analysis of the court, constituting the reasoned
justification of its decision, must be able to vindicate the
invoked principle in the broad context of other applications implied by the principle. We must have the neutral
application of a general principle—one which can be consistently invoked for other cases, even though such other
cases may involve different sympathies and allegiances.
To put this formidable insistence in a colloquialism:
what is sauce for the goose must also be sauce for the gan-
der. Take a simple and extreme example. If it is our legal
principle that a Congressional investigation must be conducted in a certain way to be lawful when J. P. Morgan is
involved, then the same principle must be observed when
an alleged Communist is involved. A court must test its
principle by considering other cases, preferably cases of
opposing interest. The principle in terms of which the
case is decided must be a principle which extends beyond
the result of that case. The decision is not simply to be
made *ad hoc*.

   As the student of moral theory will note, the philosophic analogue of Wechsler's view is Kant's affirmation
that the morality of an act resides in its conformity with

a principle which can be generalized. If it is right for me, it must be right for everyone similarly situated. (Hence the untenability of lying or suicide.) By adding this deontological note—as philosophers term it—to the current climate of utilitarian, pragmatic, and analytic thought, Wechsler has generated considerable critical discussion. Much of it is polemical, construing his position to be pre-Holmesian formalism. Many of his critics seem unaware of the modesty of his effort to achieve greater balance. He does not enter into the question of how a principled decision is also to be a sound decision and one which reflects democratic values.

As one whose professional lifetime has been devoted to clarifying and restating legal principles, Professor Wechsler would have us remember what law in its quintessential rendering means. The ways in which a judge is expected to fulfill his punctilios is a further question raised by even Levi's inability to go all the way with Wechsler.[56] Wechsler, like the rest of our commentators, brings the illumination which comes to him from his own vantage point. He links into that phase of Cardozo's approach which approved the project of the American Law Institute to undertake to make 'restatements' of the common law. Judge Friendly next brings us some pertinent caveats, based on his experience at the bar and on the bench.

Judge Henry J. Friendly has been prolific in the production of a number of juristic studies after the manner of Holmes, Cardozo, and Learned Hand. In one of his earliest papers, shortly after his appointment to the Federal bench, Friendly took Cardozo as a starting point for

56. See comment in the symposium edited by Hook, *Law and Philosophy*, 297.

his own 'Reactions of a Lawyer—Newly Become Judge.'[57]
He is at pains to have us keep in mind the all-too-human
limitations and fallibilities of a judge. Adverting to the
recent criticism by Dean (later Solicitor-General) Gris-
wold of so-called result-oriented decisions—a criticism
along the lines of Professor Wechsler's—Judge Friendly
assures us that it is not a criticism of Cardozo's 'method
of sociology,' pursuant to which we consider the relative
social desirabilities of various policies. What is being
criticized as result-oriented, as Friendly sees it, is a judge's
adherence to a view held prior to the argument of the
case before him and impervious to any argument. There
should, however, be no pretension to an 'intellectual
equilibrium' which 'cannot be expected or, in many instances, wanted.' While striving to be disinterested and
objective, the judge does not stand on what Cardozo
called 'chill and distant heights.'

While concurring with Cardozo that the judge 'should
try to make sure he is interpreting the long-term convictions of the community,' rather than foist his own convictions (which are likely at the least to be more evanes-
cent), Friendly warns us that even the best of judges will
not always realize this goal. Sometimes the community
has no 'true convictions' (as for example with a technical
legal point involving the procedural operation of the
legal system). Sometimes 'it is asking too much that a
judge suppress the basic beliefs by which he lives.'[58]
Sometimes it is even 'wrong to expect him to try.' In any
event, the judge's personal beliefs cannot be wholly ex-

57. 71 *YaleL.J.* 218 (1961), reprinted in Henry Friendly, *Benchmarks*, 1.
   There are many extended insights in chapter 4 of *Benchmarks* dealing with 'The Gap in Lawmaking—Judges Who Can't and Legislators
   Who Won't.'
58. *Ibid.* 17.

tirpated.[59] What Friendly helpfully stresses is the temporal stage in his deliberation at which the judge may most appropriately consult his own views. It is only after considering precedential analogies and the views of other judges that, Friendly believes, the judge should attempt to get at the community's views or take recourse to his own.

Judge Friendly does not believe we can expect that new research into the 'social laboratory' will be undertaken by a judge at this juncture. The court does not have the facilities or training for such an inquiry. He does not warm to the suggestion of Wasserstrom that, in considering the social utility of a proposed rule, the judge should gather the relevant sociological data. For example, are we to have a new rule which no longer excuses a wife from testifying in a trial against her husband (a privilege allowed to her because, in our system, concern for the truth is subordinated to our social concern for the sanctity of the marriage relation)? In answering this question, should we examine the data on the incidence of divorces in States allowing this marital privilege, as against those which do not? Who would go that far? (The United States Supreme Court used sociological studies on the ill effects of segregation on children in order to illustrate, illumine, and buttress its opinion in *Brown* v. *Board of Education,* not to predicate or bottom its opinion, as some commentators have supposed.)

For here we encounter all the variables and quagmires of social science methodology, not to mention the difficulty and feasibility of judicial pursuit of such data, and its value or weight if secured. None the less I have submitted that a court may seek light from any source and that a

59. *Ibid.* 21.

conduit should be provided between the universities and the courts, along the lines of Cardozo's suggestion that a bridge be established between the courts and the legislature. I have elaborated this point in my article 'Cardozo Twenty Years Later,' part of which I here reprint:

'Cardozo made a notable contribution to more rational and currently defensible law by his proposal for a "ministry of justice," which resulted in the creation of the Law Revision Commission. This Commission now makes analyses of needed changes in the law which the court may feel are too extensive to be judge-made and which, without the Commission shuttling between the courts and the legislature, might be too technical or recondite to become statutory revisions. I believe we should be carrying forward fruitfully the spirit of this insight of Cardozo were we now to give some thought to an official "ministry of information," by which the courts and the universities could be brought closer together in some "Legal Commission on Social Data." This Commission would aid the courts in their efforts to make decisions more realistically, not by the traditional manipulation of inherited abstractions, but by reference to the pertinent knowledge in the social disciplines.

'We would then have a more enlightened attempt to grasp the full import of a case in the context of the contemporary situation and to assess rival social values on the basis of fullest information. It is the rare court that in an obscenity case, say, would have before it a study in the *American Journal of Psychology* on sources of excitation to lust among adolescent boys, an awareness of the history of censorship involving even *Gulliver's Travels* and *Prometheus Bound,* the results of a questionnaire distributed among college girls to discover the incitation of their lascivious thoughts. If we want our judges to do justice we must give them the instruments. How can courts make a sound judgment on such matters—one at least which an educated man can respect—merely by cogitating on words in a vacuum? I am not, of course, suggesting the replacement or displacement of judicial judgment by such authority as social studies may have. I am merely suggesting that we facilitate and correlate such sources of illumination, insofar as a court may deem it well to avail itself of them, to the extent they may be helpful.'[60]

Judge Friendly reserves at several points the effect on the particular parties involved, as distinct from the effect on the law.[61] But what about the effect on the parties in the particular case? The new rule, says Friendly, 'must be the desirable one for the situation, not for the idiosyncrasies of the particular parties.'[62] Here he is in agreement with Llewellyn's view, in *The Common Law Tradition: Deciding Appeals* (1960), that the appellate judge should be concerned with the general situation of which the particular case is an instance. The appellate judge is naturally mindful of other similar situations, as he is expected to set out guidance for lower courts as well as for other persons (potential litigants) caught in such situations. Does this preoccupation tend to squeeze out human concern for the person who may be gored in the case being decided—a human sacrifice to a generically applicable rule?

Edmond Cahn directs the fire of his criticism at the passage in *The Nature of the Judicial Process* where

60. 13 *Record of the Association of the Bar of the City of New York* 7 (October 1958) 462–3. Reprinted by permission.
61. *Ibid.* 10, 17, 18, 21.
62. P. 21.

Cardozo remarks that the eccentricities of judges balance one another: one is a formalist, another is a latitudinarian; one looks from the viewpoint of history, another from that of social utility; one is timorous, another dissatisfied. Out of this 'attrition of diverse minds,' says Cardozo, comes eventually something of an 'average value' greater than its components. It is Cahn's criticism that we cannot comfort ourselves with this rationale when we consider the person involved in the case. Cahn calls him the 'consumer of justice.' Says Cahn:

'Revere Cardozo as we may, we cannot help retorting that averages in the administration of justice do not avail the person who is wronged grievously in his own, particular case.'[63]

Our 'sense of injustice,' Cahn asserts, prevents us from being patient at the cost of the individual sufferer, however much may be contributed to the refinement of legal doctrine.

Karl Llewellyn's scheme of appellate decision-making is based on his wide survey of actual judicial practices in the highest courts of various States today. Elsewhere, in a review of Llewellyn's masterwork, *The Common Law Tradition: Deciding Appeals* (1960), I have vouchsafed my views about his conclusions.[64] Suffice it to say here that Llewellyn reports to us, as a fruit of his extensive research, that the practice among appellate judges today is in the manner of what he calls the Grand Style (reminiscent of an older day before the formalisms which had led Llewellyn to the realist revolt). In this Grand Style, appellate opinions typically come to terms with the lines of precedent, lay down a generalization which is a sensible one for the kind of situation exemplified by the case, and afford

63. *Confronting Injustice: The Edmond Cahn Reader,* 10.
64. 109 *U.Pa.L.Rev.* 1045 (1961).

guidance for the social consequences of the future. He holds Cardozo up as an exemplar of this Grand Style. In a personal letter to me, Professor Llewellyn has himself formulated a crisp summary of the contribution he has made, as he would have put it had he been his own reviewer:

'There is, of course, nothing new in the author's insistence that a major factor in sound decision is to reach first and especially for the sense of the type-situation involved in the case. That has been good practice ever since judges began to judge, and in particular under our own Grand Style. On the other hand, the author does catch into words and into guidance for ordinary men in their everyday work what in the mere practice of the Grand Style lies more in court's fingers than on their tongues, and which perhaps could therefore more easily get lost and forgotten.'[65]

Able judges are often unable or disinclined to articulate, as Cardozo did, what it is that they are doing. That they are excellent legal craftsmen does not necessarily mean that they are jurisprudentially conscious, philosophically aware. Llewellyn is suggesting that his prime contribution lies in having singled out and expounded the pivotal emphasis on the 'situation,' and showing not only how judges do and should mould their opinions around the situation—but also showing judges how to do it. What he calls 'situation sense' (or a sense of the type-situation) is what contributes to formulating the rule of law, the generalized aspect of what is at stake.

It is of course surprising to find Llewellyn, so antinomian in his emphasis at the threshold of his career, seeking to objectify in a standardized model, toward the

65. Karl Llewellyn, letter to me from the University of Chicago School of Law, 11 January 1961.

end of his career, what must inevitably have an element of subjectivity. To Judge Charles Clark it is clear that Cardozo's 'method of sociology,' by way of contrast, does take due account of the 'empire of subconscious loyalties' in each judge's mind as he attempts to grasp the 'spirit of the age' through the inescapably human limitations of his own education and associations. Clark therefore deprecates Llewellyn's concept of a 'situation sense' and the putative provision of a map through the maze of value choices in a strongly contested case.[66]

Judge Clark's criticisms bring to the fore once again the basic point which we have encountered in our discussion of Van Voorhis and Friendly: the relation between the community's views and the judge's. It is a point which George Santayana also raised in his reading of this book when it first appeared.

In a personal letter (which he subsequently authorized me to publish) Santayana puts his finger on this point. I quote only the lines pertinent to this issue:

'Now what "ideology" guides Cardozo in determining the direction in which his conscience shall exercise a gentle pressure upon the law? I can find nothing more definite than "the social mind" or "cherished social ideals." Something psychological, then, prevalent sentiment or opinion? Or something biological or anthropological, the actual tendency which manners and morals show in their evolution?'[67]

66. Charles E.Clark and David M.Trubek, 'The Creative Role of the Judge: Restraint and Freedom in the Common Law Tradition' (1961) 71 YaleL.J. 255.
67. George Santayana, letter to me dated 8 August 1938. The questions raised by Santayana were further explored in comments pencilled in the margins of his copy of the book, which is now in the Treasure Room of the Harvard Law School Library.

When the way is open for change in the law by reference to 'ideological' factors, I have already noted (as have Van Voorhis and Friendly) that Cardozo would first look to views other than his own: to those prevalent and rooted in the community. One can sympathize with Santayana's perplexity, however, since Cardozo quite evidently did not thoroughly think through the implications of this point. In criticizing his 'method of sociology,'[68] I pointed out that Cardozo did not mean simply to reflect the sociological trends, but to embody into law, when pertinent, those he regards as desirable. We might indeed be said to have, as I remarked in my Conclusion, two separable methods here, one of which might appropriately be denominated as the 'method of ethics.'[69] Santayana has written in the margin at that point: 'This is the crux.'

Cardozo is thus indeed concerned about the 'social mind' (to use the phrase Santayana singled out), in the sense not only of current values, but of norms in the sense of 'cherished social ideals.' There may indeed come a point where the judge must decide which of these 'ideals' in the 'social mind' he will prefer when they conflict; and he may then be remitted to his own value scale. But he would not indulge his own values initially or in oblivion of those prevalent in the society of his time. The problem is of course greatly exacerbated by the diversity and clash of values in a pluralistic society undergoing rapid change like our own.

To revert to Santayana's terminology, I do not conceive Cardozo as believing in any evolutionary tendency of morals in some biological or anthropological sense. As I interpret him, he is simply concerned with the detec-

68. P. 61.
69. P. 115.

tion and assessment of prevalent opinion or sentiment.
But he does not call it 'psychological'; he calls it 'sociological.'

In replying to Santayana, I pointed out that we were
discussing common law, not Constitutional law, and that
it is, indeed, as he says, only gently that the judge's conscience normally exercises a pressure upon the common
law. What are his alternatives when impelled or compelled to exercise such 'pressure' in order to effectuate a
needed change in the law in an appropriate case within
the appropriate scope of judge-made law? Cardozo had
contended that he should be objective to the extent of
trying to ascertain what views are held by good and intelligent men, and give those views legal sanction when
they have been vigorously asserted. That may be a treacherous and unsatisfactory criterion. But at least it takes
the judge's mind out of his own confinements and out of
the official law-case reports and into the agitated opinions and social studies of his day, itself a significant advance. After thus posing the problem, I then went on to
say about Santayana's own characterizations: 'The judge
can be the legislator in Aristotle's sense, determining the
character of society, only within circumscribed limits. . . .'
It would not be merely 'prevalent sentiment' which then
moves him, in Cardozo's view, but also strong emerging
sentiment—which often moved Cardozo, as in the pioneering labor law decisions of the New York Court of
Appeals. If there is to be a reference to 'actual tendencies' perhaps it would be the tendency in the direction of
greater democracy, in the sense of a more genuine spread
of net liberty and more equal opportunity. Though his
own personal preferences might be aristocratic (as Cardozo's, like Holmes's, may in many respects be said to be),
I ventured the view that Cardozo, if pressed, would lean

toward affording expression to democratic ideals when a choice is relevantly open.

I asked if one could perhaps find an illustration of the distinction Santayana was drawing between 'prevalent sentiments' and 'evolving morals' in the protection of private property, for the former, and social controls of its uses, for the latter. This movement would not be inevitable and patterned, but experimental and empirical—in the sense Santayana himself may have meant in alluding elsewhere in his letter to an appeal to human nature and its potentialities for happiness—a natural basis being needed for all ideal fulfillments (as he has suggested in *The Life of Reason* in concurrence with Aristotle).

In his reply from Rome, on 16 October 1938, Santayana met directly the issue as I had framed it and said: 'Your interpretation of my distinction . . . is just what I should make it. . . .'

From his marginal notes in the book it is clear that he is critical of an approach which takes account only of what he calls 'public opinion' or 'standing convention.' After all is said and done, and wherever light may be sought, we are left, he reminds us, with the 'finality of conscience.'

In a wide-open situation where, for example, the judge must decide if an applicant has 'good character' or has done deeds of 'moral turpitude,' Judge Jerome Frank has proposed that the case be sent back to the trial court for the judge to take expert testimony from qualified witnesses (clergymen, philosophers, editors, sociologists?) as to what is the community's standard. This suggestion is in line with Frank's central insistence that in jurisprudence more attention be given to (and more weight be placed upon) the trial court's function. Insofar as the philosophy of the judicial process is concerned, Frank would have us surrender the blinkers which keep our gaze riveted on the appellate courts. What Cardozo calls *the* judicial process is really, Frank points out, the appellate process; and a full view of the judicial process requires us to attend to what is developed in the trial court—what he calls 'fact scepticism'—as well as the main critical preoccupation of appellate courts of review, *viz.*, 'rule scepticism.' Thereby we escape from the 'upper court myth' in which exclusive concentration upon Cardozo's writings could entrap us. If Cardozo had acknowledged the confinement of his analysis to the appellate process alone, says Frank, his books would deserve unqualifiedly the high praise they have received. But, Frank adds: 'I think they merit a marked criticism almost never voiced: unfortunately Cardozo purported, without qualification, to describe the entire judicial process. Because of his reputation, the very excellence of his teachings in the narrow appellate field, to which they legitimately pertain, has tended to dampen inquiry in a far larger field where inquiry is far more necessary.'[70]

Harry Jones, who holds the chair of Cardozo Professor of Jurisprudence at Columbia, has sought to integrate legal realism with the existential phase of contemporary philosophy, especially as expressed by leading philosophers of religion, like Tillich and Buber, and younger Catholic theologians. His essay 'Law and Morality in the Perspective of Legal Realism' is a piece of intellectual statesmanship which was badly needed.[71] The realists' liberation of law from its bondage to formal logic had led

70. Jerome Frank, 'Cardozo and the Upper-Court Myth' (1948) 13 *Law and Contemp. Prob.* 369, 373.
71. In the symposium on 'The Changing Role of the Judiciary in the Development of Law' (1961) 61 *Col.L.Rev.* 5, 799.

scholastic (natural-law) scholars to take an inimical attitude toward legal realism. Latterly, however, there has
been increasing recognition that legal realism and natural
law (whatever either of these omnibus terms may fully
mean) can at least unite in welcoming critical evaluation
as essential in judicial decision. Both reject mechanical
jurisprudence and neither can be satisfied only with formal analysis of existing legal concepts or with logical symmetry. Both are more concerned with good sense and
good morals in the affairs of men.

If philosophy is emerging from an 'age of analysis,' as
the author of that phrase has declared, into the 'age of
decision' (as the writings of humanistic existentialists like
Sartre no less than the religious existentialists suggest),
the judge may be helped by this line of philosophic development to meet his own awesome challenge of choice.[72]

As Jones has put it, the ethical implication to be drawn
from legal realism is that the 'moral dimension' is to be
sought in the 'process of responsible decision.'[73] In mak-

72. Contrariwise, one can learn much from the judicial process about the
factors involved in wise decision generally. (See the *Nomos* volume
edited by Carl Friedrich, *Rational Decision* [Atherton Press, New
York, 1964].) A European philosopher, Chaim Perelman, would have
us consider that, after having sought for centuries to model itself
after science, philosophy should now turn to the traits which it shares
in common with law. 'A confrontation with the latter would permit
better understanding of the specificity of philosophy, a discipline
which is elaborated under the aegis of reason, but a reason which is
essentially practical, turned toward rational decision and action.'
Perelman, *Justice* (Humanities Press, New York, 1967) 110. See also
Richard Brandt (ed.), *Social Justice* (Prentice-Hall, Englewood Cliffs,
1962) *passim*. Pushing for a clarification of a common ethical foundation, Professor Abraham Edel makes a ground-breaking suggestion
in *Ethical Judgment* (1955) chapter IX, 'The Theory of the Valua-
tional Base,' 293 ff., cited by Judge Bernard Botein in his 1960
Cardozo Memorial Lecture and, with his collaborator, Murray Gordon, in their book, *Trial of the Future: Challenge to the Law* (Simon
& Schuster, New York, 1963).
73. Harry Jones, 'Law and Morality in Perspective of Legal Realism'
(1961) 61 *Col.L.Rev.* 861.

ing a choice, as Jones points out, citing Tillich, both the general rule and the demands of the concrete situation must be accepted to make justice effective.[74] To which Jones adds Buber's reminder that every living situation demands 'presence, responsibility; it demands you.'[75]

The choice is made by a judge who is first of all a man and a citizen. He brings himself to the challenge of his task. He invokes such 'law' as he deems appropriate. He strives also for justice in the individual case as it comports with the generalized guidance of the legal principle involved; and he brings the case into consonance with the social currents of the day. The law is continually revised as it interacts with emerging fact situations and the changing social milieu. There is a constant fermentation as legal principles respond to the inter-relation of the moral values embodied in inherited doctrines and current social trends.

We have had plenty of emphasis heretofore on the rules as well as upon the realist challenge to the appellate courts to free themselves from rigid rule tyranny. We need today more inspection of the realities of the trial situation especially insofar as the lawsuit is a 'fact-suit.' We need more sensitive awareness of the justice to be accorded to the parties involved. We also need more attention to statutory interpretation and to the tension between the words of a statute and its social purposes. We need further utilizing of statutes as generative agencies akin to precedents. As I have elsewhere written:

'We have gone from a period of judicial hostility to statutes, as strangers in our father's house one hundred

74. See Paul Tillich, *Love, Power, and Justice: Ontological Analyses and Ethical Applications* (Oxford University Press, New York, 1954) 15.
75. See Martin Buber, *Between Man and Man* (Beacon Press, Boston, 1955) 113-4.

years ago, to a period of judicial receptivity to statutes, which judges today have domesticated into the common law (though perhaps with varying degrees of affectionate embrace).

'It is not my part to say here if men and society can be made better by more laws, or whether more emphasis should rather be placed on moral aristocracy in the individual person or social group, fostered by the elevating influences of education and religion.

'The fact is that we *have* placed great faith in legislation—as far as it goes—in our country and in our time. The complications of our society have been intensified by rapid and drastic technological developments, by accelerated trends toward an urban civilization, by social security and social welfare measures. These, combined with the rise of big business organizations and the coordinate rise of big unions, have reflected or bred social tensions, social opportunities and social realignments, which have imperatively required legislative attention. Courses in "Legislation" have now been introduced in the modern law school. "Legislative Drafting Bureaus" have been created.

'Yet there is relatively little in the juristic writings of Holmes, Cardozo and Frank (who were pre-eminently concerned with judicial law-making and judges' techniques) about judicial interpretation of statutes. And those who should know—philosophic and self-conscious judges like Breitel and Frankfurter—tell us that they have derived little help and insight from the formal maxims of statutory construction which have come down to us from the past or from the standard scholarship works on statutory construction.

'I do not intend to get into the quagmires of statutory interpretation, though every lawyer knows that more study and analysis are needed on the problems and techniques of statutory construction as a judicial art. I make reference to statutory construction only in the broadest dimension, in the context of the point which I here wish to make, which is: how statutes have been increasingly embraced into the very body of the law, increasingly integrated into a homogeneous system of law. Statutory aims and policies are now becoming generative principles, influencing ordinary common-law decisions in related fields, in the same way that the principle of a judicial precedent does. . . .

'If we go back a hundred years we find Chancellor Kent expressing the typical Blackstonian, mid-19th century hostility toward statutes, embodied in the shibboleth that statutes in derogation of the common law are to be strictly construed. It was this attitude that fifty years ago aroused the sharp condemnation of Dean Pound. In his classic article written at the beginning of the 20th century (The Common Law and Legislation, 21 Harv. L. R., 383, 1908), he advanced to an assault on the "derogation maxim" and indicated that the general attitude of the courts, as of that time, was becoming a liberal-construction attitude.

'In an effort to pierce the future, Pound had suggested that, though it might sound preposterous to lawyers of that day, he contemplated a development toward the point where statutes would not only be liberally construed by the courts, but that the statutes themselves—their aims, their principles, their policies—would constitute starting points from which judges would develop the law for an ordinary common-law case in some related field. In other words, he predicted that judges would build upon the principles of statutes as they traditionally have built upon the principles of decisional law as embodied in judicial precedents. That is to say, not only judicial precedents would have generative or creative power to decide a case, but so would statutes; statutes would be considered as having at least the *same* status of creative legal authority as a judicial precedent, with a proliferating propulsion beyond their own four corners.

'Variations upon this juristic theme were sounded subsequently by Dean Landis (Harvard Legal Essays, 1934); and in 1937 we find Justice Stone saying, in a carefully measured address on the "Common Law in the U.S.," at the Harvard Tercentenary celebration, that a *major* problem of the common law is what he called "organizing" statutes into the common law (50 Harv. L. R. 4, 13)....

'May I add, in conclusion, that, after all, it is a legal tradition of the greatest antiquity for us to absorb into the blood-stream of the common law salient statutes such as the statute of frauds. We have also inherited a little-invoked ancient doctrine of the "equity of the statute" along the very lines here discussed.'[76]

The judge goes to the whirling currents of social trends and thoughts to ascertain as objectively as he can which of them have reached a point, in a critical case, where they may properly be backed by the sanction of law and enforced by society's coercive machinery. But because of the diversity of views and tendencies in a society like ours, he must often choose among them. After he has communed with the analogies in the precedents and with his colleagues, and has sought what aid he can from the trial court and from extra-legal literature, should he not make that choice as enlightened as he himself can believe it to be and justify? Rather than capitulate to a least common denominator or some routinated folkway,

76. *New York L.J.*, 21 February 1959. Reprinted by permission.

should he not consider whether the time has not come to bring society into conformance with a perhaps higher standard, especially in terms of realizing the democratic promise of the in-built idealism of American society? The fertilizing character of the policies embodied in statutes is more likely to reflect emerging democratic values. What he will need above all is wisdom.

Wisdom is a concept common to both our roots, Biblical and Greek, and its elusive and cherished character comes to enhance and haunt our every decision. We are all keenly aware that our moral, political, and social wisdom has not kept pace with our technological and scientific advances; and that the poignant and critical need of our times is to turn our best minds toward the diminution of this deficiency.

In seeking to assay the components of wisdom, in law as in other areas, we come around to a sense of proportion —taking account of significant factors and giving to each its appropriate importance. For all of us, as well as for judges, this assessment is more difficult today because of the extent and complexity of our inter-related knowledge. Along with this allotment of values and breadth of perspective, we need a livelier awareness of the ends of human life which we are seeking to promote, together with a liberation, so far as may be, from our own idiosyncratic prejudices, and an avoidance as well of utopian impracticality. As we grow in wisdom we move from preoccupation with our own private concerns to less personal and broader interests. We become able to transcend our provincialisms and to make more disinterested judgments. 'No one can view the world with complete impartiality; and if anyone could, he would hardly be able to remain alive. But it is possible to make a continual

AFTERWORD

AFTERWORD

approach towards impartiality.'[77] But combined with striving toward impartiality, shall we not encourage engagement with the democratic ideals of which our legal system in the last analysis is itself an instrumentality?

77. Bertrand Russell, 'Knowledge and Wisdom,' reprinted in Houston Peterson and James Bayley (eds.), *Essays in Philosophy* (Pocket Books, New York, 1959), 489.

INDEX
TO THE ORIGINAL EDITION

DATE DUE

DATE DUE			
OCT 18 1971			
NO '75			
MAR 3 1 1994			
JUN 0 1 1995			
MAR 1 8 1995			
GAYLORD			PRINTED IN U.S.A.